# BUSINESS
# RESEARCH METHODS

# BUSINESS RESEARCH METHODS

**Dr S. Nakkiran**
Professor of Cooperation
AMBO UNIVERSITY, AMBO
ETHIOPIA

**Dr M. Nazer**
Associate Professor of
Commerce
Khader Mohideen College
Adirampatnam 614 701
Tamil Nadu, INDIA

**Dr Fisseha Girmay**
Asst Professor of Accounting
& Finance
Mekelle University
Mekelle, ETHIOPIA

**ABHIJEET PUBLICATIONS**
**NEW DELHI 110002**

**ABHIJEET PUBLICATIONS**
4658-A, 21 Ansari Road, New Delhi 110002
Phone: 011-23259444, 65698474
E-mail: abhijeetpublication@gmail.com

BUSINESS RESEARCH METHODS

*First Published* 2015

ISBN 978-93-5074-185-6



PRINTED IN INDIA

Published by J.K. Singh for Abhijeet Publications, New Delhi-110002, Lasertypeset by Abhijeet Typesettrs, Delhi and Printed at Asian Offset Printers, Delhi.

# Preface

Business world is crossing very many boundaries. With the impending proliferation of the effects of globalization, business activities at global are taking great leaps and bounds. Within countries, trade and development activities are taking place at pace, to suit the increasing purchasing power of the people. Competition among the business community has paved the way for quality consciousness among the consumers. Competition in business has also crossed boundaries and stands at global level. With economic liberalization, produc,tion, distribution and investment activities have been internationalized. Foreign private investment and business and industrial collaboration have made the business boom at global level. Though there may be negative sides of globalization, the positive aspects are more and benefits the global community at large. Such expansion of business at national and global levels is not without problems. When inflation or economic depression occur, they give chain reaction and will not spare any country. Many more challenges like meeting the consumer tastes, creating quality for products and services etc are certain offshoot effects of such globalization. The foremost challenges to be faced by today's managers are relating to marketing and human resource management. Problems like production, investment, finance etc. could be solved by economic forces , but the above two factors are posing continuous challenge to the managers. Here comes the role of research in business.

Research in other areas, especially in social sciences are fast expanding. New techniques are being applied, new scholars are going for model developments. Such process helps to find solutions to problems on a rational way. Because finding solutions to problems through research is rational, scientific and reliable, compared to methods like administration or legal. Research in business is lagging behind other social sciences, due to non-recognition of its values by the managers. Of late, especially after economic liberalization and globalization, the importance is gaining momentum. Business research methods cover vast areas like production, materials, finance, marketing, human resource and office. Among these functional areas of management, research relating to marketing, or what is called as Marketing Research has established its presence after the Second World War.

Present work is a modest attempt taken by the authors. This book covers various aspects of business and application aspects relating to Business Research. We have applied the methodologies that are popular with Social Science Research. Because for all Social Sciences, certain methodologies are quite common, but they differ in certain aspects like, selection of research problem, tools of data collection and statistical treatments.

Though number of books on Business Research have come out in western countries, books on this area in developing countries are rare. To fill this void we have made good attempt. We hope the readers, especially students of business and management will relish this book. Any constructive criticism is welcomed by the authors, to make further improvements in future editions.

We thank all our dear friends, whose number could not be counted, who stood behind us on various occasions to finish this book in time. Our heart felt thanks go to the Publishers, Abhijeet Publications, New Delhi, who took pains to bring out this book neatly and in time.

**Authors**

# Contents

**Sampling**



**Methods of Data Collection**

# 1

# Introduction

## Business Management

Business management is the process of the planning, co-ordination and control of a business. To survive in the long run, a business must be profitable and liquid. To do so, it must create sufficient value for its customers so that its revenues exceed its total costs. The overall task of business management is to address successfully the problems that confront a business in its role as a value-creating organization.

In addition to their problem-solving abilities and skills, business managers must have knowledge and expertise in the seven functional areas of business: production, marketing, finance, accounting, human resources, management information systems, and product research and development. Moreover, top management must be able to co-ordinate these activities within the business so as to maximize the value of the business to its shareholders and its other stakeholders, such as employees, suppliers, customers and the surrounding community.

## Business Process Management

The effects of globalization and the technical advances of the last twenty years profoundly increased the pace of change and the severity of competition in the business environment compared to the previous five decades. In response to this rapidly changing business environment, management theorists and scholars are constantly putting forth new ideas to help corporations succeed in this turbulent world. These new ideas are like the flavor of the day. One idea after another would be put forth, generating excitement in the management press, only to fade away in a few years. The uninitiated outsiders might perceive these management fads as unrelated concepts that arose independently. The truth is most of this management ideas often built on one another and shared central themes that have not changed through the years. Whether it is Total Quality Management (TQM) of the 1980s or Business Process Reengineering (BPR) of the 1990s, the one central theme common to these management ideas is the concept of business process management. Before we discuss business process management, a definition of process is warranted.

A business process is a set of coordinated tasks and activities, conducted by both people and equipment that will lead to accomplishing a specific organizational goal. And then, the phrase Business Process Management refers to a set of activities an organization implements to optimize its processes. Thus, Business Process Management (BPM) can be defined as a systematic approach to improving an organization's business processes. BPM activities seek to make business processes more effective, more efficient, and more capable of adapting to an ever-changing environment.

Business process management also encompasses software tools designed to assist firms in achieving process optimization. BPM is proving a dynamic solution to some of the most challenging process problems in business. Business process management also revolutionizing the way companies operate by boosting their efficiencies and capacities to adapt.

A business process management system used appropriately provides crucial benefits. It can cut cost, increase efficiency and enhance customer service. BPM can also drive up revenue. Designed to provide real-time visibility into business functions, business process management software is ideal for achieving a greater return from today's process-intensive industries.

More specifically, a BPM solution can reduce the time needed to complete a business process, the number of steps required to perform tasks or the number of errors made in implementing an activity. BPM may also reduce the number of employees needed to complete a job, thereby allowing a company to utilize those employees for additional growth in other areas. In addition, you can apply BPM practices to automate routine procedural tasks and improve call center performance.

### Business Organizations: Achieving and Maintaining Business Continuity

By business organizations, we do not only mean commercial organizations that manufacture and sell products or that provide, for instance, financial services. A business organization in this context is any organization that provides services or goods, either to individual customers, to other business organizations, or to the public. Examples of such business organizations include manufacturers, distribution companies, sales organizations, transport organizations such as rail roads or air-lines, utility companies such as electricity production and distribution, water, gas and telecommunications and community services such as cooperative services, tax services, emergency services, government and so on. Although not all these organizations are established to make profit, they all provide some service to somebody else, and have all built an operational structure to enable them to do so. In the context of this chapter they are all called business organizations. As all these organizations are equally at risk from the effects of a disaster that interrupts their organizations, they should consider business continuity management if they are to optimize their chance of successful resumption of business following an interruption.

### Business Dependencies and Vulnerabilities

Each business process depends on a number of critical elements. In a business process a number of persons or departments are involved, who execute one or more activities and pass the resulting information on to the next participant in the business process.

A first dependency is human resources, where a minimum number is required with the appropriate skills and knowledge to be able to execute the business activities. Other dependencies are resources and infrastructure elements. These can be logistical resources, utilities, office infrastructure, manufacturing infrastructure, information technology or financial resources. Examples of logistical resources are loading and stocking areas, transport facilities, neigh bridges and so on. The extent to which business operations depends on these critical items means that there is a higher vulnerability to business interruptions. These vulnerabilities include, for instance, single points of failures in the information technology (IT) architecture and network. When such a contingent becomes unavoidable, many or all of the critical information flows to support business operations are interrupted.

Within each business process, there are a number of key activities. When such key business activities can no longer be executed because of unexpected events, the results could be an interruption of the business process that is part of the value-chain to the customer.

Within business continuity management it is impossible to duplicate every process—this would be too expensive. Nor it is sufficient just to provide backing for one or more elements due to the interdependencies; this would be insufficient to effectively recover the full process.

To be able to provide continuity of this complex cycle when an unexpected event interrupts the chain, the business continuity plan will have to organize the business process differently by using a limited alternative infrastructure and by temporarily redefining the cycle times and deadlines.

### External Dependencies

Business organizations are not only dependent on elements within the company. No business organization is an island. Each depends on a number of external resources and outside organizations. These external resources are often beyond its immediate control. Examples are electricity, water, and telecommunication and so on. Although your organization can not control the delivery of these services and therefore can not prevent interruptions, it is your organization alone that can and will have to manage the impact on your business operations should these external dependencies fall. Likewise, the participants in the business process are both internal and external to the company. Examples are suppliers, business partners, agents, distributors, and banks, factors of invoices, insurers, and public authorities.

The business activities that provide customer service extend beyond the company boundaries. The concept of 'external enterprise' is very applicable. This means—again—that you are dependent on elements that are beyond your immediate control. You will have to handle the consequences to your business when they become unavoidable. These external dependencies are very critical for any company participating in a supply-chain.

Companies are also dependent on the execution of business activities outside their own organization. This is typically true with the increased level of outsourcing and business partnerships. Examples of hi-tech outsourcing include information and communication technology contract centers, web service and application services. Other services that are frequently outsourced are facilities management, security, cleaning, catering, transport, distribution, packaging, back-office functions and financial services. Although these external companies are responsible for their own business continuity management to resume their business, you are responsible for managing the impact on your business operations of a disaster within these companies.

Experiences show that, in many cases, the effect of an unexpected event cascades into larger impact levels. This again underlines, why, for business continuity management to be effective; it must be driven in terms of managing the business impact, rather than handling the event.

All these—internal and external—elements must be considered and will drive the business continuity management. When going through this exercise, it is important that you use a reference framework of business risks, specific for your business environment. Such a framework allows you not to dwell on symptoms or the obvious, but to focus on what is essential for your business success.

## Ethics in Business

There is no single definition of "code of ethics"; nor is there consistency in the language used to describe such a document. For example, a search of the Internet reveals the following phrases used by different companies:

- Business Ethics Policy (New York Times)
- Business Conduct Guidelines (IBM)
- Code of Business Conduct and Ethics (Ford Motor Company)
- Statement of Ethics (Wal-Mart)
- Credo (Johnson and Johnson)

To facilitate discussion, this article will use the phrase "Code of Ethics". We will define it as an official corporate document approved by the board that forms the underpinning of a comprehensive program for helping to ensure ethical behavior and decision making at all levels in the organization. Here are some suggested ways to think about a Code of Ethics, both what it is and what it is not.

A Code of Ethics is:

- A statement of the values adopted by the company, its employees and its directors. It sets the official "tone at the top" regarding expected behavior.
- A living document that can be disseminated to consumers, the media, and others, such as by being placed on the co-op's web site.
- Part of a broader, on-going program to provide guidance for ethical decision-making and to prevent misconduct. This broader program must be actively managed and should include periodic training for employees and directors, monitoring of compliance, and regular reports to the board.
- A valuable communication tool that the cooperative can use to articulate its commitment to ethical and legal compliance.

A Code of Ethics is NOT:

- The same as a Mission Statement. A Mission Statement is usually brief (under one page in length) and expresses why the company exists, in contrast, a Code of Ethics is a longer document (approximately 3-10 pages) intended to serve as a guide for day-to-day decision making. Rather than stating why the company exists, it guides employees and directors on how to act in certain situations.
- A detailed statement of how personnel issues will be handled. Co-ops usually have an Employee Handbook or similar document that addresses such issues as discrimination, sexual harassment, and employee discipline. The Code of Ethics references the Employee Handbook.
- A board policy. Boards have policies that address specific issues such as conflict of interest or standards of conduct for directors. Those policies are important and should be maintained. The Code of Ethics is a broader "umbrella" statement that applies to the entire company. The Code may make reference to specific board policies that provide additional details.
- Complete or exhaustive. It provides guidance to employees and directors for carrying out their responsibilities. But no document can address every possible situation. The

Code should specify that employees and directors must use good judgment and be prepared to raise questions when in doubt.

### Whan Belongs in a Code of Ethics?

There are many approaches and formats. There is no "one size fits all." Deciding what goes into the code will first take an examination of what key purposes you want your code to serve—whether you want it to focus on specific types of individual conduct or more general standards—and how the code will operate with existing policies for staff and board members. You'll also need to determine who will be involved in drafting the code. One approach to consider is to form an "ethics task force" or committee that includes key staff representatives. Not only does such a process help to ensure a thorough document, it also helps to make the code meaningful for employees.

Although there is no "one size" for codes of ethics, we can report on the consensus opinion of approximately 200 cooperative directors, managers and attorneys who attended recent workshops on Ethics and Governance. They emphasized the following guidelines to keep in mind when developing a code:

- It should be positive.
- It should be brief.
- It should make reference to relevant board policies and other documents.
- It should be "aspirational" in tone rather than compliance oriented.
- It should help reinforce the fact that as cooperatives, we are different.

Given these factors, the following sections might be included in a Code of Ethics for electric cooperatives:

- Cover page and statement of values
- Introduction and explanation of the purpose of the Code of Ethics
- General corporate and personal standards of conduct
- Conflicts of interest
- Confidentiality of information
- Member communications
- Financial practices and record keeping

- Legal and regulatory compliance
- Reporting of violations
- Employee and director education
- Monitoring and enforcement.

These sections might address the following:

*Cover page and statement of values:* Identifies the cooperative and the fact that this is its official Code of Ethics. Some co-ops may choose to identify specific values that express the ideals that should govern the behavior of employees and directors. Such values might include:

- Integrity and Accountability
- Safety
- Member Focus and Customer Service
- Respect
- Corporate Citizenship
- Fairness
- Honesty
- Innovation
- Environmental Stewardship

*Introduction:* Explains that the cooperative is committed to the highest standards of legal and ethical conduct, and that its employees and directors are expected to uphold those standards. It informs readers why the Code is important and the key purposes it serves. The Introduction also explains that the Code of Ethics is not exhaustive and that it provides guidance to employees and directors in how they are expected to carry out their duties. Because the Code cannot address every possible situation, employees and directors are expected to use good judgment and to raise questions (either up the chain of command or with the board) when in doubt.

General corporate and personal standards of conduct: Expresses the fact that employees and directors are expected to uphold the values of the corporation and conduct themselves in a professional and ethical manner at all times. Further, employees and directors are expected to deal honestly and fairly with consumers, suppliers and others. Specific prohibitions may include bribes, kickbacks or other forms of improper payment.

*Conflicts of interest:* Clarifies that directors and employees with decision making authority are expected to not seek any personal benefit through any arrangement with vendors or suppliers, and that they should consult the policy on conflicts of interest.

*Confidentiality of information:* Clarifies that directors and employees may not discuss or disclose confidential information with or in the presence of unauthorized persons, including family members and friends, and that they may use confidential information only for the company's legitimate business purposes and not for personal gain.

*Member communications:* Affirms that cooperative members are entitled to receive information, and communications will be honest and transparent. Many cooperatives already have policies regarding communications and access to information, that they should reference here.

*Financial practices and record keeping:* Clarifies that the cooperative complies with generally accepted accounting principles; maintains a system of internal accounting controls that will provide reasonable assurances that transactions and asset dispositions are properly recorded in order to prepare accurate financial reports and prevents and detects fraud; and has a system in place to ensure that necessary company records and documents are properly retained and secured.

*Legal and regulatory compliance:* Affirms that the company will comply with all local, state and federal laws, rules and regulations applicable to the activities of the company; that employees and directors are expected to maintain a safe and healthy work environment free from harassment or discrimination; and that the company will conduct its activities in accordance with fair business practices.

*Reporting of violations:* Explains that it is the responsibility of every employee and director to ensure that violations of laws, rules, regulations or the Code itself are reported and addressed. Explains that reports of suspected violations may be made in person or in writing, confidentially or anonymously, to the responsible designated person (e.g., to the Human Resources Manager, the CEO, the "ethics officer" or the Chair of the Board Audit Committee). Stipulates that all such reports will be investigated and appropriate corrective action taken. Calls attention to the fact that any employee (or director) who makes a report in good faith and on reasonable belief may do so without fear of harassment, retaliation or retribution, in accordance with the cooperative's whistleblower policy (if it has one).

*Employee and director education:* Notes that all employees and directors will receive a copy of the Code of Ethics and will receive training and periodic communications to ensure that they are familiar with its requirements. The cooperative may include a statement that each year every director and employee should reread the Code or, alternatively, include a form to be signed at some regular interval, (every year, every two years, etc.) indicating that each employee and director has reread the Code and refreshed his/her understanding of its components.

### Content of the Code of Ethics

Cooperatives come in a variety of forms, and a code of ethics may need to be tailored to fit your particular business. Some public companies have one code of ethics for financial officers and another for employees. However, the approach that is more common is to have a single code of ethics that covers all directors, officers, employees, including consultants. Some topics frequently covered in a code of ethics:

### Fair Dealing

- Prohibiting bribes, kickbacks or any other form of improper payment to any representative of a government, a labor union, a customer or a supplier.
- Prohibiting directors, officers and employees from accepting any bribe, kickback or improper payment.
- Prohibiting gifts or favors of more than nominal value to or from customers or suppliers.
- Limiting marketing and client entertainment expenditures to those that are necessary, prudent, job- related and consistent with company policies.
- Reflecting accurately the sale price and terms of sales for products sold or services rendered.

### Conflicts of Interest

- Prohibiting officers or directors from being hired by or involved in the management of an outside business that competes with the cooperative or does business with the cooperative.
- Prohibiting officers or directors from seeking or accepting any loans or services from the cooperative and any entity

with which the cooperative does business.
- Prohibiting officers or directors from conducting business on behalf of the cooperative with immediate family members.

**Full, Fair, Timely and Understandable Disclosure**

- Not making false or misleading entries in books and records.
- Not condoning any undisclosed or unrecorded bank accounts or assets.
- Maintaining an adequate system of internal accounting controls.
- Presenting information to members in a clear and orderly manner.

**Compliance with Laws, Rules and Regulations**

- Promoting a workplace that is free from discrimination or harassment.
- Supporting fair competition and laws prohibiting restraints of trade and other unfair trade practices.
- Conducting activities in compliance with environmental laws.
- Keeping the political activities of directors, officers and employees separate from company business.

**Monitoring Compliance with the Code of Ethics**

It does little good to adopt a code of ethics if there is no process in place to monitor compliance. Many larger companies have an "ethics officer" in order to ensure compliance. The position is usually assigned to an employee who has a number of job duties. If a cooperative does not have an ethics officer, potential violations can be reported to the audit committee chair, the human resources director or legal counsel.

Training is also an important aspect of compliance with a code of ethics. Employees, directors and officers should receive training on the code of ethics as part of new employee orientation and possibly as part of on-going training programs. To ensure familiarity, directors, officers and employees are frequently asked to read the code of ethics and sign a compliance certificate. The compliance certificate frequently states the consequences of violating the policy, including potential demotion or discharge.

**But Can You Legislate Business Ethics?**

Probably not. However, a written code of ethics can ensure that employees, directors and officers are aware of the "rules of the game" that have been adopted by your cooperative. Personnel who violate the code of ethics probably will not have a defense that "I wasn't aware of the policy."

If your cooperative does not have a written code of ethics and an employee, officer, or director engages in inappropriate conduct, the other officers or directors may be subject to criticism that the behavior could have been prevented if the cooperative had appropriate policies in place. Thus, while ethics cannot be legislated, a cooperative can establish expectations on how it will conduct its business and reduce its potential liability by enacting appropriate policies and safeguards

**Nature and Definition of Management**

Management is nothing but a process of organizing and directing the resources of an enterprise towards the achievement of certain objectives laid down by the same organisation. It is an art as well as a science, as it involves the scarce skills of human beings and it promotes knowledge, like other sciences, which may be useful to the humanity. As various theories are being build up, management is becoming a subject of attraction. It is a body of knowledge which is expanding its avenues through the experiences of various managers working under various conditions.

Efficiency of business organisations is enhanced by the application of the principles of management. Fuller utilisation of resources is the prime motive of management. As this involves the utilisation of human resources, in the beginning of this century, management science has been branded as an instrument of exploitation. Later, its salient features were properly conceived and it has got its application in all private and public sector economies. Co-operative organisations did not lag behind the application of management principles and techniques.

Scientific approach to problems and preparedness are the other features of management. Haphazard approach to solve problems has no place in scientific management. Determination of goals on the basis of thorough scrutiny of the areas and resources concerned, has also been the motto of management, which gave objectivity to the approaches. Scientific management is also alert in facing problems and finding solutions to problems as organisations have to face unexpected risk in their operations. Management techniques insure such risks by means of thorough preparedness.

Dynamism and adaptability are imbibed with the scientific management. The long standing existence of any organisation depends on the dynamism it is introducing in its operations. As the society is changing the tastes and demands of the consumers are also changing. Hence, an organisation must change its strategy of planning and techniques of production, to suit the tastes of the customers. Otherwise, the unit has to suffer for want of customers.

The science of management trains the people in the art of managing organisations. Potential managers are trained to manage organisations more scientifically. Peter Drucker the management giant viewed that, "The manager including the managing of a business, through the systematic study of principles, the acquisition of organised knowledge and the systematic analysis of his own performance in all areas of his work and job and on all levels of management. Indeed nothing else can contribute so much to his skill, his effectiveness and his performance. And underlying this theme is the conviction that the impact of the manager on modern society and its citizens is so great as to require of him the self discipline and the high standards of public service of a true professional".

## Definition of Management

*Encyclopedia of Social Sciences:* "Management may be defined as the process by which the execution of a given purpose is put into operation and supervised. The combined output of various types of and grades of human effort by which the process is effected is again known as management. Again the combination of these persons who together put forth this effort in any given enterprise is known as the management of the enterprise".

*American Management Association:* "Getting things done through the effects of other people".

John Mee: "Management is the act of securing maximum results with a minimum of effort so as to secure maximum prosperity and happiness for both employer and employees, and given the public the best possible service".

G.R. Terry: "Management is a distinct process consist up of planning, organizing, actuating and controlling, performed to determine and accomplish the objective by the people and resources".

Peter Drucker: "It is a multipurpose organ that manages, the business and manages managers and manages workers and work".

Stanley Vance: "Management is simply the process of decision making and control over the actions of human beings for the express purpose of attaining pre-determined goals".

From the above definitions, we can draw the following meaning of management:-

1. Human effort is consolidated and put to use to achieve pre-determined goals.
2. Management is an art of getting things done by satisfying the entire persons involved in the process.
3. The process of management consists of planning, organizing, staffing, directing and controlling functions.
4. It implies the maximum use of available resources.
5. Management is art as well as science. It is an art as it brings about a desired result through the application of skill. It is science, because it involves new knowledge, which is systematized through the application of scientific method.
6. It is intangible, the unseen force. Its presence is evidenced by the results of its efforts.
7. Management is universal in character. In addition to acting as a problem solving tool, it should look into the problems of the society surrounded by it.

## Features of Management

### *1. Multi-Disciplinary Approach*

Management has grown as a separate discipline drawing upon the knowledge and skills of various disciplines like economics, commerce, cooperation, finance, political science, sociology, statistics, demography, quantitative techniques, engineering, ecology, geography, biology, etc. Management uses the relevant information from these disciplines and integrates them to form a multi-disciplinary and cross functional field of study and develops a broad-spectrum approach in dealing with organisational problems.

*2. Dynamic and Relative Principles*

Management principles and systems are dynamic, open, progressive and flexible in nature—not rigid, closed or absolute. They can be adapted or modified to suit the requirements of different types of organisations and changed situations.

*3. Organised Activity*

Management is not an isolated activity but is essentially a team-work informally organised groups.

*4. Existence of Objectives*

Determination of organisational objectives and their accomplishment form the core of managerial activity.

*5. Working with and Through People*

Management is essentially leading, guiding, developing and motivating people to effective performance for attainment of common goals.

*6. Integration of Resources*

Management is integrating and balancing of all resources—both material and human—for their optimum utilisation, so as to achieve effective results.

*7. Management—Both a Science and an Art*

Management is a science because it consists of an organised knowledge and systematic body of principles. It is, however, a combination of social sciences and behavioural sciences, not an exact science like the physical or natural sciences. Management is also an art because it involves application of systematic knowledge and scientific principles for achieving the desired results in actual work situations. Science teaches one "to know" while art "to do". It may be said that management is the oldest of arts and the youngest of sciences. Management is essentially a practice, it is performance-oriented creative action.

*8. Management—A Profession*

Management has now emerged as a profession—as managers,

to be effective, must acquire the basic professional knowledge and skill in managing, through formal management education or management training; develop the right managerial attitude, sense of professional responsibility and service motive follow the professional code of ethics; and associate themselves with professional management associations or institutions.

### 9. *Universality of Management*

The basic process and the principles of management are applicable in all situations, in different organisations and countries, with such modifications as deemed necessary.

### 10. *Management—Both a Technical and a Social Process*

Management integrates, in all its decisions and actions, the technical and the social aspects, the economic and the human aspects of the organisation.

### 11. *Management Includes Administration*

Although different authors have expressed different views about the use of these two terms and many of them have mentioned several points of distinction or difference between them, for all practical purposes, management and administration are considered as the same—with regard to responsibilities, tasks and process.

### 12. *Management—A Multi-Purpose Organ*

Management is a "multi-purpose organ" of a business enterprise (which is itself a specific organ of an industrial society") that "manages a business, manages managers, manages workers and work"—to quote the inimitable words of Peter Drucker, "If one of them were omitted, we would not have management anymore—and we also would not have a business enterprise or an industrial society".

## Management As a Profession

A profession denotes certain accepted norms for its universal application. Management is one of the youngest social sciences and it is yet to be recognized as a profession. Although management does not include all the characteristics of a profession it is moving towards that direction.

## Characteristics of a Profession

(a) an organised and systematic body of knowledge, (b) a formal method of acquiring such knowledge and skill through established institutions of business management, (c) formation of management association, (d) growth of professional management consultants and (e) growing of emphasis on the ethical conduct of management personnel.

## The American Management Association stated in 1963

"Management is rapidly involving as a true profession with definable principles and with a body of reference points strong enough to differentiate manager from non-manager and to correlate basic goals for its members, regardless of the nature of their business, their geographical location or the activity with which they are affiliated".

Furthermore, the American Management Association has contended that management as a profession meets the following basic but specific characteristics:

1. It has a body of knowledge that is transferable. There are basic principles of management which can be identified, mastered and practiced. This body of knowledge is being constantly enlarged and enriched from the experience of successful management as well as from the research finding of sociologists and scientists in related areas.
2. It follows a scientific approach. There are prescribed patterns for managerial operations.
3. It requires specific skill and tools that are used in the performance of managerial duties and responsibilities.
4. It adheres to a code of ethics. A professional manager is perfect in his role and is honest in his attitude and philosophy.
5. It has a required discipline. As in the case of other professional careers, managing required a discipline for effective performance.

However, in spite of AMA's assertion of management as a profession it falls short of strict disciplinary standards of some other accepted standards. Some of these shortcomings are enumerated by Aamrine, Ritchey, and Hutley. these are:

1. Skill not fully developed. Even through there are some

principles of management that are fully established and universal in nature, it still has not evolved a complete set of techniques and skill that are universally applicable.

2. The ethical codes are not as strict as desirable-unlike medical profession and the legal profession which has very strict ethical Standards for performance, the manager still uses high-pressure tactics and unfair competition to increase the market share of their product.
3. No uniform method of entry into the filed of management—any body can proclaim to be a manager. While doctor and engineers have to go through a required course of study and need a license from a professional body to practice, no such license is required to practice as a manager. Accordingly, some managers may have a Master's degree in Business administration and others may not have any degree at all and still be able to practice as managers.
4. The objective is monetary rather than service—service to society and humanity is the basic function of a professional and the monetary reward is only secondary. For example, a doctor's objective is to save lives. Management as a professional lacks that service objective. Dalton MC Farmland says, "Management is only in part a profession. Licensing is non-existent; no large-scale movement for licensing managers is under way. No single organised group professes to speak for all manager although a number of associations assist particular groups such as personnel managers. There is no universal code of ethics, although many subgroups within management have advanced their own codes. Also, it is doubtful that concepts of service transcend the importance of salary or fees for most managers".

## Aims and Objectives of Scientific Management

1. *To determine industrial and market trends:* Industrial and market trends help assure continuous operations and employment—so essential for the sustenance of any enterprise.
2. *To assure employment security to the employee:* As a result of determination of industrial and market trends planned and balanced operations in an enterprise will assure

continuous employment to the employees.

3. *To obtain better gains for the concern and its employees:* Minimising wastes while employing scientific techniques and getting productive use of human resources and material results in increased profits for the concern which they willingly share with their employees by way of enhanced wages to them.
4. *To improve the living standard of workers:* Enhanced income to the workers leads to improvement in their standard of living.
5. *To provide better contentment and a happier life for workers:* As a result of the increased income and their improved standard of living, this takes away all aching factors from their minds and they come to lead a better contented and happier life.
6. *To render employees satisfactory conditions for work:* It is the objective of scientific management to let the employees feel satisfied and at ease so far as the conditions of their work are concerned.
7. *To provide highest opportunity for workers' employment and advancement:* Scientific management through its 'Job analysis' techniques offers the highest opportunity to an individual, depending on individual's capacity, for employment and advancement through training and development.
8. *To motivate workers for promotion to higher positions:* With the systematic training and methodical instructions that help the development of new and higher capacities, the scientific management motivates and creates, an urge within the workers' minds for reaching the higher ladder and promotion.
9. *To generate self-reliance and self-respect in workers:* With methodical job specifications and know-how techniques, the scientific management helps generating feelings of self reliance and self-respect in the workers.
10. *To develop personality, attitudes and behaviour of workers:* An atmosphere surcharged with research and evaluation free from any authority pressures as provided by scientific management helps in the development of their personality attitudes and behaviours.

11. *To building of workers' character:* Scientific management relies on the golden principle 'Work is worship' and through this impresses workers to build their character through their proper work performance.
12. *To promote equity and justice:* Scientific management aims at promoting an equitable and a justful treatment in wages and other things to all irrespective of any favour of fear.
13. *To create atmosphere of amity and mutual cooperation:* Scientific management's endeavour is ever directed to eliminate elements of friction and discord and bring about an atmosphere of amity, mutual cooperation and understanding in a given situation.

## Application of Scientific Method in Management

Scientific method is the preliminary process for research methods and research orientation. Any research methodology starts with the initiation of the learning of scientific method. The same approach is given to management also. There are seven important steps involved in the application of scientific method in management.

1. *Identifying the proposition:* This step states precisely the objectives and the investigation is directed to the achievement of a specified goal.
2. *Preliminary examination of the proposition:* This step is concerned with the preliminary examination of the propositions on the basis of information and data as available from past experience.
3. *Stating tentative solutions to the proposition:* With the help of the information and data as obtained in step (2) and adding his personnel observation, thinking, and ideas, the scientific man, hypothetically states tentative solutions to the proposition, to be accepted or rejected after controlled experimentation.
4. *Thoroughly investigating the proposition:* With the information and data of past experiences as the scientific man already possesses and the information he has collected from his controlled experimental thinking as in step (3), he is better equipped to apply his mind to a thorough examination of the proposition in its various aspects.
5. *Classifying the data obtained:* By now the scientific man

has accumulated with him quite a good volume of data for the efficient handling of this data classification is the proper means.

6. *Stating tentative answer to the proposition:* Now the stage has come when the scientific man's efforts will be directed to find a tentative answer to the proposition. This is to be done by him through a careful and intelligent interpretation of the classified data as available with him through the inductive and deductive reasoning and methods.
7. *Stating answer to the proposition after adjustment:* This is the stage when the scientific man is seized of the proposition. After marking necessary adjustments as a result of the interpreted data findings the scientific man is now ready with the answer to the given proposition and he delivers the answer.

**Skills Needed in Management**

1. Technical skill—ability to use specific knowledge, methods or techniques in performing work. This is of great importance to managers at lower levels. A foremen has to be well up in the methods of production, an accounts officer in the preparation of balance sheets and so on.
2. Human relations skill—capacity to understand, work and get along with people. This is needed by managers at all levels and to a greater extents by those at the levels of supervisors who deal with the rank and file.
3. Decision making skill—involving the power of judgment to evaluate alternative courses of action and select the best course among them. This is necessary at all levels of managers, although the gravity of the decision involved, the importance of the issue dealt in, vary from level to level.
4. Analytical skill—This is closely related to decision making skill. It requires ability to use logical and scientific methods for probing into problems, finding out the critical factors and assessing them in the context of opportunities, constraints and threats. This skill is required to a greater extent at upper levels of management.
5. Communication skill—ability to explain policies and

procedures, issue instruction, listen to problems and grievances, and so on. It is required at all levels, in a greater degree at upper levels.

6. Conceptual skills—This is the ability to think in abstract terms to form image and ideas to visualise and understand the future and to discern relationships and indications among the elements of a system and changes there in.
7. Administrative skills—This is the ability to get things done by implementing decisions and plans and to act in a very pragmatic manner. Carrying the system as per the procedures, policies and programmes, also falls within the scope of administrative skills.
8. Social skills—Social skills are basically behavioural and interpersonal. It involves the ability to understand the people and to create interpersonal relations on healthy dimensions. Building a team, getting the people towards the organisational objectives and at the same time meeting out the psychological requirements of the people falls within the scope of social skills.
9. Research orientation—Today's management and managers must recognize the role and importance of research in decision making and using it as a problem solving tool. This warrants the managers at all levels to acquire the skils of research methods and the application of certain statistical tools.

## Manager and Management Development

The word manager has been used in a variety of ways by others. To some, the term manager means top executive, to others a manager is any person who supervises other employees. But the organizational structure of a firm contains number of echelons, each level possessing the designation of manager. In every sense, a manager is a key person and responsible for the day-to-day affairs and for the ultimate success of an organization. One way of understanding what manager do is to examine the functions of management. The process of management consists of planning, organizing, staffing, directing, and controlling. Planning comprises of looking ahead of the future, setting goals, and figuring out policies, procedures, and methods of achieving these goals. The decision-making process forms the important process of planning. Organizing involves the breaking down of the total work to be done into jobs, groups, and departments and establishment of workable relationships between these units. It includes such elements as grouping of activities, setting-up jobs, determining authority and responsibility relationships, setting-up patterns of communication, delegating and the use of staff. Staffing refers to the process of recruiting and selecting people to run the enterprise. Direction is the motivation and leading people to achieve the desired goal. It integrates the personal goals of the employees with the objectives of the enterprise. The control function includes measurement of work performed, comparison of actual performance with a pre-determined standard and taking corrective action to ensure that performance meets standard.

Today's managers are expected to learn and orient themselves towards research methods. Research is a problem solving tool and it will help them to take right type of managerial decisions. Many managers have created a negative attitude towards this science, which is unacceptable to the dynamic world.

### Personal Characteristics of Managers

A manager, in addition to his professional abilities, must have certain personal characteristics, which are mentioned below.

1. Intelligence—A manager must have adequate intelligence to take quick decisions and to deal with problems. During certain critical situations they should use their intelligence for crisis management through spot decisions.
2. Education—Manager should also have the minimum required education in the particular profession as well as managerial education.
3. Broad interest—He must have broad interest to develop the organization to which he is heading.
4. Desire to manage—He must completely devote to the organization and he must take further interest to promote the enterprise.
5. Ability to communicate—He must be able to communicate freely and frankly with his superiors and subordinates.
6. Integrity and honesty—Managers have to deal with financial and other material resources and they should have integrity and honesty towards men and materials.
7. Delegation—Using the subordinates effectively, allocating decision-making and other responsibilities to the appropriate subordinates.

8. Control—Establishing procedures to monitor and regulate process, tasks or activities or subordinates and job activities and responsibilities; taking action to monitor the results of delegated assignments.
9. Initiating—Making attempts to influence events to achieve goals; self starting rather than passive acceptance; taking actions to achieve goals beyond those called for.
10. Tolerance—Stability of performance under pressure or stress.
11. Adaptability—Maintaining effectiveness in varying environments with various tasks, responsibilities, or people.
12. Tenacity—Staying with a position or plan of action until the desired objective is achieved.

### Types of Managers and their Tasks

Generally, in all organizations, the management level is divided into three, namely, lower management (first-line managers), middle management, and top management.

The lower management (line-managers) direct non-management employees and they do not supervise other managers. Such lower level management managers are called as supervisors and foremen.

Middle management—Middle managers direct the activities of lower level managers. Their principal responsibilities are to direct the activities to direct the activities that implement their organizational policies and to balance the demands of their managers.

Top management—Top management is responsible for the overall management of an organization. These people are called as executives. They establish operating policies and guide the organization's growth and development. Top managers are also called by various names like chief executive officers (CEO), general manager, or manager. The top managers have to undertake liaison activities, monitoring activities, and the role of a negotiator.

With regard to the personal characteristics and skills needed, for various levels of managers, they vary from level to level. At the lower level management, technical skills are needed. Human skills are also needed here for the frequent interaction with the subordinates. At the middle management level, human skills are very essential and the conceptual skills gain importance. At the top management level, conceptual and design abilities and human skills are especially valuable.

### Business/Management and Social Responsibility

Business organisations have to shoulder certain social responsibilities, because they are part of the society and society has invested heavily for the business. Investments on infrastructure, transport, communication, etc are beneficial to the business also. Hence, the business in turn must repay several things to the society.

There are many strong grounds why business should be responsible to society.

(1) Business exists in society and as part of it. It must, therefore, observe the ideals and norms of society.

(2) It is society which supports business, provides it with resources, purchases its products and so on. Doing good to society means just repayment of its debt.

(3) The effluence of many businesses positively damages the air and water of the surrounding locality. They are duty-bound to repair the damage. They must take preventive measures as well.

(4) The Government grants protection, maintains law and order, which enables business to carry on its activities in an unfettered way. Business must pay its dues to the Government so that the Government can run and perform its functions.

(5) Workers help production by contributing their labour. They deserve fair treatment and just reward.

(6) Business should make society better and stronger in its own interest. It flourishes best under a system of private enterprise. But organised society may modify or even break up the existing order if it fails to get its dues from business, if its expectation continue to be ignored by it.

University of Texas Professor S. Prakash Sethi has identified three stages of social responsibility of the businesses. They are

1. Social obligation
2. Social Responsibility
3. Social Responsiveness.

Social obligation refers to corporate behaviour designed to deal only with legal requirements and competitive market factors.

Social responsibility according to him refers to corporate behaviour that complies with contemporary values norms and expectations of the society.

Social responsiveness is the third stage of the corporate behaviour, wherein the management it expected to anticipate various changes and to take appropriate preventive action.

### Arguments for and Against Social Responsibility

Rationale for the business organisations to fulfil certain social responsibilities are listed hereunder:

1. Business enterprises are sub systems of the larger society. To fulfil their economic objectives, they will have to draw from the various resources which the society has got. Since it is depending on the society to utilise the various resources that it requires to fulfil its economic objectives, it is quite logical for the enterprises to be responsible to the society.
2. When the business enterprises accept social responsibility then the same will get reflected in all their managerial decisions. If that is so, the operations of the enterprises will always produce something beneficial to the society.
3. Business enterprises because of their operations build up for themselves tremendous amounts of social power. This social power, logically speaking, ought to be matched with social responsibility. Otherwise, there is a threat of the same being misused.
4. Acceptance of some amount of social responsibility will also legitimise the commercial and economic objectives of the business.
5. One of the professional requirements to manage any business enterprise is to be sensitive to the social environment. Social sensitiveness is difficult to pick up unless otherwise business enterprises are made to have some social responsibilities.
6. The business enterprises could not grow and diversify unless otherwise the economic and societal environment is conducive to their development. The said environments can be made conducive only when the business enterprises make some effort towards it. To make such efforts the enterprises must fulfil some social responsibilities.

7. To changing societal environment will naturally force the Government to enact laws so as to make the business enterprises to have social responsibilities. Hence it is always better for the business enterprises to make some social initiation on their own account and to have some social responsibility before it is enforced on them.

Certain view points against Social Responsibilities of the Business are listed hereunder:

1. Since most of the business enterprises are funded by the public, in order to safeguard the economic interest of the investing public, business enterprises must concentrate only on achieving its economic objectives.
2. The managers in the business enterprises normally have competence only to manage the maquagerial activities pertaining to their organisations. They may lack social skills to fulfil the social responsibilities.
3. Accepting social responsibilities may lead to diluting economic goals. Under the guise of fulfilling certain social responsibilities, the business enterprises may tend to run the businesses on inefficient lines.
4. Accepting social responsibility would also increase the cost of the business operation, because, then the enterprises would be expected to invest in certain activities which may not be directly relevant to their normal business operations.
5. If business enterprises are expected to have social responsibilities since that concept is a vague one, many entrepreneurs who want to start industries and to contribute to the economic system of the country may have their own fear to start business. Because they may think that they may not be able to stand up to the larger expectations of the society.

### Business Research

Business is the study of various aspects of running a business organization. That organization may be a sole enterprise, Partnership firm, Joint stock company, Multi-national firm, Government owned public sector organizations or Cooperative organizations. The study of business research is closely related to the study of managerial aspects of organizations also. Here in our book, we have interchangeably used the terms Business and management. Business research methods have incorporated all problems relating to business as well as the study of Managerial aspects relating to the functions of management namely, Planning, Organising, Staffing, Directing and Controlling.

**Why to Study Business Research?**

Business research may be defined as "a systematic enquiry whose objective is to provide information to solve managerial problems".

The complex decision making process in organizations have made the process on research an important input. The following are several reasons for managers to use research inputs:

1. In every decision number of variables are to be considered and to choose the best.
2. More knowledge exists in every field of management, to go for the suitability of needs rational approach.
3. Global and domestic companies are facing severe competition and they are in a position to reduce cost and increase competencies through research findings.
4. The quality of theories and models to explain results is improving.
5. Governments are very aggressive in protecting the interests of citizens and consumers.
6. There is information growth through web sites and the quality of these information is to be improved through research.
7. The shareholders, customers and the general public are more concerned about their respective interests, which calls for regular research about their perspectives.
8. Organisations are increasingly plasticizing data mining, learning to extract meaningful knowledge from volumes of data contained within internal databases.
9. Computer advances have allowed businesses to create data warehousing, where vast arrays of collected data are ready for mining.
10. Techniques of quantitative analysis take advantage of powerful computing capabilities.
11. The number and power of the tools used to conduct research have increased, commensurate with the growing complexity of business decisions.

## A Researcher's Participation in Decision Making

A researcher and a manager are two different portals and their minds must meet to make use of the research findings for managerial decision making. A manager has practical field knowledge, where as a researcher may not have managerial exposure. A researcher is not expected to participate in the decision making, due to the following reasons:

1. The researcher may spoil the process objectivity. He may try to influence his personal views.
2. The researcher would weigh the research findings heavily in selecting a course of action, in contrast the manager can evaluate and weigh the significance of research findings in the context of experience and the broad policy considerations associated with a decision.

While many researchers are sufficiently management oriented, many managers are not sufficiently research oriented. This inhibits their active participation in various stages of research. Some managers are of the view that the researcher is clairvoyant regarding the nature of decision situation, the course of action that appear reasonable, the objective to be accomplished and the information needed to reduce the decision uncertainty. Some times managers do not provide enough information or do not communicate properly with the researchers. So, a manager can view research with right perspective:

1. The managers can use research as a way to gain visibility and power to in the organization.
2. Research can be used to justify decisions already made. If the research decisions contradict the decision, the manager can simply ignore it altogether.
3. Research can be used as a promotional tool like advertising.
4. Research can serve to soothe an anxious manger tat 'something is being done'

But some managers view research with suspicion and threat to their decision making process:

1. Some managers view research as a threat to their personal status as decision makers. They fear that research information may conflict with or invalidate their knowledge gained from experience and judgment.
2. The absence of systematic planning process in many organizations may contribute to lack of common

organizational objectives for managers. In the absence of clear orgasitational objectives , the managers will substitute their own objectives, which may mislead the organization. Research may be seen as a way to support one's in this struggle for power. Managers who believe that research will enhance their position will favour it. While others will oppose it.

3. Some managers are unable to work effectively with,understand and use the skills of researchers. They must respect their professional integrity.
4. Research personnel, like the marketing research team must keep close contact with the managers.

Studies conducted by the Marketing Science Institute of USA have identified several observations regarding the effectiveness of the manager-researcher interaction:

1. Researchers love a surprise. Managers do not like surprises, when they are surprised, they tend to reject research.
2. Researchers like to explore. Managers prefer to confirm. Researchers should be sensitive to managerial "comfort zone".
3. Technical quality does not speak for itself. Working together influences perceptions of technical quality and creates trust in the research results.
4. Political acceptability of research results is perceived by researchers as a major consideration for use. An effective working relationship between researcher and manager can enhance political acceptability.
5. Manager-teacher interaction, of all variables studied, has the highest total influence on research use. Open and frequent communications with managers are vital to research effectiveness.
6. Good horizontal relationship (teaming researchers with product managers) are more important than vertical relationships.
7. Involvement in the strategic planning process separates more effective from less effective research departments. But most research is tactical and researchers feel excluded from strategy formulation.
8. Managers expect research to come up with innovative solutions or courses of action. Research is not perceived

as doing so. More involvement in strategy formulation might help.

9. Smooth planning and delivery of research services have a strong influence on management satisfaction. On the other hand, researchers perceive managers as making sudden changes in data needs, priorities or deadlines.

## Why Business/Management Research is Distinctive?

Till recently management as a science was drawing resource and strength from other social sciences/disciplines like psychology, economics and sociology. Many scholars are skeptical about management as a discipline to stand alone. But management research poses some unusual problems which are not often encountered by other social sciences. Compared to other fields, management filed has more challenges to face, as it is the life blood to run corporate firms. Here comes the distinctive nature of management research.

1. *The practice is management is diverse:* in spite of vast developments that are taking place in the field of management, managers need to work across technical, practical and functional boundaries. They need to draw knowledge from other disciplines like psychology, economics, statistics etc. the dilemma for the researcher is whether to examine management from the perspectives of one discipline or to adopt an inter-disciplinary approach. We are in a position to make research in management more independent of other disciplines by developing acceptable methodologies.
2. *Managers are always busy:* They are unlikely to allow the researchers access to data from their organizations, unless they get some benefit out of such research. This means access to data will be very difficult with conditions like confidentiality and publication. Their time is also precious. So the researchers have to find new ways of collecting data.
3. *Management requires both thought and action:* Very many managers judge the ability of research positively. So the research methods need to take into account the practical consequences that may cause with or without the guidance of research.

## Why Some Managers Like Research?

Though a section of the managers are skeptical about the potentials of research, many like to accommodate research to their purposes. Because:

1. The sponsor manager may gain political support for a new idea that he wants to initiate. The presence of a researcher may give credibility to his new idea.
2. The manager may want to demonstrate to the insiders of his organization the success of a venture with which he has been associated.
3. When the manager is facing attacks from insiders, the research can show how precious the decision or the idea.
4. The manger may wish to test some new ideas against some external validation, by using the researcher as a sounding board.

## Managerial Values of Business Research

We have argued that research facilitates effective management. At the Ford Motor Company a Marketing Manager stated, "Research is fundamental to everything we do, so much so that we hardly make any significant decision without the benefit of some kind of marketing research. The risks are too big." Managers in other functional areas have similar belief about research in their specialist.

The prime managerial value of business research is that it reduces uncertainty by providing information that improves the decision making process. The decision making process associated with the development and implementation of a strategy involves three interrelated stages:

1. Identifying problems or opportunities,
2. Selecting and implementing a course of action, and
3. Evaluating the course.

Business research by supplying managers with pertinent information may play an important role by reducing managerial uncertainty in each of these stages.

*Identifying problems or opportunities:* Before any strategy can be developed, an organization must determine where it wants to go and how it will get there. Business research can help managers plan strategies by determining the nature of situations by identifying the existence of problems or opportunities present in the organization.

*Selecting and implementing a course of action:* After the alternative courses of action have been identified, business research is often conducted to obtain specific information that will aid in evaluating the alternatives and in selecting the best course of action.

*Evaluating the course:* After a course of action have been implemented, business research may serve as a tool to inform managers whether planned activities were properly executed and whether they accomplished what they were expected to accomplish. In other words, business research may be conducted to provide feedback for evaluation and control of strategies and tactics.

## Scope of Business Research

The scope of business research is limited by one's definition of "business". Certainly research in the production, finance, marketing, or management areas of a for-profit corporation is within the scope of business research. A broader definition of business, however, includes not-for-profit organizations. For example, Utility companies such as Electricity production and distribution, Water, Gas and Telecommunications and Community services such as Cooperative services, tax services, emergency services, the Indian Certified Public Accountants Association, and the Nehru Zoo. Each of these organizations exists to satisfy social needs and they require business skills to produce and distribute the services that people want. Business research may be conducted by organizations that are not business organizations. The federal government for example, performs many functions that are similar, if not identical to those of business organizations. Federal managers may use research techniques for evaluative purposes much the same way as managers at Baggage Or Marti Car Company.) The term business research is utilized because all its techniques are applicable to business settings.

Business research covers a wide range of phenomena. For managers the purpose of research is to fulfill their need for knowledge of the organization, the market, the economy or another area of uncertainty. A financial manager may ask, "Will the environment for long term financing be better two years from now?" A personnel manager may ask, "What kind of training is necessary for production employees? Or "What is the reason for the company's high turnover?" A marketing manager may ask,"How can I monitor my sales in retail trade activities?" Each of these questions requires information about how the environment, employees, customers, or the company will respond to executive decisions. Research may be one of the principal tools to answering these practical questions. Here below, we site some of the important areas of research in Business/Management research:

*1. The Company or the Organization*

a. Objectives and philosophy
b. Policies and procedure
c. Products and services
d. Organizational structure and organizational dynamics
e. Plant facilities
f. Financial picture
g. The labor agreement and union management relations

*2. Management Principles and Techniques*

a. Organization principles
b. Financial planning and management
c. Management information systems
d. Production planning and control
e. Methods analysis and work measurement
f. Personnel management
g. Wage and salary administration
h. Cost analysis and control
i. Statistics and probability
j. Operations research
k. Data processing and computers
l. Marketing
m. Risk management

*3. Human Relations*

a. Fundamentals of human behavior
b. Motivation
c. Group dynamics
d. Attitudes
e. Conflict resolution
f. Managing change
g. Patters of management
h. Concepts of leadership
i. Power, authority, influence

j. Communication
k. Personnel management responsibilities of supervision in such areas as selection, training, pay administration, counseling appraisal, discipline, and grievance handling.

### 4. *Economic, Social and Political Environment*

a. Business ethics
b. Economic system
c. Relations with local, state and federal governments
d. Community relations
e. Social responsibilities
f. Legal framework for business
g. Business operations in foreign countries
h. Environmental issues
i. Consumerism

### 5. *Organizational and Production Problems*

a. *Low productivity:* This is an area, which needs greater concentration on the part of the organization. Enough return should come to the organization in the form of total production. Productivity per employee must alone enhance total production. A low productivity of an employee can signal the training needs.
b. *High cost:* An organization has to keep its cost of production to a lower level to increase its profit and make the product competitive in the market. So high cost of production will warrant the need to give training to the employees.
c. *Poor material control:* The material manager should see that materials are not wasted, or over stocking is not made and huge investment is not locked on materials.
d. *Excessive scrap and waste:* Raw materials are always scarce and sometimes costly. So the production manager and materials manager must ensure that the use of raw materials will not lead to huge scrape and waste.
e. *Excessive labor management strife:* This is an important area to be taken into account in any organization. The labor management relations must be cordial and any strain may lead to closing of the unit and production will be affected.
f. *Excessive grievances:* Any employee will have grievances of his own relating to his job and family. His grievances

in the factory must be set right by the organization. Research can help both the organization and the employee to solve the grievances.

g. *Poor discipline:* Employees should work with discipline in their units. So that total production and productivity will increase. Research can help to find out the causes for poor discipline and remedial measures could be suggested.
h. *High employee turnover:* employee turnover means changing the job or switching to various jobs by an employee.
i. *High absenteeism:* Absenteeism comes in the form of taking leave by the employee frequently and at times when the presence of the employee is needed. Such absenteeism can be controlled by research, which can explain the results of absenteeism to the employees.
j. *Delayed production:* Production schedule of an organization must be reached perfectly to face competition, meet the demands of the consumers and to meet the export needs.

**Business Basics of an Organization**

To make the business research a success, any organization must have certain basic philosophy about its own. Adequate funds must be allotted for research, a separate section for research must be created. Or research can be combined with the R&D Department. The following basics are needed to make business research a success :

1. Alignment—The key to getting the basics right is making sure that everyone has the same understanding of the current situation and that everyone is moving towards that direction for the future. Without alignment no company can make progress and no training department can provide effective training.
2. Philosophy—A philosophy is a statement of what the company stands for. It is a set of values and beliefs by which actions can be judged. A philosophy makes it clear which behaviors are appropriate and which are not unacceptable.
3. Mission—A mission is a statement of what a company has to do. A mission should describe what is done for whom in such a way that it cannot be confused with any others' mission.
4. Assessment—Assessment is very much about the

understanding where the company is today, and determining the reasons for both success and failure.

5. Vision—A vision is a picture where the organization wants to be in future. By describing the future, a vision can exert a strong pulling force, which helps keep the organization aligned.
6. Goals—Goals are quantitative figures such as sales, profit, and market share. Without goals, the vision will remain a dream.
7. Policies—A policy is a medium to long range course of action comprising a goal and a strategy. A strategy is the means of achieving a goal.
8. Policy deployment—It is a process of ensuring that the company's policies for quality, cost, and delivery are understood throughout the company. Policy deployment is a cyclical process. Progress against goals should be checked, the reasons for any deviation diagnosed and the policies modified in the light of the diagnosis.

### Business Research is a Global Activity

International business refers to all those business activities which involves cross border transactions of goods, services, resources between two or more nations. Transaction of economic resources include capital, skills, people etc. for international production of physical goods and services such as finance, banking, insurance, construction etc.

International transactions generate trillions of dollars in yearly global sales. And virtually every nation engages in significant international business, whether it is the United States, Namibia, India, Ethiopia, China, or Tonga (in the south pacific). In many areas, the marketplace has a wide variety of foreign firms competing with domestic firms.

Whether a firm is small or large, operates solely in its home nation or both domestically and abroad, markets goods or services, and is, profit or nonprofit driven, it needs to grasp key international business concepts and to devise a proper strategy. This means having a broader business perspective.

Thus, the idea that global business is the exclusive preview of large corporations must change. Too many smaller companies are missing opportunities for growth through exports. Promoting goods and services in large international markets often results in profitable sales for those with the innovation, competency, and willingness to make use of help available from state and federal agencies. Despite increased overseas opportunities some businesses are not interested in exporting because they are comfortable in the domestic economy. This situation is dangerous because the global economy—brings competition from unexpected places. Likewise, companies that conduct business in foreign lands must understand the particular nature of those markets and determine whether they require customized business strategies.

Business research, like all business activity, has become increasingly global. Research in international business aims to make empirical and applied research on issues relating to international business decisions and in helping a firm to address issues related to global customers, markets, and competition. That is, business research is undertaken to help you run your business, either for business development or to improve operational efficiency in the global market.

### The Business Research Process: A Quick Glance

The following section of this chapter provides a quick glance at the whole process to acquaint you with the various tasks you need to understand to carry out your study, thus giving you some idea of what the business research journey involves.

Business research involves systematically gathering, recording and analyzing information about specific issues related to the production and marketing of goods, services, organizations, people, place, and ideas. The business research process consists of a series of activities: defining the issue or problem to be studied, examining secondary data (previously collected); generating primary data (new); if necessary; analyzing information; making recommendations; and implementing findings.

The research process is very similar to undertaking a journey. As with your drive, for a research journey there are two important decisions to make. The first is to decide what you want to find out about or, in other words, what research questions, issues or problems you want to answer; you then need to think how to go about finding their answers. The path to find answers to your research questions constitutes research methodology.

There are practical steps through which you must pass in your research journey in order to find the answer to your research questions. (Figure 1-5 shows the 8-step model). The sequence of these steps is not absolute. With experience you can change it. At each operational step in the research process you are required to choose from a multiplicity of methods, procedures and models of research methodology which will help you to achieve your objectives.

## Steps in Planning a Business Research Study

### *I. Formulating a Research Problem*

The main function of formulating a business research problem is to decide "what you want to find out about". Issue (problem) definition is statement of the topic looked in to via business research. With out a focused definition, irrelevant and expensive data which will confuse rather than illuminate may be gathered. A good problem definition directs the research process to correct and analyze appropriate data for the purpose of decision making.

### *II. Conceptualizing a Business Research Design*

The main function of a business research design is to explain "how" you will find answer to your research questions. The business research design sets out the logic of your inquiry. A research design should include the following: the study design per se and the logical arrangements that you propose to undertake, the measurement procedures, the sampling strategy, the frame of analysis time-frame.

### *III. Constricting an Instrument for Data Collection*

Any thing that becomes a means of collecting information for your study is called a "research tool" or a "research instrument". For example, observation forms, interview schedules, questionnaires and interview guides are all classified as research tools.

### *IV. Selecting a Sample*

The basic objective of any sampling design is to minimize with in the limitation of cost, the gap between the values obtained form you sample and those prevalent in the population.

The underlying premise in sampling is that, if a relatively small number units is selected it can provide with a sufficiently and high degree of probability a fairly true reflection of the sampling population that is being studied.

There are three categories of sampling designs:

1) Random/probability sampling designs
2) Non-Random/probability sampling designs
3) "mixed" sampling designs

### *V. Writing a Research Proposal*

This "over all plan" tells a reader about your research problem and how you are planning to investigate; and is called a research proposal. Broadly a research proposal's main function is to detail the operational plan "for obtaining answers to your research questions.

A research proposal must tell you, your research supervisor and a reviewer the following information about your study:-

- what you are proposing to do;
- what you plan to proceed;
- why you selected the proposed strategy;
- a statement of the objective of the study;
- a list of hypothesis, if you are testing any;
- the study design you are proposing to use;
- the setting for your study;
- the research instrument(s)you are planning to use
- information on sample size and sampling design;
- information on data processing techniques;
- an outline of the proposed chapters for the report
- the study's problems and limitations, and
- the proposed time-frame

## Steps in conducting the Business Research Study

### *VI. Collecting Data*

At this stage you actually called the data. For example, depend up on your plans, you might commence interviews, mail out a questionnaire, conduct nominal /focused group discussions or make observations.

*Secondary Data*

The secondary consists of information not collect for the issue or problem at hand but for some other purpose; this information is available with in a firm or externally. Whether secondary data fully resolve an issue or problem or not, their low cost and rather fast accessibility, mean that primary data should not collected until a thorough secondary data search is done.

*Primary Data*

Primary data consists of information gathered to address a specific issue or problem at hand. Such data are needed if secondary data are insufficient for proper business decision to be made. If a firm decides primary data are needed, it must device a research design—which outlines the procedures for collecting and analyzing data. After a research design is detailed, data are then collected.

***VII. Processing Data***

The way you analyze the information you collected largely depends up on two things:

1) Type of information:- descriptive, qualitative, quantitative or attitudinal
2) The way you want to communicate your findings to your readers (texts, graphs, and tables). There are two broad categories of report—qualitative and/or quantitative approach.

*Data Analysis*

In data analysis, the information on questionnaires or answers forms/ schedules is first edited, coded, classified, tabulated, and then analyzed. Editing refers to the cleaning of the data collected. Coding is the process by which each completed data form is numbered and response categories are labeled. Tabulation is the calculation of summary data for each response category. Analysis is the evaluation of responses, usually by statistical techniques as they pertain to the specific issue or problem under investigation.

*Recommendation*

Recommendations are suggestions for a firm's future actions that are based on business research findings. They are typically presented in written form to business decision makers. The report must be written for the audience that reads it. Thus, technical terminology must be defined.

*Implementation of Findings*

A research report represents feed back for business analysis, who are responsible for using findings. If they ignore the findings, research was little value. If they base decisions on the results, then business research has a greater value and the organization benefits in the short and long run.

## *VIII. Writing a Research Report*

Writing a research is the last and, for many, the most difficult step of the research process. Thus report informs thee world what you have done, what you have discovered and what conclusion you have drawn form your findings. Your report should be written in an academic style and be divided in to different chapters and/ or sections based upon the main themes of your study.

Remember that, there are several ways of collecting and understanding information and finding answers to your questions, problems or business issues – research is one way. The difference between research and other way of obtaining answers to your questions, problems, issues or phenomenon is that in a process that is classified as research, you work within a framework of a set of philosophies, use methods that have been tested for validity and reliability, and attempt to be unbiased and objective.

# 2

# Definition of Research and Social Research

## Introduction

Human civilization has grown from stage to stage and now has reached a stage where one can enjoy the fruits of scientific advancement and material welfare. Such results are the outcome of new findings, efforts and hard work of few people. In the absence of such beep enquiries many of our problems would not have been solved. Still we have to solve many problems and researchers are striving hard to find solutions. Hence, research has become the part of our life and continued to co-exist with our civilization.

Research is not the exclusive preserve of a chosen few. Any individual belonging to any field of activity can undertake research. Intensive study, deep analysis and reflective thinking are the basic ingredients of research. Application of scientific tools and accepted steps and procedure are essential for an ideal research. It must have utility to the society; result in new findings and, or truth must be brought out.

## Need for Research

As the human society is expanding in terms of its material wealth, problems associated with such expansion also develop in various fields. To study such problems of varied nature and find solutions to such problems, research serves as an essential aid. It is the only scientific way of analyzing a problem. Besides, research is essential for the researcher to acquire and familiarize himself with various tools of research. Research tools and techniques are also refined from time to time. It is the duty of a researcher to keep himself abreast with the latest development in his field of research. As evaluation is one of he important aspects of private or public sector projects, research will have immense value to evaluate the failure or success of the project or the programme. Based on such evaluation the project can be aligned in a right direction. Hence, research has occupied a rightful place in all Government departments, industrial concerns and business organization. Majority of the concerns have started separate department called 'Research and Development Wing' to evaluate the programmes, to find solution to problems and to make new discoveries..

## Scientific Method

The scientific method is the process by which scientists, collectively and over time, endeavor to construct an accurate (that is, reliable, consistent and non-arbitrary) representation of the world.

Recognizing that personal and cultural beliefs influence both our perceptions and our interpretations of natural phenomena, we aim through the use of standard procedures and criteria to minimize those influences when developing a theory. As a famous scientist once said, "Smart people (like smart lawyers) can come up with very good explanations for mistaken points of view." In summary, the scientific method attempts to minimize the influence of bias or prejudice in the experimenter when testing an hypothesis or a theory.

### *I. The Scientific Method has Four Steps*

1. Observation and description of a phenomenon or group of phenomena.
2. Formulation of an hypothesis to explain the phenomena. In physics, the hypothesis often takes the form of a causal mechanism or a mathematical relation.
3. Use of the hypothesis to predict the existence of other phenomena, or to predict quantitatively the results of new observations.
4. Performance of experimental tests of the predictions by

several independent experimenters and properly performed experiments.

If the experiments bear out the hypothesis it may come to be regarded as a theory or law of nature (more on the concepts of hypothesis, model, theory and law below). If the experiments do not bear out the hypothesis, it must be rejected or modified. What is key in the description of the scientific method just given is the predictive power (the ability to get more out of the theory than you put in; see Barrow, 1991) of the hypothesis or theory, as tested by experiment. It is often said in science that theories can never be proved, only disproved. There is always the possibility that a new observation or a new experiment will conflict with a long-standing theory.

### *II. Testing Hypotheses*

As just stated, experimental tests may lead either to the confirmation of the hypothesis, or to the ruling out of the hypothesis. The scientific method requires that an hypothesis be ruled out or modified if its predictions are clearly and repeatedly incompatible with experimental tests. Further, no matter how elegant a theory is, its predictions must agree with experimental results if we are to believe that it is a valid description of nature. In physics, as in every experimental science, "experiment is supreme" and experimental verification of hypothetical predictions is absolutely necessary. Experiments may test the theory directly (for example, the observation of a new particle) or may test for consequences derived from the theory using mathematics and logic (the rate of a radioactive decay process requiring the existence of the new particle). Note that the necessity of experiment also implies that a theory must be testable. Theories which cannot be tested, because, for instance, they have no observable ramifications (such as, a particle whose characteristics make it unobservable), do not qualify as scientific theories.

If the predictions of a long-standing theory are found to be in disagreement with new experimental results, the theory may be discarded as a description of reality, but it may continue to be applicable within a limited range of measurable parameters. For example, the laws of classical mechanics (Newton's Laws) are valid only when the velocities of interest are much smaller than the speed of light (that is, in algebraic form, when $v/c << 1$). Since this is the domain of a large portion of human experience, the laws of classical mechanics are widely, usefully and correctly applied in a large range of technological and scientific problems. Yet in nature we observe a domain in which v/c is not small. The motions of objects in this domain, as well as motion in the "classical" domain, are accurately described through the equations of Einstein's theory of relativity. We believe, due to experimental tests, that relativistic theory provides a more general, and therefore more accurate, description of the principles governing our universe, than the earlier "classical" theory. Further, we find that the relativistic equations reduce to the classical equations in the limit v/c << 1. Similarly, classical physics is valid only at distances much larger than atomic scales (x >> 10-8 m). A description which is valid at all length scales is given by the equations of quantum mechanics.

We are all familiar with theories which had to be discarded in the face of experimental evidence. In the field of astronomy, the earth-centered description of the planetary orbits was overthrown by the Copernican system, in which the sun was placed at the center of a series of concentric, circular planetary orbits. Later, this theory was modified, as measurements of the planets motions were found to be compatible with elliptical, not circular, orbits, and still later planetary motion was found to be derivable from Newton's laws.

Error in experiments have several sources. First, there is error intrinsic to instruments of measurement. Because this type of error has equal probability of producing a measurement higher or lower numerically than the "true" value, it is called random error. Second, there is non-random or systematic error, due to factors which bias the result in one direction. No measurement, and therefore no experiment, can be perfectly precise. At the same time, in science we have standard ways of estimating and in some cases reducing errors. Thus it is important to determine the accuracy of a particular measurement and, when stating quantitative results, to quote the measurement error. A measurement without a quoted error is meaningless. The comparison between experiment and theory is made within the context of experimental errors. Scientists ask, how many standard deviations are the results from the theoretical prediction? Have all sources of systematic and random errors been properly estimated? This is discussed in more detail in the appendix on Error Analysis and in Statistics Lab[1].

## III. Common Mistakes in Applying the Scientific Method

As stated earlier, the scientific method attempts to minimize the influence of the scientist's bias on the outcome of an experiment. That is, when testing an hypothesis or a theory, the scientist may have a preference for one outcome or another, and it is important that this preference not bias the results or their interpretation. The most fundamental error is to mistake the hypothesis for an explanation of a phenomenon, without performing experimental tests. Sometimes "common sense" and "logic" tempt us into believing that no test is needed. There are numerous examples of this, dating from the Greek philosophers to the present day.

Another common mistake is to ignore or rule out data which do not support the hypothesis. Ideally, the experimenter is open to the possibility that the hypothesis is correct or incorrect. Sometimes, however, a scientist may have a strong belief that the hypothesis is true (or false), or feels internal or external pressure to get a specific result. In that case, there may be a psychological tendency to find "something wrong", such as systematic effects, with data which do not support the scientist's expectations, while data which do agree with those expectations may not be checked as carefully. The lesson is that all data must be handled in the same way.

Another common mistake arises from the failure to estimate quantitatively systematic errors (and all errors). There are many examples of discoveries which were missed by experimenters whose data contained a new phenomenon, but who explained it away as a systematic background. Conversely, there are many examples of alleged "new discoveries" which later proved to be due to systematic errors not accounted for by the "discoverers."

In a field where there is active experimentation and open communication among members of the scientific community, the biases of individuals or groups may cancel out, because experimental tests are repeated by different scientists who may have different biases. In addition, different types of experimental setups have different sources of systematic errors. Over a period spanning a variety of experimental tests (usually at least several years), a consensus develops in the community as to which experimental results have stood the test of time.

## IV. Hypotheses, Models, Theories and Laws

In physics and other science disciplines, the words

"hypothesis," "model," "theory" and "law" have different connotations in relation to the stage of acceptance or knowledge about a group of phenomena.

An hypothesis is a limited statement regarding cause and effect in specific situations; it also refers to our state of knowledge before experimental work has been performed and perhaps even before new phenomena have been predicted. To take an example from daily life, suppose you discover that your car will not start. You may say, "My car does not start because the battery is low." This is your first hypothesis. You may then check whether the lights were left on, or if the engine makes a particular sound when you turn the ignition key. You might actually check the voltage across the terminals of the battery. If you discover that the battery is not low, you might attempt another hypothesis ("The starter is broken"; "This is really not my car.")

The word model is reserved for situations when it is known that the hypothesis has at least limited validity. A often-cited example of this is the Bohr model of the atom, in which, in an analogy to the solar system, the electrons are described has moving in circular orbits around the nucleus. This is not an accurate depiction of what an atom "looks like," but the model succeeds in mathematically representing the energies (but not the correct angular momenta) of the quantum states of the electron in the simplest case, the hydrogen atom. Another example is Hook's Law (which should be called Hook's principle, or Hook's model), which states that the force exerted by a mass attached to a spring is proportional to the amount the spring is stretched. We know that this principle is only valid for small amounts of stretching. The "law" fails when the spring is stretched beyond its elastic limit (it can break). This principle, however, leads to the prediction of simple harmonic motion, and, as a model of the behavior of a spring, has been versatile in an extremely broad range of applications.

A scientific theory or law represents an hypothesis, or a group of related hypotheses, which has been confirmed through repeated experimental tests. Theories in physics are often formulated in terms of a few concepts and equations, which are identified with "laws of nature," suggesting their universal applicability. Accepted scientific theories and laws become part of our understanding of the universe and the basis for exploring less well-understood areas of knowledge. Theories are not easily discarded; new discoveries are first assumed to fit into the existing theoretical framework. It is only when, after repeated experimental tests, the new phenomenon cannot be accommodated that scientists seriously question the theory and attempt to modify it. The validity that we attach to scientific theories as representing realities of the physical world is to be contrasted with the facile invalidation implied by the expression, "It's only a theory." For example, it is unlikely that a person will step off a tall building on the assumption that they will not fall, because "Gravity is only a theory."

Changes in scientific thought and theories occur, of course, sometimes revolutionizing our view of the world (Kuhn, 1962). Again, the key force for change is the scientific method, and its emphasis on experiment.

### *V. Are there Circumstances in which the Scientific Method is not Applicable?*

While the scientific method is necessary in developing scientific knowledge, it is also useful in everyday problem-solving. What do you do when your telephone doesn't work? Is the problem in the hand set, the cabling inside your house, the hookup outside, or in the workings of the phone company? The process you might go through to solve this problem could involve scientific thinking, and the results might contradict your initial expectations.

Like any good scientist, you may question the range of situations (outside of science) in which the scientific method may be applied. From what has been stated above, we determine that the scientific method works best in situations where one can isolate the phenomenon of interest, by eliminating or accounting for extraneous factors, and where one can repeatedly test the system under study after making limited, controlled changes in it.

There are, of course, circumstances when one cannot isolate the phenomena or when one cannot repeat the measurement over and over again. In such cases the results may depend in part on the history of a situation. This often occurs in social interactions between people. For example, when a lawyer makes arguments in front of a jury in court, she or he cannot try other approaches by repeating the trial over and over again in front of the same jury. In a new trial, the jury composition will be different. Even the same jury hearing a new set of arguments cannot be expected to forget what they heard before.

## Definitions of Research

The strict definition of scientific research is performing a methodical study in order to prove a hypothesis or answer a specific question. Finding a definitive answer is the central goal of any experimental process.

Research must be systematic and follow a series of steps and a rigid standard protocol. These rules are broadly similar but may vary slightly between the different fields of science.

Scientific research must be organized and undergo planning, including performing literature reviews of past research and evaluating what questions need to be answered.

Any type of 'real' research, whether scientific, economic or historical, requires some kind of interpretation and an opinion from the researcher. This opinion is the underlying principle, or question, that establishes the nature and type of experiment.

The scientific definition of research generally states that a variable must be manipulated, although case studies and purely observational science do not always comply with this norm.

We have given below some of the generally accepted definitions of research by well-known authors.

Encyclopedia of social science: "It is the manipulation of things, concepts or symbols for the propose of generalizing and to extend, correct or verify knowledge, whether that knowledge aids in the construction of a theory or in practice of an art."

Francis Rummel: "Research is a careful inquiry or examination to discover new information or relationships and to expand and to verify existing knowledge."

From the above definitions we can simplify the meaning of research:

### *1. It is an Enquiry or Examination Seeking Facts*

To find out the truth a researcher can spend any number of years and may come out with the truth through his findings. Such enquiry or examination must be conducted deeply. No shallow enquiry is called research. Such deep enquiry must probe deep into the problem. Why? How? When? Are some of the questions the researcher must pose to himself in the course of his research.

### 2. *Research Aims at Finding New Truth or Knowledge and/or it Can Confirm the Established Truth or Knowledge*

When Problems occur daily in our life, they provide inspiration to find out new truth. Even the established truths or knowledge or theories can be proved or disproved by research. A truth which was relevant in 18th century may not be relevant to the happenings of today. Hence, it can be disproved.

### 3. *The Purpose of Research is to Find Out Solutions to Problems*

If a researcher does not come out with any solution to the problem under enquiry, it is not research: it is "Pseudo research".

### 4. *Research Involves Use of Accepted Scientific Tools and Statistical Methods*

Before a researcher engages himself into the task of research, he must acquire a fair knowledge of the methods and techniques of research.

## Characteristics of Research

Research being a fact finding inquiry, has certain characteristics of its own. It involves scientific procedures and techniques. As social problems can be studied from various angles, the social research should not depend on a single tool or method of research.

The following are some of the characteristics of research as pointed out by John Best:

i. Research gathers new knowledge or data from primary or first hand sources. It is not research when one merely relates or reorganizes what is already known or what has been written. Research places emphasis upon the discovery of general principles.
ii. Research is expert, systematic and accurate investigation. There is no place for approximations and ambiguities in research.
iii. Research is logical and objective, applying every possible test to verify the data collected and the procedures employed. The researcher constantly strives to eliminate personal feeling and preference.
iv. Research endeavors to gather original data in quantitative terms if possible and to express them as numerical measures. Research is patient and unhurried. The research

is willing to exert painstaking effort, suspending judgment to permit the data and logic to lead to a sound conclusion. He realizes that significant findings do not come as a result of hurried and careless procedures.

v. Research requires courage. The researcher should be willing to follow his procedures that may be unpopular and bring social disapproval.

vi. Research is carefully recorded and reported. Every term is carefully defined, all procedures are described in detail, all limiting factors are recognized, all references are carefully documented and all results are objectively recorded.

### Objectives or Purposes of Research

The objectives or purposes of research are varied. They are:

1. Research extends knowledge of human beings, social life and environment. Scientists and researchers build up the wealth of knowledge through their research findings. They search answers for various types of questions: What, Where, When, How and Why of various phenomena, and enlighten us. The bodies of knowledge have been developed by research in general and pure or fundamental research in particular.
2. Research brings to light information that might never be discovered fully during the ordinary course of life. For example, marketing research could result in discovery of new uses for an old product
3. Research establishes generalizations and general laws and contributes to theory building in various fields of knowledge. Our knowledge of separately known events is connected together to draw generalizations and general laws. Law of gravitation, Law of Demand, and principles of organization such as unity of command and scalar principle, the theory of consumer behaviour and motivation theories are some examples for such generalizations, laws and theories.
4. Research verifies and tests existing facts and theory and these help improving our knowledge and ability to handle situations and events, Merton argues: "Empirical research goes far beyond the passive role of verifying and testing

theory... Research plays an active role, it performs at least four major function ... It initiates, it formulates, it deflects, and it clarifies theory."

5. General laws developed through research may enable us to make reliable prediction of events yet to happen.
6. Research aims to analyze inter-relationships between variables and to derive causal explanations: and thus enables us to have a better understanding of the world in which we live.
7. Applied research aims at finding solutions to problems ... socio-economic problems (e.g., social unrest, unemployment, poverty) heath problems, human relations problems in organization and so on. Thanks to the fruits of research, we have better quality of life, longer life span, better control over events.
8. Research also aims at developing new tools, concepts, and theories for a better study of unknown phenomena.
9. Research aids planning and thus contributes to national development.

## Ethics in Research

Ethics is some sort of morality any one or any business has to meet. The most common way of defining "ethics": norms for conduct that distinguish between acceptable and unacceptable behavior. Another way of defining 'ethics' focuses on the disciplines that study standards of conduct, such as philosophy, theology, law, psychology, or sociology. One may also define ethics as a method, procedure, or perspective for deciding how to act and for analyzing complex problems and issues.

In research it has greater meaning and any researcher has to follow certain accepted norms, rules and regulations from the beginning of conducting the research to the ending of the programme.

There are several reasons why it is important to adhere to ethical norms in research. First, norms promote the aims of research, such as knowledge, truth, and avoidance of error. For example, prohibitions against fabricating, falsifying, or misrepresenting research data promote the truth and avoid error. Second, since research often involves a great deal of cooperation and coordination among many different people in different disciplines and institutions, ethical standards promote the values that are essential to collaborative work, such as trust, accountability, mutual respect, and fairness. For example, many ethical norms in research, such as guidelines for authorship, copyright and patenting policies, data sharing policies, and confidentiality rules in peer review, are designed to protect intellectual property interests while encouraging collaboration. Most researchers want to receive credit for their contributions and do not want to have their ideas stolen or disclosed prematurely. Third, many of the ethical norms help to ensure that researchers can be held accountable to the public Fourth, ethical norms in research also help to build public support for research. People more likely to fund research project if they can trust the quality and integrity of research. Finally, many of the norms of research promote a variety of other important moral and social values, such as social responsibility, human rights, animal welfare, compliance with the law, and health and safety. Ethical lapses in research can significantly harm human and animal subjects, students, and the publicity.

## Ethical Principles to be Followed in Research

### *Honesty*

Strive for honesty in all scientific communications. Honestly report data, results, methods and procedures, and publication status. Do not fabricate, falsify, or misrepresent data. Do not deceive colleagues, granting agencies, or the public.

### *Objectivity*

Strive to avoid bias in experimental design, data analysis, data interpretation, peer review, personnel decisions, grant writing, expert testimony, and other aspects of research where objectivity is expected or required. Avoid or minimize bias or self-deception. Disclose personal or financial interests that may affect research.

### *Integrity*

Keep your promises and agreements; act with sincerity; strive for consistency of thought and action.

### *Carefulness*

Avoid careless errors and negligence; carefully and critically examine your own work and the work of your peers. Keep good records of research activities, such as data collection, research design, and correspondence with agencies or journals.

*Openness*

Share data, results, ideas, tools, resources. Be open to criticism and new ideas.

*Respect for Intellectual Property*

Honor patents, copyrights, and other forms of intellectual property. Do not use unpublished data, methods, or results without permission. Give credit where credit is due. Give proper acknowledgement or credit for all contributions to research. Never plagiarize.

*Confidentiality*

Protect confidential communications, such as papers or grants submitted for publication, personnel records, trade or military secrets, and patient records.

*Responsible Publication*

Publish in order to advance research and scholarship, not to advance just your own career. Avoid wasteful and duplicative publication.

*Responsible Mentoring*

Help to educate, mentor, and advise students. Promote their welfare and allow them to make their own decisions.

*Respect for Colleagues*

Respect your colleagues and treat them fairly.

*Social Responsibility*

Strive to promote social good and prevent or mitigate social harms through research, public education, and advocacy.

*Non-Discrimination*

Avoid discrimination against colleagues or students on the basis of sex, race, ethnicity, or other factors that are not related to their scientific competence and integrity.

### *Competence*

Maintain and improve your own professional competence and expertise through lifelong education and learning; take steps to promote competence in science as a whole.

### *Legality*

Know and obey relevant laws and institutional and governmental policies.

### *Human Subjects Protection*

When conducting research on human subjects, minimize harms and risks and maximize benefits; respect human dignity, privacy, and autonomy; take special precautions with vulnerable populations; and strive to distribute the benefits and burdens of research fairly.

Following are some of the ethical issues to be considered in collecting data from the respondents:

*Informed consent*—In social or business research, we use human beings to collect data in the form of opinions. Their consent must be obtained before collecting data from them. This freedom to participate or to decline, is basic and it includes freedom to withdraw at any time from the participation. One can not compel them to give data or response. Which may lead to exploitation, which is deemed to be an unethical practice.

*Invasion of privacy*—When we collect data relating to the personal behaviour of respondents, their privacy should not be affected. Concealed observers,cameras,microphone etc without the consent or knowledge of the respondents are invasion of privacy.

*Confidentiality*—The ethical researcher holds all information that he or she may gather about the respondents in strict confidence, disguising the participant's identity in all records and research reports. No one should be in a position to threaten the respondent's anonymity nor should any information be released without their permission.

*Knowledge of outcome*—The respondents have a right to receive an explanation about the results or the outcome of the research. The researcher may explain the results and their significance orally or in writing or through publishing them through relevant research journals.

These are "other deviations" or practices which form as

acceptable research practices and include:

- Publishing the same paper in two different journals without telling the editors
- Submitting the same paper to different journals without telling the editors
- Not informing a collaborator of your intent to file a patent in order to make sure that you are the sole inventor
- Including a colleague as an author on a paper in return for a favor even though the colleague did not make a serious contribution to the paper
- Discussing with your colleagues confidential data from a paper that you are reviewing for a journal
- Trimming outliers from a data set without discussing your reasons in paper
- Using an inappropriate statistical technique in order to enhance the significance of your research
- Bypassing the peer review process and announcing your results through a press conference without giving peers adequate information to review your work
- Conducting a review of the literature that fails to acknowledge the contributions of other people in the field or relevant prior work
- Stretching the truth on a grant application in order to convince reviewers that your project will make a significant contribution to the field
- Failing to keep good research records
- Failing to maintain research data for a reasonable period of time
- Making derogatory comments and personal attacks in your review of author's submission
- Not reporting an adverse event in a human research experiment
- Wasting animals in research
- Rejecting a manuscript for publication without even reading it
- Sabotaging someone's work
- Making unauthorized copies of data, papers, or computer programs

### Advantages of Keeping Ethics in Research

Cohen,Manion and Morrison pointed out the following advantages of fashioning a personal code of ethics in research:

1. Such a code establishes one as a member of the wider research community having shared interest in its values and concerns.
2. A code of ethics makes researchers aware of their obligations to their subjects and also to those problem areas where there is general consensus about what is acceptable and what is not. In this sense it has clarifying value.
3. When one's professional behaviour is guided by a principled code of ethics, then it is possible to consider that there may be alternative ways of doing the same thing., ways that are non-ethical of less ethical should be confronted by a moral challenge.
4. A balanced code can be important factor in researcher's perception of the research situation and as such, may assist them in their need to anticipate and prepare.
5. A code of practice validated by their own sense of rightness will help researchers to develop an intuitive sensitivity that will be helpful to them in dealing with the unknown and unexpected.
6. A code of ethics will bring discipline to researcher's awareness. It should be their aim to strike a balance between discipline and awareness.

## Stages of Keeping Ethics in Research

The following are the three stages of keeping ethics by a researcher:

### *Status of Research*

#### *Initiation of Research*

Pursue research maintaining openness to unanticipated results: do not pursue research intended to reach a pre-determined conclusion. Many methods and techniques used in research may be appropriately used to clarify or justify pre-determined positions, but that is not research.

Researchers and sponsors should come to a mutual agreement on the research objectives and data sources at the outset.

Make any sponsor-imposed limitations on the research explicit in the contract prospectively; do not pursue research if the limitations are not acceptable to the researcher.

Sponsors should assume responsibility to promote ethical research standards by setting reasonable objectives and deliverables as well as giving the researcher freedom to analyze the data and report conclusions as the researcher sees fit.

### *Conducting Research*

There should be no fraud or fabrication in research, regardless of the purposes for which the research will be used.

Maintain objectivity in conducting research and analysis; whenever possible, use measures and methods that are widely-accepted and reproducible.

Record the methods and measures of research and analysis, making this information available to legitimate requests, such as confirming or replicating the reported results.

### *Reporting Research*

Authors should be free to report data and results within 2 months (but no longer than 6 months) after the research has concluded; any restrictions on this timing must be disclosed.

Any sponsor-imposed changes in the reporting of results that distort or misrepresent the research findings are unethical and should not be accepted by the researcher.

Differences in opinion between the researcher and the sponsor about the interpretation of data should be appropriately managed; if differences remain after the researcher and sponsor endeavor to agree upon conclusions, differences should be disclosed whenever the data are reported. Further disagreements should be resolved through a peer review-like mechanism consisting of appointments by both parties of people with relevant expertise.

Researchers should endeavor to make their methods transparent and available to peers for replication or confirmation of results.

All reporting of research results should specify who sponsored and financed the research, as well as their role and involvement in the research at any point.

Work originally intended for advocacy or similar purposes (rather than as research) should be identifiable as such.

Researchers must be explicit about their other roles and interests when reporting results and must not conceal the possible limitations of the research.

# 3

# Social Research

Pauline Young: "Social Science Research is a systematic method of exploring, analyzing and conceptualizing social life in order to expand, correct or verify knowledge whether that knowledge aids in the construction of theory or in the practice of an art."

## Meaning and Definition of Social Research

Rummel: "It is devoted to a study of mankind in his social environment and is concerned with improving his understanding of social orders, groups, institutions and ethics."

M.H. Gopal: "It is the scientific analysis of the nature and trends of social phenomena of group or in general, of human behaviour so as to formulate broad principles and scientific concepts."

From the above-accepted definitions the following meaning of social research is derived:

### *i. Social Research is the Study of Man's Behaviour Towards the Society he Lives*

It encompasses the study of social phenomena covering the economic, political, educational, administrative and related aspects of social life, as also the social groups and institution.

### *ii. Social Research Aims at Discovery of New Facts*

The Scientific research techniques are applied to find out truth reasoning of relationships of various kinds of human behaviour.

As P.V. Young aptly puts it, "Research is devoted to discover new facts or verify old facts."

### *iii. Social Research Assists in the Understanding of Evolution of New Theories*

Every research highlights some broad principles, establishes some scientific truths and analyses their sequences, inter-relationship and casual explanations. This results in expansion of knowledge, improvement in the understanding of social phenomena and in the evolution of new theories.

### *iv. Social Research Involves the Use of Scientific Methodology*

"Research also implies the development of new scientific tools, concepts and theories which would facilitate reliable and valid study of human behaviour."

The social research is a process which goes through all these stages of research from sensing a problem till finding solutions and applying them, which are the ingredients of research. Yet it has certain unique methods and logical problems. In social surveys human beings are the sources of data. The attitudes of respondents and their environment, honesty, personal values and biases of the research, will alter research decision considerably.

## Type of Social Research

The Social research may be broadly classified into following three categories:

### *1. Studies Which Aim at Discovery of Facts*

Such fact finding studies aim at an accurate assessment of the conditions prevailing. They are based on the empirically gathered primary data.

### *2. Studies Which Aim at Interpreting the Already Available Information*

They are based on the secondary data. Such studies are more concerned with the scientific interpretation of the data than merely content with presenting the data.

### *3. Theoretical Type of Research*

Such researches are also called pure research. They neither

depend on primary data nor on secondary data. They make contributions to the realms of the theory and add to the existing literature on the subject by way of new interpretation or a different approach to the problem.

### Importance of Social Research

The overall objective of any social research is to find solution to the problems of human society. Naturally, social research is concerned with the study of human society, human organizations and human behaviour. Such problems are broader in nature and fall in the domain of disciplines like Psychology, Sociology, Education, Administration, Commerce etc. The importance of social research as instrument of development has been increasing.

There has been a significant shift in the emphasis on social research due to the following reasons:

1. The desire to bring about more precision in social research methods and techniques, so as to make them more amenable for better scientific treatment and statistical analysis is on the increase.
2. Greater emphasis has been placed on improving the quality of research in its different facts – practical, theoretical and methodological. Such improvement is inevitable to make the research matching to the complex social reality.
3. The need for depth and clarity of the study of social phenomena enhances the role of research as a method of seeking explanations to the unexplained social phenomena.
4. Research has a greater role in proving solutions to immediate problems faced by the community.
5. Research not only helps to evolve new techniques and methods but also standardizes them. Such standardized techniques are capable of reproduction.
6. Social research also aids in formulating normative standards, which are useful in framing socio-economic plans, for comparison and for evaluation of such plans.
7. Knowledge building is an important aspect of humanity. Research makes contributions for the expansion of knowledge horizon, as available knowledge on socio-economic conditions, problems and institutions are very limited.
8. The policy and programme oriented research supports the planners and administrators and aids decision making.

# 4

# Concepts, Proposition and Theory

## Concepts

Concepts are those expressions, which a researcher may use very often in research studies. Again we can say that, a concept is a generally accepted collection of meanings or characteristics associated with certain events, objects, conditions, situations and behaviours. Classifying and categorising objects or events. that have common characteristics beyond any single observation create concepts.

Social science researchers' view that mere dictionary definition of concepts is not useful or it will not serve the purpose. Young points out that, "it was realised that dictionary definitions do not suffice for scientific studies." So the researcher has to give, "working definition" or "operational definition".

### *Sources of Concept*

Concepts that are in frequent usage have been developed over time through shared experience. The following are the sources of concept:

1. *Personal experience:* For experienced researchers and social scientists it is easy to form concepts. Because they come across new observations and new phenomena. They can very easily name such new set of activity.
2. *Continued observation.:* Another way of forming a concept is by means of continued observation. New observations

or new happenings may lead to new behaviour and such things are to be named.

3. *Borrowing from other languages.* A particular language may borrow concepts from other languages. English language has borrowed huge number of concepts from languages like French, Latin, Greek, etc

## 1.2 Characteristics of Concepts

The significance of concepts stems from their ability to transfer information in the form of images about experiences in the empirical world. By means of concepts researchers can transmit their experience to others. Useful concepts represent generalized abstraction regarding empirical phenomena. The usefulness of concepts is evaluated by the extent to which they permit meaningful classification of objects or traits.

Some of the characteristics off the concepts are noted below;

1. Concepts are symbols which we attach to the bundle of meanings that we hold.
2. Concepts represent only one part of reality. That is, we abstract only certain meanings or implications out of the object for our use.
3. Thus different people hold different concepts of the same thing. for example book for a student differs for a publishers merchandise. to the transporter it is a physical object.
4. Concepts also represent various degrees of abstraction. For example, a calculator at first level of abstraction is considered as a mechanical devise, at the higher level it may be considered as one of a class viz, calculators, at the third level it may be considered as an office equipment. Each of these levels of concept abstraction is useful for one purpose or another.

## Uses of Concepts in Research

1. *Problems of research can be expressed:* By using the right concept, we can focus the research problem on the right perspective. The real meaning of a research problem can be expressed by using right concepts.
2. *Avoids repetition and over explanations:* In a research project a problem is to be discussed very often and repeated

reference is to be made. Under such circumstances, by using the right concept we can avoid lot of repetitions, which can save the time of the researcher.

3. *To frame the objectives:* One of the important research activities is to frame objective to the research problem. Framing of objectives is a sensitive task of researcher and he must coin right words to express the correct meaning of the objectives. Here comes the using of relevant concepts
4. *To frame hypothesis:* While framing hypothesis to the research proposal, concepts come to the help of the researcher. The effectiveness of hypothesis is reflected by the usage of appropriate concepts.
5. *To find out relationship between variables:* One of the purposes of the researcher is to find out the relationship between the independent variable and dependent variable. Using the right concepts makes the comparison and correlating process easier.
6. *Basis for communication:* Concepts form the basis for communication for the researcher. The researcher can express his ideas and innovations, easily to the audience by using the relevant and clear concepts.

## Propositions

Concepts are the basic units of theory development. However theories require an understanding of the relationship among concepts. Thus one reality is abstracted into concepts; the researcher is interested in the relationship among various concepts. Propositions are statements concerned with the relationship among concepts. A proposition explains the logical linkage among certain concepts by asserting a universal connection between concepts. A proposition states that every concept about an event or thing either has a certain property or stands in a certain relationship to other concepts about the event or thing.

Propositions have close relationship to theory building. A theory is an abstract from observed reality. Concepts are one level of abstraction. When we think about theories,. we are at the highest level of abstraction because we are investigating the relationship between propositions. Theories of net work of propositions and its verification are the fundamental aspects of research. A hypothesis is a hunch or belief or speculation about the phenomenon. It is based on common sense, theory or empirical facts. Scientific research is mostly understood today as a process of forming hypothesis and checking it by means of observed data. The observed data is found to be inconsistent with the hypothesis, the hypothesis is rejected and if there is an agreement it is accepted. Thus, when a proposition is tested, it reinforces the theory.

# 5

# Hypothesis

Formulation of hypothesis and its verification are the fundamental aspects of research. A hypothesis is a hunch or belief or speculation about the phenomenon. It is based on common sense, theory or empirical facts. Scientific research is mostly understood today as a process of forming hypothesis and checking it by means of observed data. The observed data is found to be inconsistent with the hypothesis, the hypothesis is rejected and if there is an agreement it is accepted. Thus, when a proposition is tested, it reinforces the theory.

## Definition

Goode and Scates: "A hypothesis is a shrewed guess or inference that formulated and provisionally adopted to explain observed facts or conditions and to guide in further investigation."

Walter R. Brog: "Hypotheses reflect the research worker's guess as to the probable outcome of his experiment and they place clear and specific goals before the researcher and provide him with a basis for selecting sample and research procedures to meet these goals."

Rummel: "A Statement capable of being tested and thereby verified or rejected."

Goode and Hatt: "A hypothesis states what we are looking for. What facts are assembled; ordered and seen in a relationship, they constitute a theory. The theory is not speculation, but built upon fact. Now the various facts in a theory may be logically analysed, and relationships other than those stated in the theory can be deduced. At this point there is no knowledge as to whether such deductions are correct. The formation of deduction, however constitutes a hypothesis, if verified it becomes a part of a future theoretical construction."

M.H. Gopal: "It has been defined as a tentative solution posed on a cursory observation of known and available data, and adopted provisionally to explain certain events and to guide in the investigation of others. It is in fact, a possible solution to the problem."

## Functions of Hypothesis

From the above definitions we are able to infer three main functions of hypothesis. They are:

1. To test theories
2. To Suggest theories
3. To describe social phenomena.

### *1. To Test Theories*

The relationship between theory and hypothesis is very close indeed. Theories are based on facts, which if elaborated becomes hypothesis. Theories need to be tested in as a tool of explanation for some events. The theories lend themselves for empirical test only if the facts, proposition and assumptions implied in them are split up into specific hypothesis.

### *2. To Suggest Theories*

Another function of hypothesis is to suggest theories. Theory is derived out of hypothesis an is considered as elaborate hypothesis. In other words hypothesis when refined becomes a theory. Carter V. Good observes that, "There is no sharp line of demarcation between hypothesis and theory, since the basic difference is one of complexity and the extent of testing against the evidence. In its early stages or testing a theory usually has been called as hypothesis checked against the data and their logical implications toward a successful conclusion, it may become known as a theory." Goode & Hatt say that "every worth wile theory permits the formulation of additional hypothesis. These, when tested, are either proved or disproved and in turn constitute further tests of the original theory."

### *3. To Describe Social Phenomena*

When a hypothesis is tested, it explains the phenomenon

associated with it. This phenomenon may be new or not known earlier. Neither a theory nor a hypothesis is involved in such test. Any common sense knowledge or belief is put to empirical test to determine its validity. Hence, new knowledge is gathered. Goode and Hatt observe that, "a hypothesis looks forward. It may prove to be correct or incorrect. On any event the hypothesis is a question put in such a way that answer of some kind can be forthcoming."

## Importance of Hypothesis

In addition to putting the theory to test, a hypothesis has to perform certain other functions. In many ways, it is a guiding point to a research. Young observes that "formulation of the hypothesis gives definite point to the enquiry, aids in establishing direction in which to proceed and helps to delimit the field of inquiry by singling out the pertinent facts on which to concentrate and by determining which facts should be set aside, at least for the time being. The use of hypothesis thus prevents a blind search and indiscriminate gathering of data which may later prove irrelevant to the problem under study." Hence, to collect the needed data hypothesis serves as a forerunner of time and keep the research away from considerable amount of confusion. Prof. Northtrop also views that, the functions of hypothesis is to direct research for finding out order among facts. The suggestions formulated in any hypothesis may be solutions to the problems.

Hypotheses have also certain practical values to society. Besides serving as a means for seeking solution to various social problems, they help in understanding the social phenomena in their proper perspective and refute certain 'common sense' notions about human behaviour.

## Type of Hypotheses

### *1. Descriptive Hypotheses*

These are propositions that describe the characteristics (such as size, form or distribution) of a variable. The variable may be an object, person, organisation, situation or event. Some examples are:

"The rate of unemployment in India is higher than that of USA."

"Public enterprises are more amenable for centralised planning".

### 2. *Relational Hypotheses*

These are propositions which describe the relationship between two variables. The relationship suggested may be positive or negative correlation or causal relationship. Some examples are:

"Families with higher incomes spend more for recreation."

"Upper-class people have fewer children then lower class people."

Causal hypotheses state that the existence of, or a change in, one variable causes or leads to an effect on another variable, and the latter becomes the dependent variable.

### 3. *Working Hypotheses*

While planning the study of a problem, hypotheses are formed. Initially they may not be very specific. In such cases, they are referred to as, 'working hypotheses' which are subject to modification as the investigation proceeds.

### 4. *Null Hypotheses*

These are hypothical statements denying what are explicitly indicated in working hypotheses. They do not, now were ever intended to exist in reality.

They state that no difference exists between the parameter and the statistic being compared to it. For example, even though there is a relationship between a family's income and expenditure on recreation, a null hypothesis may state: "There is no relationship between families income level and expenditure on recreation."

Null hypotheses are more exact. It is easier to reject the contrary of an hypothesis than to confirm it with complete certainty. Hence, the concept of null hypotheses is found to be very useful.

### 5. *Statistical Hypotheses*

These are statements about a statistical population. These are derived from a sample. These are quantitative in nature in that they are numerically measurable, e.g., "Group A is older than Group B"

### 6. *Common Sense Hypotheses*

These represent the common sense ideas. They state the existence of empirical uniformities perceived through day to day observations. Many empirical uniformities may be observed in business establishments, the social background of workers, and the behaviour patterns of specific groups like students, e.g., "shop-assistants in small shops lack motivation.

### *7. Complex Hypotheses*

These aim at testing the existence of logically derived relationships between empirical uniformities. For example, in the early stage human ecology described empirical uniformities in the distribution of land value, industrial concentrations, type of business and other phenomena.

### *8. Analytical Hypotheses*

These are concerned with the relationship of analytic variables. These hypotheses occur at the highest level of abstraction. These specify relationship, between changes in one property and changes in another. For example, the study of human fertility might show empirical regularities by wealth, education, region and religion.

This level of hypothesizing is the most sophisticated mode of formulation and contributes to the development of 'brilliant' abstract theories.

## Characteristics of Hypothesis

Goode & Hatt in their book, "Methods in Social Research", discuss the following characteristics of hypothesis:

### *1. Hypothesis must be Defined Clearly*

The definition should be commonly accepted. Further these definitions should be communicable rather than be the product of a 'private world'.

### *2. Hypothesis Should Have Empirical Reference*

Science concept mush have an ultimate empirical reference. No working hypothesis can embody moral judgements. Such statement as "Criminals are no worse than businessmen" are no more usable or working hypothesis. In other words, while a hypothesis may study value judgements, such a goal must be separated from a moral preachment or plea for acceptance of ones values.

*3. The Hypothesis must be Specific*

The operations and predications indicated by it should be spelt out. The possibility of actually testing the hypothesis can be appraised. Hence, it must be specific in terms of its purpose, clarity and testability. Such specific formulations have the advantage of assuring that research is practical and significant.

*4. Hypothesis Should be Related to Available Techniques*

These are some aspects of the hypothesis which may make its formulation worth while. If the problem is significant enough as a possible frame of reference it may be useful whether or not it can be tested at the time. So a researcher must review the articles on the subject being studied and prepare a list of various techniques used. If one is unable to find any discussion on techniques, it is better to make a research on the necessary techniques.

*5. The Hypothesis Should be Related to a Body of Theory*

Any research must help to refute, quality or support any existing theory or social relation. A science can be cumulative only by building on an existing body of fact and theory. It cannot develop if each study is an isolated survey.

## Origin of Hypothesis

As society grows, cultural patterns continue to change and socio-economic milieu undergoes a constant transformation. Such changes in socio-economic relations, human behaviour, values and attitudes provide ample scope for identification of hypothesis.

*1. The General Culture in Which a Science Develops, Furnishes Many of its Basic Hypothesis*

Cultural values sever to direct research interests. Today's science has developed to a great dimension due to the function of culture. Folk wisdom also serves as another source of hypotheses. For example, in Western society race is through to be an important determinant of human behaviour. This can be used to frame hypotheses.

*2. Hypotheses Originate in the Science Itself*

Scientists continuously discuss current research and through it, important areas for further research are located. Through this interaction modes of thought, concepts and problems develop. These in turn suggest further hypotheses.

### *3. Analogies are Often a Source of Useful Hypotheses*

The success of a system in one discipline can be used in other discipline also. The hypotheses that resulted in the development of human ecology, for example, were an application of established theory in the field of plant and animal ecology.

### *4. Hypotheses are also the Consequence of Personal, Idiosyncratic Experience*

Not only do culture, science and analogy attract the formulation of hypotheses but also the way in which the individual reacts to each of these is also a factor in the statement of hypotheses. Therefore, the individual experience of the scientists contributes to the hypotheses.

## Testing of Hypothesis

A knowledge or a fact could be accepted only when it has validity. The validity of such knowledge could be accepted only when it is tested with regard to its usefulness or truth. Hence, to accept hypotheses, which are merely hunches or guesses, as facts, they are to be tested. Testing hypotheses means subjecting them to some sort of empirical scrutiny to determine if they are supported or refuted by what the researcher observes.

Robert Bales states that the following questions should be asked about hypotheses before they are tested:

1. Are the terms, empirically specific, so that the concepts or variables can be distinguished in concrete situations?
2. Is the relationship between variables such that it could be verified or nullified by means of empirical operations?
3. Is there any prior evidence as to the truth or falseness of the relationship?
4. Can an appropriate study design be devised?
5. Are the variables context-bound (e.g., restricted to play group or gang) or could they be equally well applied to other interaction situations (e.g., work group or family)?
6. Are the generalizations 'culture-bound' or can they be also applied realistically to other cultures?

7. If other relevant factors or subject to change in the course of the observations, are they adequately specified and enumerated, so that the observer can ascertain whether, they have changed during the period of observation?
8. Is the generalisation a part of the theoretical system from which it could be deducted as well as being verified by the proposed empirical induction?
9. Is the empirical system that is constructed sufficiently precise and articulates to permit predictions in concrete situations?

Black and Champion, in their book, "Methods and Issues in social Research," specify two prerequisites to test hypotheses which are given below:

1. A real social situation is needed that will suffice as a reasonable testing ground for the hypotheses.
2. The investigator should be make sure that the hypotheses are testable.

After these conditions are fulfilled the researcher collects data, processes them and based on these findings he has to support or refute the hypotheses. Unbiased judgement and professional ethics are the guiding principles to avoid subjectivity.

### Problems in Formulating Hypotheses

A researcher has to come across several problems in formulating hypotheses. It is as difficult as finding out a research problem or identifying a suitable theory. The following are some of the difficulties in formulating hypotheses as pointed out by Goode and Hatt in their book, "Methods in Social Research".

1. Absence of a theoretical framework.
2. Lack of ability to utilize that theoretical frame work logically.
3. Failure to acquaint with available research techniques so as to aboe to phrase the hypotheses properly.

The researcher must bear in mind that he has to formulate a good, definite, and testable hypothesis. At the beginning stage, when one is not familiar with various processes of research, the formulation of a sound hypothesis would be somewhat difficult. He may frame some formulations, and can say that they are hypotheses. But they may not have the testability.

### *Is Hypothesis Necessary?*

This is a controversial issue; and there is no categorical opinion on this. Hypotheses give purpose and direction to the research. One of the main objectives of hypothesis is to test a theory as well as to formulate a theory. When we have adequate theory in a science the need to formulate a hypothesis is sometimes questioned. M.H. Gopal in his book, "An introduction to Research Procedure in Social Sciences" says that while hypothesis is useful it is not always indispensable. In physical sciences which are very highly developed, the hypothesis is most often necessary. In social sciences, research may be conducted without formulating hypotheses. Only in certain types of studies hypotheses are needed. P.V. Young also holds the same view.

# 6

# Theory

A theory is set of propositions which can be tested. In other words it 'is a coherent set of hypotheses'. When a set of hypotheses is accepted after testing its truthfulness, the next stage of its growth is theory.

A theory is again to be proved or disproved. Pauline Young defined the nature of a theory as, "it is the gradual outgrowth of constructive study of the accumulated sorted facts, empirically verified over a period of time, until consistent generalizations or logical principles can be formulated."

## Purpose of Theory

Theory building is a part of social research and social scientists have laboured hard through centuries to build theories in various social sciences. As the very purpose of social research is to study human behaviour, it also becomes the very purpose of theory. Theory should not only study the human behaviour but also it must explain the relationship between various variables. Theory must also serve to predict the behaviour of human beings, and explain the courses. The explanation may be in the form of statements. Human behaviour and their inter-relationship of a set circumstance may vary to other and a theory can help to compare places and circumstances.

## Role of Theory

Theory has a greater role to play in society. For social scientists and social researchers it is of immense value and it gives an orientation to them. A researcher who has grip over theories of his field can formulate hypothesis easily and he can proceed his research in order and smoothly. Goode and Hatt explain the role of theory as follows:

### *1. Theory as Orientation*

These veterans feel that theory, 'narrows the range of facts to be studied'. Any phenomenon, or problem can be studied in different ways. What in needed and what is not needed can be oriented properly by theory. Beating round the bush can be avoided. "Each science and each specialization with a broader field abstracts from reality, keeping its attention upon a few aspects of given phenomena rather than upon all aspects. Only thus can the work of science be reduced to manageability. The board orientation of each field, then "focuses upon a limited range of things while ignoring or making assumptions about others."

### *2. Theory as Conceptualization and Classification*

Terms and concepts that are commonly used must be defined properly in order to understand their range, depth, implication and connotations. This is called as conceptualisation and classification. Theory helps the researcher to define them and classify them properly. Every science is organised by a structure of concepts, which refer to the major processes and objects to be studied. It is the relationships between these concepts which are stated in 'the facts of science'. Such terms make up the specialised vocabulary that the scientist uses normally. It is clear that if knowledge is to be orgained, there must be some systems imposed upon the facts which are observable. As a consequence, a major task in any science is the development of systems of classification, a structure of concepts, and an increasingly precise set of definitions for these terms.

### *3. The Task of Summarising*

Another important role of theory is to summarise what is already known about the object of study. Summarising of facts is necessary to arrive at generalisations and to find out relationships between variables.

### *4. Theory Predicts Facts*

If theory summarises facts and states a general uniformity beyond the immediate observations, it also becomes a prediction of facts'. By predicting facts through theory, it acts as guideline for the researcher to collect data and to shape his research.

### *5. Theory Points to Gaps in our Knowledge*

Like predicting the facts, theory identifies the gaps that has been left by others or in the particular area of research. One of purposes of researcher is to find the gap in the particular area of research and theory comes to the help of the researcher in identifying the gap in particular research areas.

## How are Theories Generated?

There two methods through which theory can be built. The first method is deductive reasoning At the abstract conceptual level theory can be developed with deductive reasoning by going from a general statement to specific assertion. Deductive reasoning is the logical process of deriving a conclusion about a specific instance based on known general premise or something known to be true. Foe example, we know that all managers are human beings. If we also know that A is manager, then we can deduce that A is a human being.

Inductive reasoning is the logical process of establishing a general proposition on the basis of observation of particular facts. All managers that have ever been seen are human beings, therefore all managers are human beings.

Over the course of time, theory construction is often the result of a combination of deductive and inductive reasoning. Our experiences lead us to draw conclusions that we are trying to verify empirically by using the scientific method.

## Utility of Theory in Research

Theory helps the researcher in the following ways:

1. Theory suggests problems for the researchers. Before venturing into the research work, the primary duty of a researcher is to go through all the relevant theories relating to the particular field of research. This process helps the researcher to identify problems of research.

2. Theory helps to test hypothesis. One of the means of testing a hypothesis is to subject it to the verification of the relevant theory.
3. Theory provides a conceptual model for delimiting the scope of the study.
4. Theory helps the selection of variables. In a research problem there are two variables available to the researcher, namely, independent variable and dependent variable. Theory is useful to identify the right type of variables needed for the research problem.

However there are certain general principles, regarding the use of theory in research. They are:

A. A knowledge of the existing theories in one's area of research. One should be familiar with all the theories available in the field.
B. Concepts are the crucial components of theory and their clear definition and operationalisation are essential to the designing of the study.
C. A complete understanding of the relevant hypotheses, relating to the field of study is also a precondition for the usage of theory.

## Contribution of Research to Theory

The relationship between theory and research is mutual and interdependent. The research work already done in the specific areas help develop theories. Other aspects of the role of research in theory building are as follows:

1. *Research initiates theory:* Many of the findings of a research work may lead to the formulation of theories. Research in social sciences led to the contribution of lot of theories in relevant areas of study. Theories like leadership, motivation, organization etc are the outcome of number of research undertaken in these fields.
2. *Reformulation of an existing theory:* Any theory developed by researchers is subject to verifications and changes. Successive researchers have challenged the past theories and the existing theories and changes have been introduced.
3. *Research tests an existing theory:* One major function of empirical research is to test the hypothesis deduced from

existing theories. If a hypothesis is not proved by research, the theory from which the hypothesis is deduced is reexamined and tested.

4. *Research refocuses theory:* Empirical research may give a new focus to the existing theory. When the process of proving and disproving a theory goes as a continuous process, refocusing the old theory becomes inevitable.

# 7

# Organizational Features of Cooperatives and Need for Research in Co-Operatives

## Organizational Features of Cooperatives

1. *Cooperatives are associations of human beings:* Cooperatives are formed by members to solve their economic problems. In that process they have to mobilize capital. It is subordinated to human interests. Capital is not allowed to dominate in cooperatives over human beings.
2. *Democracy in cooperatives:* Cooperative management strictly follows the principles of democracy. All are equal here and 'one man one vote' principle is followed. No single individual is allowed to dominate, by virtue of large number of shares held by him.
3. *Service motive:* Service is the motive and not profit in cooperatives. In doing such service, efficiency is emphasized in cooperative management. P.R. Dubhashi, has viewed that "the principle of efficiency is vital in cooperative management. But in so far as the market mechanism of private enterprise, turns the principle of maximum efficiency into maximum profit, it becomes in compatible with the cooperative management and needs modification".
4. *Equality:* Equality is practiced in cooperative management.

All members are given equal opportunity to enjoy the benefits of cooperative and they can exercise equal control without any narrow rise to the level of the president of a National Federation through his leadership.

5. *Application of principles of cooperation:* Cooperatives have to first follow the principles of cooperation laid down by ICA, then they have to go for applying the management process. It has to keep a balance between these two. Weeraman States that "the proper application of cooperative principle is necessary for the success of the movement, for cooperative principles are those which are essential, that is absolutely indispensable to the achievement of cooperatives movements role".
6. *Different aims system:* Cooperatives have to satisfy the aims of different people composed under its management. They are members, office bearers, personnel and government, so it has to harmonize the interest of these complex aims system and to maintain a balance.
7. *The Control Process:* In cooperatives, the members are users and owners. Varied interests of members must be bet with at most efficiency. In that process cooperatives should not loose their control over factors of production. Prof. Laidlaw, stresses that, "it is a business organization in which the components of ownership – use – control are integrated by being all vested in one body of people, the members".
8. *Cooperative management is governed by cooperative legislation:* The cooperative societies Act of respective states directly and indirectly control the management of cooperatives. The Registrar of cooperative societies is assigned with enormous powers to interfere in the management of cooperative institutions.
9. *Integrating government policies:* In countries like India cooperative movement had its origin with initiative of government. In the Planning process, specific roles have been assigned to the cooperatives. Here the cooperatives have to sacrifice some of their autonomy and freedom.
10. State (government) interference is quite common in the management of cooperatives in countries like India. Boards are very often dissolved to suit the political convenience of ruling parties.

11. *Cooperatives strive to introduce professional management in their administration:* In that process they have to face so many hurdles and interferences. Without minding that large sized cooperatives and processing cooperatives go a head with professional management.
12. Tools and techniques of management applied by cooperatives vary from society-to society- primary cooperative societies, with smaller area of operation and smaller area of transactions offered to use only elementary tools whereas bigger cooperatives use latest and sophisticated techniques of management.
13. *It is an art as well a science:* It is an art as it effects changes or accomplishes goals by deliberate efforts. It is a science as cooperative management strives to acquire body of knowledge through observation, speculation and forecasts, which are capable of verification.
14. *Practice of cooperative management is based on knowledge and responsibility:* Entire gamut of management technique are applied under various situations to get things done, at lesser cost and at the cost of giving enough training and experience to the people concerned.
15. *Cooperative management involves group effect at all levels:* It combines the efforts of all individuals and bodies (Board, general body, etc.) at every stage of activity. At the culmination, the Board and executive sit together to discharge responsibilities.
16. *Economic liberalization:* Last decade saw the liberalization of the economy world over. The implication was that, private sector has been given a free hand. Till recently, cooperatives have been enjoying lot of privileges from government and they have to loose such privileges in during course. Cooperatives have to adjust themselves to the changing economic climate.
17. *Competition:* Cooperatives are given thorough competition by private and public sector organizations. They have to improve their operational efficiency by means of using modern management techniques. Otherwise they cannot survive in the competition.

## Need for Research in Co-Operatives

In all economics, co-operatives occupy a significant place. Lot of money has been invested in co-operatives. Co-operative have touched all types of economic activities. Research is needed to improve their performance, viability, efficiency and customer attraction. Other aspects are as follows:

### 1. *Co-Operation is an Academic Discipline*

In addition to being an economic organization, co-operatives have become an academic discipline. All universities, institutes, and educational bodies are teaching co-operation, as a subject of higher learning Teaching should go with Research Teaching and research are inseparable.

### 2. *Co-Operation is a Latest Social Science*

There are various social science like history, economics, commerce, management, sociology, etc., that study human behaviour. Cooperation has become one of the latest social sciences. It needs theory building to develop it as a full-fledged social science. Lot of research is to be undertaken in the field of co-operation for this purpose.

### 3. *To Study the Growth of the Movement*

World co-operative movement is nearly 160 years old and in India its is nearing a century. As a movement, it has past history, present and future performances. They face day to day problems and problems of long term nature. Research on co-operation is needed to make it a prosperous movement.

### 4. *To Build Theories*

Theories are basis for any science. Advancement of knowledge is possible by means of building theories. Co-operatives lack theories. Present Theories are related to other social sciences like economics and management. Hence to build Theories research alone can help.

### 5. *To Solve Problems*

As economic organizations, co-operatives face lot of problems relating to organization, management, operations, etc., There are various ways of solving problems. But solving problems through research is more scientific and reliable. Hence, research in needed for co-operatives.

### *6. To Study Human Behaviour*

Co-operation is also a behavioral science. Studying of human behaviour in co-operatives occupy a strategic place. Because co-operative are dealing with members, leaders, customers and officials. Study of the behaviour pattern of these people is needed to contribute each one's efforts to the success of their co-operatives. Research methods like case studies can do good role here.

### *7. To Identify Variables of Problems*

A problem is surrounded by various variables. Social research has two types of variables namely independent variables and dependent variables. Association between these variables should be identified to solve the problem. Research will help to identify variables associated with problem.

### *8. To Organize New Co-Operatives*

New co-operatives are organized by members very often. Before organizing a new co-operative, its viability, survival scope, future, etc., must be viewed carefully. By means of undertaking research studies like feasibility studies, we can assure their success.

### *9. To Evaluate Successful and Failed Co-Operatives*

In the field of co-operation successful co-operatives as well as dormant societies exist. Research is needed on both types of co-operatives. Research on successful co-operatives can help to find out the factors for success and that can be emulated by other co-operatives. Like wise, by studying the dormant or failed societies, causes for their failure could be ascertained and solutions could also be found to revive them.

### *10. Forecasting*

Co-operatives have to forecast their future, demand, uncertainties, decision-making, etc., Forecasting is needed to face competition, problems and future. Social research has lot of forecasting techniques that can be applied to co-operatives.

### *11. Sales Management*

All producers co-operatives and distribution co-operatives need to concentrate on this area to improve their sales turnover and customer attraction. Methods like marketing Research can be helpful to the co-operatives in this context.

### *12. For Expansion*

Co-operatives have to expand their business operations to serve more customers, to increase viability and to face competition. They may go for opening new offices and branches. Research can predict the success of such branches.

### *13. Performance Evaluation*

Co-operatives need to evaluate their performance once in few years. Such evaluation is needed to measures their strength and weakness. For such stock taking, research has immense use to co-operatives.

### *14. Customer Attraction Measures*

Co-operatives are members and users Organizations. Research, is needed to improve their performance, image and to add new customers.

### *15. To Build Models*

Model building is an exercise, through which one successful effort can be followed by others. This warrants the application of management and statistical tools. Research can help the co-operatives to build new models.

# 8

# Classification of Research—Pure and Applied

Social research has been classified in several ways depending on the purpose for which it is undertaken, the extent to which it satisfies the scientific procedures or the method of collection of data, the control factor involved and the purpose of research. There is no hard and fast rule in the classification. It is more for the sake of promoting better understanding or for the sake of convenience. The classifications are not mutually exclusive and often overlap. There are several ways of classification of research on the basis of field, purpose, place, method of data collection, application and control factor.

## METHODS OF RESEARCH

The common way of classifying social research is on the basis of the purpose for which it is conducted, or its application value. Four major types of Research namely, Pure Research, Applied Research, Action Research and Evaluation Research fall under this category.

### Various Types or Methods of Research—Why?

As knowledge is expanding new problems are confronted by researchers, presuming that old problems have been settled or solutions have been found for old problems. Fresh problems may start from old problems or a fresh or due to the proliferation of knowledge. Mankind has to answer questions that are raised very often and such answers must be in the form of solutions. A problem can be attacked from many angles and many researchers may try to find a solution to a single problem when it becomes a daring necessity.

Having one method of research we cannot study all social problems. Hence:

1. Various methods of research in social science is needed to study and find solutions to various social problems which may have various dimensions.
2. When society grows or changes, problems are ought to arise very often. Such problems may be new one or old one. We need different yardsticks to measure such problems.
3. Having one method or type of research we cannot study a social problem relating to a past as well as present. Likewise having one method of research one cannot study a problem relating to the present and future.
4. Hence, we have different types of social research to study social problems relating to the past, present and future.
5. In sciences other than social sciences we can accurately predict the future. But in social science research prediction or forecasting is little difficult as this field of research deals with human behavior, which is unpredicted and not constant. Even this difficulty is overcome now by means of introducing new tools in social research.

## Pure Research

Pure research or fundamental research is the research that is understood in its most original and formal sense. It draws its pattern and spirit from physical sciences and has represented a rigorous structured type of analysis. Gathering knowledge for knowledge sake is termed as pure or basic research. Many scientific inventions such as invention of steam engine or invention of electricity fall under this category. Several economic theories like consumers' surplus, indifference curve analysis also belong to this category

### *Aims of Pure Research*

Goode and Hatt list the following aims of Pure Research:

1. By developing general principles, theory offers solutions to many practical problems.
2. Pure research helps to find the central factors in a practical problem.
3. Research as an answer to problems may become a standard procedure for the administrator.
4. Theoretical research develops many alternative solutions, with the result that alternative costs may be weighed and ultimately reduced.

### *Features of Pure Research*

*1. General Principles*

General principles are the quintessence of knowledge and forms the basis or foundation for nay field of knowledge for nay field of knowledge. Without framing general principles a discipline or knowledge cannot be expended or elaborated, Principles are also the basic yardsticks to measure the growth of knowledge in a particular field. General principles are core to pure research.

*2. Central Factors*

Any social or economic or cultural problem would be surrounded by certain key problems. Pure research helps to locate such key factors.

*3. Standard Procedure*

By building new theories solutions to problems become a standardized one. "Pure research may have an effect upon the pattern of administrative procedure, as the practitioner learns of its utility. This development has not been a common one, but both government and business organizations have begun to utilize 'research and planning units' to evaluate the techniques which have been applied in the past and to develop new solutions to old as well as new problems.

*4. Alternative Solutions and Cost*

In the initial stage the cost on pure research may look heavy, but in the long run the benefits will neutralize the cost. . Consequently, after a time there are many solutions for a given type of problem, with different main and subsidiary consequences. We are thus permitted to choose the best solution for our practical problem."

## Applied Research

The applied research is a development aid and is directed towards the development of human society. It is need based and aims at solving immediate problems. It is completed in a short span of time. Its findings are evaluated on the basis of local applicability, not in terms of universal validity. It is empirical and man-centered.

Stouffer in his study on "After thoughts of a contributor to the American Soldier." Points out the contributions of applied research to social science:

1. By providing the kind of convincing evidence of the usefulness to society, which is necessary to continuing support.
2. By utilizing and developing techniques which can also be made to serve the so-called basic research.
3. By providing data and idea which may speed up the process of generalisation.

### *Aims of Applied Research*

*1. Applied Research Can Contribute New Facts*

New facts may come out with the result of new works undertaken by scientists. "New facts may lead to the initiation, rejection and reformulation of theory or to its clarification and redefinition."

*2. Applied Research Can Put Theory to the Test*

Applied research offers an opportunity to test the validity of existing theory. It attempts the diagnosis of a situation and a solution."

*3. Applied Research may Aid in Conceptual Clarification*

Often concepts have become unclear and need clarification. Different interpretation by different people leads to confusion. Applied research can help to clarity concepts. "A concept exhibits its vagueness most sharply when we begin to define the procedures and operations for dealing with it in research."

*4. Applied Research May Integrate Previously Existing Theory*

The solution to a problem may require integration of many

theoretical as well as applied investigations in several fields. Applied research can easily integrate theories.

**Difference Between Pure Research and Applied Research**

| *Pure Research* | *Applied Research* |
|---|---|
| 1. It is undertaken primarily for gathering knowledge; and is based on the assumption that all knowledge is potentially useful. | It is utilitarian and is primarily undertaken for the betterment of humanity. Knowledge is applied to concrete problem. |
| 2. The sphere of activity of pure research is wide. It is broad based and more abstract in nature. | Applied research is confined to narrow fields and is more specific in nature. |
| 3. It involves long-term. Protracted and time-consuming process. | It is short-term, time bound and result oriented. |
| 4. It involves huge financial out lay. | The financial outlay is relatively limited. |
| 5. It aims at understanding the social phenomenon i.e., diagnostic. | It aims at finding solution to social problems i.e., therapeutic. |
| 6. Pure research takes up problems understood by scientists i.e., it is scholastic and elitist in nature. | Problems understood by common people are the subject matter of applied research. |
| 7. Pure research is based on theoretical abstractions and speculations. | It is based on practical application and empirical method. |
| 8. Pure research aims at developing theories by discovering broad generalization or principles. | Applied research is need based and is applied to immediate problem solving effort i.e., ameliorative. |

Here below find good discussion on various types of research, which are brought under either Pure research or Applied research:

### *(i) Problem Oriented Research*

One of the classifications of social research is 'problem oriented research.' Any research is problem oriented. A researcher can come across problems during the course of his research or he can seek the very problems for the sake of it. In such research the duty of the researcher would be to devote more of his attention towards magnifying the problem rather than finding solution to such problem. One can find problems from an issue or from a phenomenon or from a happening. Culling out the crux of the issues, which are amenable for research itself is a take and forms part of finding a problem. All problems cannot be considered to be research problems or all problems will not have the properties of a problem. In other words any social problem worth studying must have 'viability'. It should enthuse the researcher to kindle his originality and must create a 'curiosity about unknown'. The problem must also be pragmatic and must have 'social relevance'. It should not stop with satisfying the ego of the researcher. The problem must also lead him to come out with pragmatic solutions.

A problem can be called as a research problem only when it satisfies the following conditions:

1. The problem must have viability of potentiality to stand as a research problem. It should satisfy the norms of scientific inquiry.
2. The problem must have social relevance. The study should be useful to the society and must draw the attention off all concerned.
3. As far as possible a research problem must be 'virgin' in nature and must not be touched by others. So the researcher must find out the gap in his area of research.
4. There must be 'felt need' for research over the problem. Such problem must be in need of further elaboration and exploration. A compelling situation must arise to study a problem.
5. A research problem must come out with pragmatic solutions to the issues. The user of the problem must be many.
6. A social research problem must be up-to-date or relevant to the current social happenings.

While selecting a 'problem oriented research' the researcher can consult experts of the field, policy makers and researchers who are doing research already in the field. Duplication of work must be avoided.

### *(ii) Performance Evaluation Studies*

Such type of research studies are the outcome of our planned economic development. After the Second World War, Governments have started vying with each other in proclaiming themselves as welfare Governments. Such Welfare Governments have started spending more money for public welfare and economic development. Expenditures. As huge money is spent on public welfare, it has become necessary to evaluate the benefits of such expenditures. According to Baker, "the purpose of evaluation research is to evaluate some social activity, which has been set up to address and ameliorate a social problem." The objectives of performance evaluation studies are:

1. To know whether the money is spent as per the guidelines laid down.
2. To know whether the priority in outlay has been given to the pressing socio-economic problems.
3. In the case of industrial and agricultural outlays, whether importance is given to lay down the infrastructure development, thereby in the long run the country should attain self sufficient in basic needs.
4. In the case of technology development, whether we can match the speed of advanced countries and keep up the tempo of growth continuously.
5. To evaluate each programmes and to verify whether the programmes have benefited for whom they have been introduced.
6. To find out the pitfalls that come across in implementing programmes.
7. Whether the schemes have been implemented through the course laid down or any deviation occurred?

**Areas of Performance Evaluation Studies**

Performance Evaluation studies are conducted on the following socio-economic areas:

***1. Field of Agriculture***

Agriculture being the primary sector of our economy, it is necessary to see that it is contributing its share to the national wealth and income. We have to verify whether agriculture is doing justice to its dependents by way of increasing their income. It is also necessary to verify whether the input industry is set on the right lines and farmers are able to get needed inputs like seeds, fertilizers, pesticides and machineries for the right price.

***2. Field Of Industry***

Industry being the prime mover of the economy must solve economic problems like unemployment, scarcity of goods, earning of foreign exchange problems like unemployment, scarcity of goods, etc. Evaluation is needed on the above fields and based on the evaluation studies remedial measures must by suggested to solve the problem faced by industries.

*3. Poverty Alleviations Schemes*

Government have introduced various poverty alleviation schemes at State and Central levels. Such schemes are subsidized by the tax payers money. Hence, it is necessary to evaluate the efficiency of such schemes and to ascertain whether the benefits have reached the right people. IRDP and PDS are such programmes which need continuous evaluation and monitoring.

*4. Welfare Schemes*

Welfare schemes like health, sanitation, housing, environmental protection, etc., have occupied important place in the public expenditure of developed as well as developing countries. Evaluation studies are needed to increase the quality and quantity of such schemes to all citizens.

*5. Educational Schemes*

Countries like ours have invested heavily on education from primary level to universities level. Education is made compulsory to all citizens and is made free upto a level. Such costs are borne by the state and expenditure made on various heads must be evaluated to know whether we are also to remove illiteracy, whether depressed sections have been access to professional education, whether the type of education that we impart is relevant to the society and whether we are keeping pace with the advanced countries in improving the quality of our education.

**Type of Evaluation Studies**

There are three types of evaluation studies:

*1. Periodic Evaluation*

This evaluation is undertaken giving an interval say one year, two years or five years. As prescribed gap is allowed we can detect deviations or loopholes and can rectify them in the next evaluation.

*2. Concurrent Evaluation*

Such studies are a continuous process and are akin to social audit. Mistakes or deviations can be found out and feedback could be provided to correct deviations.

*3. Terminal Evaluation*

Such studies are undertaken after a project or scheme is over. There is little scope to correct deviations under such studies. But such studies would be useful when new schemes are launched.

Baker (Doing social research) gives four types of Evaluation Research:

(i) *On going Programme Evaluation:* This is undertaken simultaneously when the programme is going on.
(ii) *Cost Benefit Analysis:* This seeks to assess whether the benefit of a programme or social strategy is worth its cost.
(iii) *Community Impact Assessment:* This is to find out the effect of a new policy on the community.
(iv) *Time-Series Analysis:* Evaluating a programme after every particular interval.

**(iii) Impact Studies**

Impact studies are those studies which are undertaken to study the positive or negative results of certain variables. The effect of adding a variable or the effect of eliminating a variable is studied. Impact studies are also undertaken to find out the results or effects of a scheme before it was introduced and after it was introduced. It is also undertaken to know the position before and after a particular period of year.

***Variables and Impact***

Studying of one type of variable or the other is a social process and research studies can point out the type of impact or the level of impact. In social research two types of variables are available for researchers, namely independent variables and dependent variables.

Independent variables cause effect or impact over dependent variable. One or more independent variable can cause effect on a dependent variable. Age, income, size or the family, size of land holdings, etc. are independent variables. Phenomena like savings, expenditure, borrowings, repayment etc., are dependent variables. Usually one dependent variable is caused or effected by one or more independent variables.

*Impact 'Before' and 'After' a Scheme*

Second type of impact studies are undertaken while a scheme is introduced. When a scheme is introduced the socio-economic conditions that prevailed before the introduction of the scheme were measured, quantified and noted with statistical details. After the introduction of the scheme due gap is given say two years, five years or ten years. Then again the socio-economic changes are measure as to know whether the scheme has produced any results positive or negative. To improve the living conditions of weaker sections many schemes are introduced. Through impact studies we can know the benefits of such schemes on such groups.

*Impact Over a Period*

By choosing a particular year as 'Base Year' we can study the impact of schemes before and after that period. Socio-economic developments are studied before and after our independence.

**Uses of Impact Studies**

Impact studies have the following uses:

1. For planners and policy makers such studies help to understand the effects of specific programmes implemented.
2. Through such studies we can identify the factors which contributed to the success of a scheme or which have not contributed anything or which have negatively contributed to the growth.
3. When a new product is introduced in the market, impact of it on other products or existing products could be studied and later a safer passage could be introduced.
4. If a company wants to increase its market share, it can be done so through the results of impact studies.

*(iv) Action Research*

Action research or policy research, as it is sometimes called, is a type of applied research. There is thin line of difference between the two. Through several authors consider both these types of research as one and the same. Social scientists have differentiated action research from the larger field of applied research. Action research aims at contributing to the practical concerns of the people in an immediate problematic situation. It not only experienced by the community as unsatisfactory. Another significant feature of action research is that it is frequently carried out on the request of a client organisation that hopes to solve some problem. The action research is carried out in the setting of a functional organisation. As against the 'neutral' and 'objective' elements of classical research, action research is less elitist and provides for intervention, and participation to bring about certain desired changes.

There is close collaboration between the sponsoring organsiation and the research agency. The organisation, sponsoring the research to some extent participate in planning and carrying out the research. In the action research the theory is not only tested and applied in a given set of conditions, it is also modified according to the local prevailing conditions. It adopts to the local prevailing conditions and change that takes place in the community. The action research makes full use of the available materials on fundamental and applied research and helps in testing the hypothesis in the varying field situations as well as formulation of new hypothesis.

## Definition and Meaning of Action Research

Stephen M. Corey of Columbia University, an authority of this subject defines Action Research as "an attempt to get the scientific approach to practical problems used at the grass root level".

Action Research is a type of evaluation study. It is launched to solve a problem or for improving the existing situation.

### *Features of Action Research*

1. It is nothing but bringing a trained mind on the solution of problems in our day to day life situations.
2. It can be applied to a variety of situations such as class room teaching, management, social work, extension work etc.
3. It enables one to think better to identify problems and analyse the reasons for them and to solve them.
4. Action research seeks to bridge to gap between theory and practice, knowledge and behaviour.
5. It is more effective and easy to administer.
6. It is less elitist and provides for intervention and participation.

7. It makes full use of the available materials on pure and applied research and helps in testing hypothesis in the varying field situations as well as formulation of new hypothesis.

*Objectives of Action Research*

1. To find immediate solutions to problems by being pragmatic in approach.
2. To discover new facts by altering certain conditions based on practical experience.
3. To test a theory and if possible to modify it according to local conditions.

## Starting Point of Action Research

Unlike other methods of research, availability of time is a constraint for Action Research. The researcher has very less time at his disposal. Hence, he is in a position to give a quick start to his work. But at the same time he must be cautious in the quality of wok and outcome of his research. Hence, he must make a cautious and at the same time purposeful starting.

'Self Questioning' and resultant 'Genuine Discontent' is the starting point of actions research. Smug self-satisfaction is a sure sign of stagnation and stunted growth. On the other hand 'self dissatisfaction' based on the learning desire for self improvement is a most valuable attitude and guide. In the words of Peter Drucker, such genuine discontent is "the most real expression of pride in job and work, and of responsibility". Responsibility, not smug satisfaction, is the only thing that will serve. To perform one has to be dissatisfied, to want to do better. To perform one has to take responsibility for one's own actions and their impact. Action research serves this objective of peak performance eminently well.

## Action Research Design

Action Research has the following steps:

1. The first step is to identify the problem area.
2. The second step is to pinpoint a problem.
3. The third step is to identify the problem causes or the problem. This is known as 'Problem Analysis', and much importance is attached to this step in Action Research.
4. The fourth step is Action Hypothesis. It must be related

to Action Research which the researcher wants to take. It should be based on central not peripheral causes. One must be specific about what one want to do and be clear about what might happen.

5. The fifth step is framing Action Research Design. This consists of (a) Base line data (b) Sources of data, (c) Tools for data and (d) Action Programme and Time chart.
6. The sixth step is the periodic assessment of Action Research project.
7. The last step is the Evaluation of the project. This is a very important stage and Action Research studies the following questions as proposed by Proscot Hinkle:
   - (i) What is it that has charged?
   - (ii) How much has it changed (extent)?
   - (iii) How quickly has it changed (rate)?
   - (iv) What where the conditions before and after the change?
   - (v) What occurred during the transition?
   - (vi) What was the stimuli that induced change?
   - (vii) Through what mechanisms did change occur?
   - (viii) What brought stabilization at a particular point in change?
   - (ix) Can directionality be observed in the change?

These questions indicated the problem areas which can be the focus of evaluation. These areas are:

- (a) Impact of the programme on intended recipients.
- (b) Extent of the programme's effect on the intended receipients.
- (c) Time involved in bringing about the impact of effects.
- (d) Before-after measures of the variables which are supposed to undergo change.
- (e) Indentification of the events and processes that took place between the before-and after-measures.
- (f) Analysis of the subject-matter or content of the programme.
- (g) Organisational, structural and operational aspects of the programme.
- (h) Factors in the change introduced.
- (i) Direction of the changes observed relative to the objectives of the programme.

## Criteria for Action Research

The common criteria for a good Action Research Design could be:

(a) It must be sufficiently specific so as to enable him to take action immediately.
(b) It must be such that it could be completed within a couple of months.
(c) If must be such that the research could be completed with the available facilities.
(d) It must be such that the co-operation of people concerned is easily available.
(e) It must be clearly related to one of the causes.
(f) It should be such that it does not isolate the administrative requirements.
(g) The success of Action Research depends on the co-ordination ar.d report fo the sponsoring agency and the research agency.
(h) The method of investigation adopted in Action Research must be suitable to the filed situation by integrating local knowledge in the research process.

### *(v) Feasibility Studies*

While analysing the scope for starting new firms or organsiations, we have to think scientifically about the scope, viability, survival instincts, etc. of the proposed unit. Such scientific assessment can be provided by a "Feasibility study". A feasibility study can predict te success or failure of an organisation. A feasibility study can assess the deposit and other resource potencial of a proposed bank. The level of competition and strategies to woo the customers can also be drawn. It can also fix indicators for success like break even analysis, credit deposit ratio, profit ration etc., A feasibility study can not lead us to failure. A ten per cent margin of probability of success or failure can be given. A cent per cent success of the study can be ensure provided the implementers take the scope, suggestions and strategies true to the spirit of the feasibility study.

Feasibility studies are essential in the field of industries. "Feasibility studies indeed have gained considerable importance in recent years specially in developing countries seeking to harvest their natural resources for rapid industrial development. In fact prospective entrepreneurs like very much to know and perhaps, the various aspects of their selected industry before investing their capital in such a venture. Sufficient and requisite knowledge of feasibility studies may help them immensely in this regard. Such studies also help the promotional agencies to know the viability of a proposed industrial venture so that they may counsel prospective entrepreneurs better.

Moreover, if some of the personnel of the promotional agencies learn how to make feasibility studies, then it may create confidence in them as they would be collecting all the particulars concerning a particular industry. The confidence, in turn, will help them to convince other.

***Feasibility studies would then help the following***

(i) Persons interested in starting industries but appear to be baffled to identify the product and or products to be produced by them;

(ii) Persons who are already in the industry line i.e., they have already been entrepreneurs but are interested to have entry into new lines of products, products of which they like to make a systematic study that will help them to know whether new entry/entries would be economically viable or not;

(iii) State and Central Government proposing to start new industries specially in backward areas may do it well to undertake feasibility studies to examine the strength or weaknesses of their proposals because large public money may be involved in the process and hence, a prior thorough study to examine economic feasibility in this regard may be highly desirable.

(iv) Different departments/institutions/organizations etc., in the State as well as in the center connected with economic and or industrial development in the country may undertake feasibility studies to prepare a list of identified products which may be economically viable and the same may be handed over to the prospective entrepreneurs so that they may examine the product or products which they may like to start to produced in their new enterprises. Such a list may be of immense value to the prospective entrepreneurs in identifying their products.

(v) Consultancy organisations may be developed to be specialised in the technique of feasibility studies and such a specialised skill may be sold to the customers to ease out their problems of identifying the product/products specially because such an identification demands a skill that may be termed as 'specialised skill' that needs training, know-how aptitude, resource, personnel, time, etc., to prepare such feasibility reports: and

(vi) Some university/colleges/research organisations are found in recent times undertaking feasibility studies in developing countries and these studies would be enriched more if a scientific methodology is adopted in such studies.

### A Model of a Feasibility Study on Starting a Cooperative Marketing Society

Co-operatives can be confronted with the need for such an analysis, for example, if a new society or a new branch is to be established, if new activities are to be undertaken, etc. In a wider sense a similar study, though perhaps not so elaborate, should precede any decision which could decisively alter the course of a society.

In smaller matters this analysis can be prepared and assessed by the society's staff or, in the case of societies to be formed, by a pre-co-operative study group of prospective members, but in most cases a qualified economist or engineer, or both, have to be consulted. Within the co-operative sector this type of extension service can usually be contacted through central business organizations, auditing associations or government departments. In some instances feasibility studies are also carried out by international organizations involved in co-operative extension work or by private consulting firms.

In most cases the study is carried out according to a schedule similar to the following:

#### *1. Terms of Reference*

In this preface it should be established on whose authority the study is being made, and the exact objectives it is to pursue. For the further course of the study it is important that this purpose is clearly stated. It should also include the course the study will follow and the source of information on which it will rely.

### 2. *Introduction*

The introduction must present the background information to the project:

(a) General aspects which may affect the project, such as the relevant legislation, the structure of local administration, income statistics, etc., and a general description of the area where the project will be carried out, its geographical factors, climate, communication system, people and customs. In the individual case it may also include specialized information, in rural projects, for example, about soil qualities, rainfall, land tenure and utilization, average farm size, methods of farming, etc.

(b) The scope for development or the need for new facilities, at present as well as in the future, by showing the faults and disadvantages of the present set-up or situation, or by proving, by way of market analysis, the room for expansion.

(c) The suggested target for expansion or the proposed capacity of any new facilities.

(d) The possible approach or method to be used and, if necessary, a comparison of several methods, and the planned location of any facilities.

(e) The time schedule for the realization of the project considering the recruitment and training period for any new staff, the delivery period for any new machinery and the construction time for any new buildings required as well as the most favorable time to start the project with regard to the market.

(f) The size of membership related to the set targets and the possibility of attracting new members.

(g) The expected response from present or prospective members, especially whether they realize the necessity of the project and are willing to co-operate, or what steps can be taken to enlist their collaboration.

### 3. *Market Analysis Research*

The key questions that should be answered in the Market Analysis section of the feasibility study are presented below.

(a) What is the current or projected demand for your proposed products or services? In other words, how many units can you reasonably expect to sell each month?

(b) What are the target markets for this product or service? What demographic characteristics do these potential customers have in common? How may of them are there?

(c) What is the projected supply in your area of the products or services needed for your project?

(d) What competition exists in this market? Can you establish a market niche, which will enable you to compete effectively with other providing this product or service?

(e) Is the location of your proposed business or project likely to affect is success? If so, is the identified site the most appropriate one available?

The market analysis should be conducted first because it is critical to the success of the business. If you cannot substantiate through research that adequate demand for your product or service exists, or if you cannot obtain sufficient quality to meet expected demand, they you project is not feasible. You should not continue to the next step in the feasibility study.

### 4. *Organizational Issues*

(a) What organizational structure is the right one for you?

(b) Who will serve on the board of directors?

(c) What qualifications are needed to manage this business?

(d) Who will manage the business (if possible)?

(e) What other staffing needs does the co-op have? How do you expect staffing needs to change over the next 2 – 3 years?

### 5. *Technical Requirements*

(a) The feasibility of using the existing facilities and the present staff for the new task and the possible changes to be made for their adaptation.

(b) Any new facilities and manpower needed and their availability

   (i) land and buildings, their size design, outlay and equipment.

   (ii) machinery, type, make, capacity.

   (iii) transport, type, capacity.

(iv) manpower, required skill and experience, recruitment plan.

*Key Questions to Answer Include:*

(a) What are the technology needs for the proposed business?

(b) What other equipment does your proposed business need?

(c) Where will you obtain this technology and equipment?

(d) When can you get the necessary equipment?

(e) How much will the equipment and technology cost?

### 6. Capital Outlay and Finance

(a) the total cost of the project assessed according to a detailed list of the costs of any building, machinery or vehicles needed and, if possible, accompanied by tenders of the relevant suppliers.

(b) The required rate of finance calculated on the basis of the expected average lifetime of the invested assets.

(c) The source of finance available for the purpose of the project.

The following financial aspects are to be considered.

(a) *Start-up Costs:* These are the costs incurred in starting up a new business, including "capital goods" such as land, buildings, equipment, etc. The business may have to borrow money from a lending institution to cover these costs

(b) *Operating Costs:* These are the ongoing costs, such as rent, utilities, and wages that are incurred in the everyday operation of a business. The total should include interest and principle payments on any debt for start-up costs.

(c) *Revenue Projections:* How will you price your goods or services? Asses what the estimated monthly revenue will be.

(d) *Sources of Financing:* If your proposed business will need to borrow money from a bank or other lending institution, you may need to research potential lending sources.

(e) *Profitability Analysis:* This is the "bottom line" for the proposed business. Given the costs and revenue analysis above, will your business bring in enough revenue to cover operating expenses? Will it break even, lose money or make a profit? Is there anything you can do to improve the bottom line?

### 7. *Analysis of Operating Costs (Includes Salary, Taxes, Interest, etc.)*

(a) The breakdown of the expected operating cost including the proportional overhead expenses calculated for various levels of output or development.
   (i) based pm estimated costs
   (ii) by comparison with a society which has already carried out a similar project taking into account the cost variations caused by differences in size, location, structure of membership and efficiency in management.

(b) The comparison of differing methods with respect to operating costs.

### 8. *Analysis of Expected Benefits*

The assessment of added revenue gained from the project or of the expected decrease in cost or improvement in service.

### 9. *Final Assessment*

(a) The comparison of the increased operating cost with the additional revenue expected (break-even graph).

(b) The influence of the new project on the overall profitability of the society.

(c) The reasons which would make the project feasible despite a decrease in profitability, for instance, the long-term effect on the development of the society.

### 10. *Appendix*

The appendix should include all those documents, statistics, tenders, drawings to which the text of the feasibility study refers.

Example: Study of the possibilities of expanding a co-operative marketing society

(a) what is the present economic situation of the society?
   (i) area of operation, membership.
   (ii) Activities, turnover.
   (iii) Management and staff.

(iv) Balance sheet and other records.

(b) Is there scope for an expansion of the established activities?

*(i) By Increasing the Membership:*

- Are there farmers in the area of operation who are eligible for membership but who are not yet members?

What is the degree of competition from other marketing institutions in the area?

What can the society do to attract these farmers despite competition? Can it improve services or give better prices?

*(ii) By Increasing the Area of Operation:*

- Are there co-operative marketing societies already working in adjoining areas? If so, is an amalgamation feasible of possible?
- What other marketing institutions have established themselves in the adjoining areas, and could the society competed with them?
- What effect would the increased average distance between member and society have on he marketing costs?

*(iii) By Increasing the Turnover Per Member:*

- Are the present members completely loyal to the society? If not, what can be done to improve this situation? Does the possibility of introducing delivery contracts exist?
- Can the society initiate a scheme by which he members increase their production, e.g. new farming methods?

(c) Is an expansion along the current lines desirable? Can the market absorb more produce without a significant fall in price?

(d) Is there scope for expansion by taking up new activities?

(i) by marketing other farming products not yet covered?

- What other crop or animal product is produced in the area in sufficient quantity to give a basis for organized marketing?
- For which of these products is there a suitable market?
- What competition would the society have to face in this field?

(ii) by taking up other activities such as credit, supply, or other services:

- For which of these activities is there a sufficient demand among members or prospective members?
- What competition would the society have to face in any of these fields?

(e) Would the society be able to cope with an expansion in connection with:

*(i) Top Management?*

- Is the present management capable of taking on additional functions? If not, are there suitable facilities for further training? And would the present management be able and willing to undergo such training?
- Is the present management willing to shoulder new responsibilities? If not, would and increase in salary act as an incentive?
- Would it be possible and feasible to replace the present management with more experienced persons?

*(ii) Staff?*

- Is the present staff adequate in quantity and quality to cope with an increase in work and duties?
- Are there staff training facilities?
- Can the society recruit additional experienced staff?

*(iii) Facilities?*

- Are the present facilities of the society adequate for additional functions with regard to space, equipment and transport?
- What new investments would be necessary? And what would be the cost?
- What are the possibilities of securing the necessary finance?

What sources are available?

(e) How would the increased costs compare with the additional revenue? Is the overall profitability of the society maintained, increased, decreased or endangered?

# 9

# Types/Methods of Research

## THE HISTORICAL RESEARCH METHOD

### Meaning

The term 'history' has been derived from 'Historia', which means learning or acquiring knowledge through research. History is the record of past events. It is complete, accurate meaningful record of man's achievements. Allan Newins[1] says that history is an integrated narration or description of past events or facts, written in spirit of critical inquiry to find out the whole truth. History helps us to study the society, its structure, functions and processes. A social scientist gets insight into the past through history. Past always contains elements of the present. Past, present and future are all well inter-linked. As pointed out by Carter V. Goode "History embraces the entire field of the human past and is as board as life itself. Our human past includes many areas of social experience and activities is to collect information about the past events and to analyse them correctly. He is concerned with an accurate account of a particular happening, stressing the location and the date. That is, it works out "an accurate record of how, when and where the event started; how it progressed and how and when it ceased. The historian explains the event by describing the conditions which led unto it and out of which it grew."

The historical method consists of heuristic criticism, synthesis and exposition. Originally developed by the philologists during the age of Renaissance, when they laid down rules for the purpose of dealing with classical and sacred texts, the historical method was adopted by the Benedictines of France during the seventeenth century. Even today historical method has greater significance for social research. There are a number of social problems which are to be studied with historical background. Historical studies have made important contributions to various social science disciplines. In the field of rural development, economics, sociology, co-operation, politics, education and psychology, many studies are essentially historical in approach. For instance, History of Co-operative thought, History of Co-operative Development, Evaluation of Pancyayat Raj System, Pattern of Leadership Development, History of Social Legislation etc. In all these studies historical data have greater relevance.

### Meaning of Historical Research

Historical Research has been defined by Walter R. Borg in the following words: "Historical research is the systematic and synthesis of objective location, evaluation, and synthesis of evidence in order to establish facts and draw conclusions concerning past nevents."

According to Shiek Ali "Historical research is digging into the past in order to re-enact the past in its entirety, to reconstruct the past event as fully as they must have happened, to explain the meaning and significance of those events, to correct the wrong notions so long prevalent, if any, and to elaborate, analyse, synthesise and philosophise the ideas in the light of the knowledge we possess."[6]

Robert G. Murdick of Florida Atlantic University says the "Historical Research is concerned with establishing the occurrence of unique events. Although one phase of historical research consist only of determining past events, the ultimate phase deals with the interpretation of such events in the past and present, the establishment of pattern of relationship and the starting point of projecting trends."[7] Historical research is essential for both basic and applied research in social sciences. The main aim of historical research, according to Frederick Lamson Whitney, is to apply the method of reflective thinking to social problems, still unsolved, by means of discovery of past trends of event, fact and attitude. It traces lines of development in human thought and action in order to reach some basis for social activity.[8] P.V.Young describes historical method as the induction of principles through research into the past and social forces which have shaped the present. The explanations of the present derived from historical inquiries are sometimes called "genetic studies." Historical research like all other research is not just concerned with digging up facts. Evaluation and interpretation are integral parts of legitimate research. The historical researcher must concern himself with critical evaluation of source documents in terms of authority, content and meaning and interpretation of records in terms of general laws, trends or hypothesis.

Historical Research has been defined by Walter R. Borg in the following words: "Historical research is the systematic and synthesis of objective location, evaluation, and synthesis of evidence in order to establish facts and draw conclusions concerning past events."

### *Sources of Historical Research*

The major sources of historical data are as follows:

1. Printed books, papers, literature and magazines
2. Documents
3. Remains
4. Materials of cultural history and of analytical history
5. Diaries
6. Memories
7. Confessions
8. Autobiographies
9. Sacred achieves
10. Covert diplomatic agreements
11. Statistical materials
12. Suppressed inventions
13. Personal letters
14. Personal accounts
15. Personal sources of authentic observers and witnesses
16. Artistic materials, historical paintings. Portraits, charts, maps etc.

### *Conditions Necessary for Historical Research*

Although the historical method appears to be simple in its application it is in a way much more complicated then some of the other methods. Historical method demands experience and competence.

The following are the conditions necessary for historical research:

1. Selection of a topic for research – The researcher must be capable of choosing a suitable topic for his research. The subject selected may be related to a region, period, trend or a person.
2. The researcher must have a great deal of social insight and historical orientation. Mastery of sources in another requirement for a historical researcher. He must also have the capacity to digest and master materials.
3. The historical researcher must posses an imagination of the topic chosen for research.
4. The researcher must have knowledge of related social science. This would enable him to analyze the topic in its proper perspective.
5. A wide educational background is a must for an effective use of the his historical method. This background would enable him to understand the topic in an inter-related manner.
6. The researcher must have familiarity with the general field of his topic and his clarity regarding his own objectives. He must also have a thorough knowledge about the work already done in the field.
7. Historical research demands experience and competence not only in assembling data but also in relating them to the major influencing conditions and in assessing their significance in the particular context.
8. The researcher must have an objective approach in analysis. He must take both an analytical and synthetic view of the facts. He has to take an overall view of the facts. He has to take an overall view to assess the true relationship between the events themselves and between the events and the environment.
9. The researcher must be in a position to know his own limitations in understanding and interpreting the events. This position would make him receptive to new ideas and knowledge put forth by more intelligent and experienced persons.
10. The researcher must be aware of the limitations in the historical sources, that he uses in his study. This fact will

induce him to probe further into the matter.

11. Availability of good library facilities.
12. Availability of adequate grants.
13. Favorable arrangements for work, with necessary tools such as computer services, calculating machines, artists to draw graphs maps etc.

As pointed out by P.V. Young, when, how and under what circumstances to use any or all of these sources depends to a great extent on the discretion of the researcher, his interest, the purpose and the scope of his study and the availability of these sources. It is always advisable for a historical researcher before consulting and drawing upon historical documents, to consult a historian and explain the purpose and the scope of his study and get his suggestions as to methods of gathering and interpreting these sources.

In historical research, if the approach is to be objective, it is essential that the data are reliable, relevant and adequate. It should also help effective evaluation of the past. P.V. Young says the historical data are reliable and adequate for social research: (i) when they are presented as complexes of social forces, (ii) when social phenomena meaning fully depict intricate social process, (iii) when sets of inter-relationships— psychological, economic, education, political, religious— contribute to a unified whole a configuration or complex pattern.

## Evaluation of Historical Data

In historical research, related documents provide the sole source of information. The documents are "reports of events consisting of impressions made on some human brain by past events and consciously or deliberately recorded for the purpose of transmitting information.[11] The evaluation of the documents is of crucial importance to enable the researcher to place each bit of information in its proper perspective and draw sound conclusions. The evaluation of historical evidence is usually known as 'Historical Criticism'. Historical Criticism is generally divided into two groups namely (a) External Criticism or Heuristics which means inciting to find out (b) Internal criticism or Hermeneutics or Interpretative Criticism. The main aim of these two types of criticism is to pronounce whether a given idea is acceptable as a fact or not. Events, occurrences and happenings as presented in the records may or not conform to reality, for they might have been distorted, twisted or misrepresented. Thus, through these methods the authenticity and creditability of the data are tested.

### External Criticism(Heuristics)

This is concerned with the genuineness of the document words. External criticism deals with data relating to form and appearance rather than meaning of contents. External criticism is sometimes called lower criticism because it is a preliminary or preparatory step providing the data to be used in the second phase known as internal criticism. In testing the genuiness of a document the problem of external criticism involves the question of authorship and his qualification as a reporter, factor or conditions that may have influenced the production of the document, such as time, place, purpose and circumstances of compositions and the extent of which the document reads true to the origin. In determining the truth and value of the document, the researcher has to see the question of authorship, his personality, character, position, general qualifications as a reporter, alertness, character bias special qualifications and or disqualifications as a reporter of ht a matter, interest in the events, his technical knowledge foe learning and reporting the events, the method of writing document from memory, after consultation with others, the data and year of documentation and such other details.

### Internal Criticism (Hermeneutics)

Internal criticism is nothing but evaluating the accuracy and value or worth of the statements within the document. In other words it is testing the creditability of the data. This process is also called higher criticism. A historical researcher must put his documentary evidence to the test of truthfulness as well as competence. Carter V. Good says that many authentic or genuine documents may not be completely accurate or truthful and require the process of internal criticism in the form of textual criticism as well as investigation of such factors as the competence, good faith, position and bias of the author of the document.14 Internal criticism involves a scientific examination of the relevance of the data, correction of errors and rejection of the information that is found wanting. Internal criticism is much more difficult than external criticism because it involves evaluating the writer, his bias and the possible motives for distortion. This evaluation requires wide knowledge, practical experience and training in psychology.

Internal criticism is of two types – negative criticism and positive criticism. Negative criticism is to examine the circumstances in which a person wrote the document, whether he was in a position to ascertain the truth and to reveal the real story and whether he was guided by motives or bias. Positive criticism seeks to find out whether the contents of the documents are true or otherwise. In historical research, both negative and positive criticism are essential.

### *Conditions Necessary for Historical Research*

Although the historical method appears to be simple in its application it is in a way much more complicated then some of the other methods. Historical method demands experience and competence. The following are the conditions necessary for historical research:

1. Selection of a topic for research – The researcher must be capable of choosing a suitable topic for his research. The subject selected may be related to a region, period, trend or a person.
2. The researcher must have a great deal of social insight and historical orientation. Mastery of sources in another requirement for a historical researcher. He must also have the capacity to digest and master materials.
3. The historical researcher must posses an imagination of the topic chosen for research.
4. The researcher must have knowledge of related social science. This would enable him to analyse the topic in its proper perspective.
5. A wide educational background is a must for an effective use of the his historical method. This background would enable him to understand the topic in an inter-related manner.
6. The researcher must have familiarity with the general field of his topic and his clarity regarding his own objectives. He must also have a thorough knowledge about the work already done in the field.
7. Historical research demands experience and competence not only in assembling data but also in relating them to the major influencing conditions and in assessing their significance in the particular context.

8. The researcher must have an objective approach in analysis. He must take both an analytical and synthetic view of the facts. He has to take an overall view of the facts. He has to take an overall view to assess the true relationship between the events themselves and between the events and the environment.
9. The researcher must be in a position to know his own limitations in understanding and interpreting the events. This position would make him receptive to new ideas and knowledge put forth by more intelligent and experienced persons.
10. The researcher must be aware of the limitations in the historical sources, that he uses in his study. This fact will induce him to probe further into the matter.
11. Availability of good library facilities.
12. Availability of adequate grants.

Favourable arrangements for work, with necessary tools such as computer services, calculating machines, artists to draw graphs maps etc.

***Steps Involved in Historical Research***

The steps involved in historical research are discussed below:

*1. Selection of the Problem*

The first and foremost problem of a historical research is identification of an appropriate topic for study. It must be understood that all problems may not lend themselves for historical analysis. The selection of a suitable topic/problem/area depends on the researcher's intellectual caliber, skill, aptitude, interest, training, courage, imagination and wide reading. The selection of a topic also depends on the availability of adequate time data and financial sources.

*2. Formulation of Hypothesis*

The next step is formation of suitable hypothesis for the study. A hypothesis directs our search for the order among facts suggest explanations for certain facts and guide in investigation.

*3. Preparations for Collection of Data*

The researcher must make necessary arrangements for

collection of relevant and adequate data for his study. In the beginning he has to prepare an exhaustive bibliography on the subject and sketch out an outline. In historical research unlike other forms of research, the investigator must deal with data that is already in existence. Therefore, he must identify the sources of data. There are primary and secondary sources. While gathering data he must go through all the sources available and make a note of the related facts. Effective note-taking procedure is very important in historical research

*4. Evaluation of Data*

The next step is criticism of data. This is nothing but testing and evaluating the authenticity and accuracy of data collected through primary and secondary sources. The evaluation of historical data is known as historical criticism.

*5. Organization of Data*

After the data has been evaluated, it is necessary to organize it into meaningful form.. The data may be arranged on a thematic or topical basis with reference to the contents, on a chronological basis with reference to the period and date of happening and on a geographical basis with reference to places or to combine different processes. This arrangement is necessary not only to draw conclusions and to present them logically but to discard the irrelevant facts. This process of course requires sound thinking, wide reading, greater imagination and good training.

*6. Interpretation and Writing Report*

After the data has been arranged and systematized, the researcher must have a mental outline of his report. The outline serves as a working plan. It is the blue print of the entire research work. It helps the research to arrange his ideas effectively.. The division of headings must be according to a logical order. Weakness in the logical organization of a report of historical research suggests weakness in the logical organization of a report of historical research suggests weakness in the research's understanding and analysis of the problem.

***Usefulness of Historical Research***

Historical research is an attempt to make a diligent and systematic enquiry or investigation into a subject in order to discover facts and or revise the known facts and or put the facts into theories. Historical research is useful both for theoretical and practical purposes. It has made important contributions to various branches of social sciences. Historical method include study of life histories, history of various organizations and institutions. Historical research enables us to get an accurate knowledge of the past. When we analyze the past and present, it is possible to predict the future. It helps in choosing suitable policy or action among a number of alternatives. Through historical study, it is possible to study the development of a particular idea, concept philosophy etc.

## CASE STUDY

### Introduction

One of the simplest methods of social research is case study. By means of analyisng a case the researcher can study the entire life history of the unit. It goes deep into the problems and the interaction between factors is noted by measuring the intensity of influence by one variable over the other. John Best says that, "case study is concerned with everything that is significant in the history or development of the case. The purpose is to understand the life cycle or an important part of the life cycle of an individual unit. This unit may be a person, a family, a group, a social institution or an entire community. The case method probes deeply and intensively, analyses interaction between the factors that produce change or growth. It emphasizes the longitudinal or genetic approach showing development over a period of time."

Case study is very useful for business research. If we want to study the growth and development of a company it is an ideal method of research. Or if we want to study a particular problem of a company deeply, say labour unrest, absenteeism or industrial sickness, this method of research will help the researcher in many ways. It takes less time to collect data and less experience than other methods of research like survey. Any beginner of social research can attempt case study and then he can go for other methods of research.

Mr. Herbert Spencer Mr. Frederick Le play and Dr. William Healey, were the pioneers of case study method. The French Social reformer Frederick Le Play's (1806-1882) study on the standard of living of families was kind of case-study. Dr. William Healey, another pioneer of the case study used this method to study juvenile delinquency covering a large number of cases, i.e., constituting the juvenile delinquents as the population of the study.

A case study is deep and intensive study of a particular social unit. It also a diagnostic study oriented towards finding out what is happening and why is it happening and what can be done about it. Some experts refer to its as insight—stimulating study. It is also known as historical genetic method and holistic approach. A case study covers all aspects of social unit. It also seeks to determine social process; it reveals the complexity of factors and indicates their sequences and inter-relationships.Case study, says Cahrles H. Cooley "deepens our perception and gives us a clearer insight into life." According to Pauline V. Young; "Case study is a method of exploring and analysing the life of social unit – be that unit a person, a family, institution, cultural group or even entire community." Mr. William J. Goodge and Mr. Paul K Hatt write that "case study is a way of organising social data so as to preserve the unitary character of the social object being studied." According to F.L. Whitney, "case study is a complete analysis and report of the status of an individual subject with respect as a rule to specific phases of his total personality." Mr. James A. Black and Mr. Dean J. Champion write that case studies are usually characterized as thorough examination of specific social settings or particular aspects of social settings, including in varying details psychological descriptions of persons in those settings.".

A case study is deep and intensive study of a particular social unit. It also a diagnostic study oriented towards finding out what is happening and why is it happening and what can be done about it. Some experts refer to its as insight – stimulating study. It is also known as historical genetic method and holistic approach. A case study covers all aspects of social unit. It also seeks to determine social process; it reveals the complexity of factors and indicates their sequences and inter-relationships

## Significance of Case Study

1. Case study helps in formulating valid hypothesis. Study of relevant literature and case study are the two potent sources of hypothesis.
2. It helps in framing questionnaire or schedule. By knowing the characteristics of individual units we can prepare the tools in a right way.

3. It aids in sampling. By studying individual units thoroughly the researcher can put them in definite class or type and it helps in perfect classification of the sample.
4. It locates deviant cases. Deviant cases are those units, which go against a hypothesis.
5. Case study enlarges the range of personal experience of the researcher. Under case study the whole range of subjects life is studied and the range of knowledge is enlarged. With this gain the researcher gets an intimate knowledge of many aspects of the unit.
6. As case study covers the entire life of the unit, it is inclusive and intensive in nature. Hence, there is a possibility of studying various aspects of a problem.

### *Characteristics of Case Study*

The characteristics of the case study method are as follows:

1. Case study is a deep, detailed and intensive study of a social unit.
2. It is a comprehensive study.
3. It is a method of qualitative analysis.
4. In case study, all the variables and traits are linked with one another.
5. It is a flexible method.
6. In case study there are changes for wide variety of units to be selected.
7. It preserves wholeness of the units, i.e., it is an approach which views any social unit as a whole.
8. In case study the complex factors are studied; and finally
9. Traits are the subject matter of the study.

Precautions Essential in Choosing an Object of Case Study. The following are the precautions, which are essential in choosing an object of case study.

1. Selection of typical and representative unit.
2. Identification of situations and problems.
3. Time to be covered—the phase of life cycle.
4. Unitary character of the unit—breadth of data, levels of data, use of indices and types.
5. Quantity of data.
6. Availability of data and its reliability.
7. Cost to be incurred.

8. Time to be spent.
9. Researcher's courage, interest, skill and training in research.
10. Possibility to repeat case study.

If these precautions are carefully adhered to by the researcher, the case study will be valid and useful.

### *Sources of Data*

In case study the information may be collected from varied sources such as:

1. Life histories
2. Personal records
3. Personal documents
4. Personal letters
5. Confessions
6. Biographies
7. Interviewing individuals
8. Observations.

### *Steps Involved in Case Study*

The various steps involved in any case study are as follows:

#### *1. Selection of Cases and Identification of Situation*

The researcher has to decide, which unit has to be taken up for study? What aspect or what period of life of unit can be studied? What are the situations in which unit exists? All these questions should be answered first. The researcher therefore, has to choose representative and typical units. The selection of such units of course depends on the ability and skill of the research.

#### *2. Gathering and Recording of Data*

While gathering data, the researcher has to keep in mind the continuity, breadth and level of data to preserve the completeness and validity of data, a broad array of facts have to be collected. . The data should be complete and up to date and of easy reference.

#### *3. Interpretation and Reporting of Data*

Interpretation is an objective judgment based on background knowledge of a situation-appraisal of an event. It is the search for the broader meaning of the research findings. It is the deeper sense of the investigation. It places a particular event in the larger flow of events. It is the color, the atmosphere, the human element that gives meaning to a fact. It is in short setting sequence and about all significance. The facts collected must be clarified, explained and interpreted.

The findings have to be adequately reported in order to make it more valuable to the public. Reporting the research findings to the public is thus an important part of any type of social investigation.

### *Usefulness of Case Study*

As cases study is a deep and diagnostic study, it has been praised as a useful research technique. The following are some of the specific advantages of the case study.

1. Case study helps to probe the entire life span of a social unit intensively and to analyze the complex factors that are influencing the social unit. It indicates their sequences and inter-relationships. It also covers a wide range of information about the cases.
2. Case data are vivid, absorbing and tend to reproduce a person's social attitudes and values.
3. Case study facilitates to understand everything about a social unit and the variety of habits, traits and qualities combined in a social unit.
4. Case study helps to secure detailed information about the growth of the unit, group structure, individual life pattern etc.
5. The relationship between individual and society is well brought out in the case study.
6. Its techniques are often used in pure research, sociology and economics with a view to develop certain theories and broad principles.
7. Case studies are indispensable for the research and administrative purposes.
8. It is also easy to generalize cases with case study and helps to prepare a plan of action for treatment.
9. Case study is followed for comparison, classification, analysis and for the formulation of hypothesis leading to further research.
10. Case studies also help the researchers to frame schedule and questionnaires.

11. Case data are useful to pure research in furnishing clues for further research.
12. They are also useful for diagnosis and other practical case-by-case problems.

*Limitations of Case Study*

Though case study method has contributed much to the social research, some social scientists have raised some objections against the value and validity of case studies. Following are some of the limitations commonly attributed to case studies.

1. Case study does not provide universal, impersonal, and common aspects of a phenomenon.
2. There is a tendency for a researcher to draw generalization after studying a few cases, which may not be relevant to all situations.
3. There is a tendency to over emphasis the unique or unusual events, which are seldom comparable.
4. The subjective data collected do not lend themselves to quantitative check.
5. It is costly, time consuming and wasteful in certain cases where the objectives are limited.
6. It is generally viewed that case study is loose and unsystematic and the generalisation drawn from a few cases are not always accurate.
7. In the case study method, there is a temptation to ignore the basic principles of Research Design.

*Survey Method*

Social surveys, says P.V. Young in her book "Scientific Social Surveys and Research," are as old as the history itself. The ever growing socio-economic and other problems in the human society stimulated the social scientists to engage the study of those problems and to find out the causes and to take remedial measures. Several economists, sociologists, anthropologists, social reformers and social scientist have conducted a number of different types of surveys either independently or in collaboration with Government or research institutions. Those include, general specific and census surveys. The social scientists thus attempted to use social survey technique to gather facts in a systematic manner right from the earlier periods.

*Early Surveys*

P.V. Young writes in the above noted book that Herodotus had recorded about a survey of population and wealth in Egypt in 300 B.C. A reference was found about the ideas of social investigation in the Doomsday Book of William the conqueror in the eleventh century. According to Mark Abrams the social surveys of today have their methodological roots in the enquiries carried out by three men namely Charles Booth, B.Seebohm Rowntree and Professor Arthur Bowley. But one of the earliest attempts was made by John Howard, a famous English philanthropist and prison reformer in the second half of the 18th century. He studied the conditions of prison and prisoners. He also employed a variety of techniques to gather a specific body of facts. Another pioneer in this field was the French social reformer by name Frederic Le Play, who in the middle of the 19th century methodically studied 1000 working class family budgets. He was the first to use inter-disciplinary approach in social surveys. He gathered the facts through personal interviews and observation. The English reformer and statistician Mr. Cherles Booth conducted a survey in 1886 on poverty of labourers in the East side of London. This was also a pioneering work in social surveys. His survey includes the aspects like income, hours and conditions of work, housing, standards of living, number of children, size of household in relation to size and type of dwelling, type and frequency of sickness, leisure activities, and club and union membership. In 1899, B.S. Rowntree made a study of the city of New York and again in 1939 to evaluate the changes in the standard of living of the people. Thus, he first introduced the method of comparative study in social survey. He obtained the required facts directly from the working class families by using interviewers. His most important contribution was that the gave far greater precision to the concept of poverty. He was the first sociologist to draw attention to the cyclical pattern of poverty. Mr. Rowntree's approach thus varied in methodological aspects from that of Mr. Booth. His study was published under the title 'Poverty': A study of Town Life. Yet another important social survey was initiated by Prof. Arthur Bowley, a famous statistician in 1912. He studied the working class conditions in reading, for the first time through random sampling technique. Bowley's important methodological contribution was his application of the principles of random sampling, which came to act as decisive stimulus to social surveys. Later in almost all the poverty surveys the same method was used. Professor Bowley had also introduced comparative studies and varied methods of investigation in social surveys. In 1928, Ford undertook a study in Southampton following the methods of Professor Bowley and the same was published under the title "Work and Wealth in a Modern Port". Again in 1928, Sir Hubert Llewelyn Smith one of the associates of Booth conducted a study on the changes in the working of socio-economic life of London labourers. He illustrated the results through charts, maps etc. In 1935, Rowntree initiated a second survey in New York and again a follow-up survey in 1950 in the same place in collaboration with G.R. Lavers. The findings were published under the title "Poverty and Welfare state". This study received greater public attention at that time. In the middle of thirities, survey activity began to receive greater importance in many fields. The establishment of the Government Social Survey in 1941 was one of the noted developments in the field of social survey in Great Britain. This organisation initiated a number of studies in the field of town planning, housing, sickness, consumption expenditure, national income, nutrition, health, industry, mining, education, employment, colonial affairs and industrial research on noise, light, heating in domestic dwellings, on road traffic problems etc. Further, opinion, market, population, urban life, rural life, audience, travelling, family expenditure, social mobility, political behaviour, old age, juvenile delinquency, industrial relations and moral surveys were initiated at different places in Great Britain by the individual social scientists, the Government and the research organisations. It must be also noted that several independent research establishments emerged which as commercial bodies, have specialised in the planning and execution of social surveys on behalf of Government or of any one who liked to use survey method in tackling problems. The work of these specialised research bodies played a significant part in social research in Great Britain.

As in England, in the USA, several socio-economic surveys were initiated by the social scientists since 1890. The first study of those kinds giving an account of tenement conditions in New York with clear explanations appeared in the year 1890. The next important social inquiry into housing conditions of the state was conducted by the New York Tenement House Commission in 1900. Similarly, the slum conditions were surveys in 1902. Another important study under the title, "The jungle describing the working conditions of the meat-packing labourers, exploitation by the industrial monster" was published in 1906. This study was very helpful for enacting the first social legislation namely "Pure Food and Drug Act". In 1907 the Russel Sage Foundation was established with a view to improving the social and living conditions in the USA, and separate department of surveys was created by the Foundation in 1912. This was another development in the history of survey movement in the USA. In 1909, the Pittsburg Survey – "A study of the Effects of Urbanisation was initiated by Paul Kellogg with the help of trained social economists and professional social workers. A noted feature of this survey was the introduction of the inter-disciplinary approach to study the effects of urbanization. This was an elaborate and a systematic study whose findings were published in six volumes. Later, on the advice of the Russel Sage Foundation, a series of small studies related to social problems were undertaken in a number of communities. In 1914, the Springfield Survey – "A Study of Social Conditions of an American Small City" was undertaken by Shelby Harrison of Illinois State. This enquiry touched the primary aspects of the city life and analysed the important social problems. For the successful completion of the survey, Shelby Harrison, not only enlisted the support of different agencies and individuals but employed publicity campaign before his field work, to mobilize interest and secure co-operation from the people. He also used exhibits to explain the city's problems.

In 1935, Sir John Boyd Orr, undertook the first modern systematic examination of consumption and standard of living of people. In 1938, Alfred C. Kinsey and his associates conducted a survey on the sexual behaviour of Americans. The chief objectives were to collect sufficient informations to describe American sexual behaviour and to establish that factors account for individual differences in sexual behaviour and for group differences among the various major segments of the population. This study covered a sample of 5300 persons. The survey Division of the Office of War Information of the U.S. Government in 1943 initiated a survey to establish certain facts about the nature and extent of industrial absenteeism in war industry and to determine some of the factors leading to such absence. This survey covered a sample of 1800 respondents, representing 100 workers systematically from 18 different plants. Further, a survey on prejudice and personality was made in 1944. The National Association of Broadcasters Commissioned a national survey on the understanding the acceptance of radio by the public in 1945. The main object was to assess the strength and weakness of the radio industry to ascertain where radio stands with the public, in order to blue print a sound plan of action for the future of broadcasting. The sampling size of the survey was 2500. In 1946, "An Enquiry into the thinking of Americans about the Atomic Bomb and International Affairs", was planned by the Committee on Social Science Research Council and conducted by the American Institute of Public Opinion. A sample of 3000 persons were covered under this study.

The surveys conducted earlier thus stimulated the American social scientists to recognize the survey as a realistic and scientific method of studying the characteristics of the American life. Later a number of individual, regional and national surveys were conducted in different parts of the country. The growth of private and government research bodies was another noted development in the survey research. The individual researchers as well as research establishments studied systematically the problem of social security, economic conditions, employment and unemployment, wages, health, housing, child welfare services, crime and delinquency. Individual researchers, colleges and universities began to use survey research as an important method in all social science disciplines. Today the social survey plays a significant role in the formulation of national policy and it is recognized that social surveys are indispensable for mobilizing the forces of community in tackling social problems.

The review of social surveys initiated in Great Britain and the USA revealed that the social scientists had used improved devices and techniques for the selection of samples, obtaining information from the respondents and for analysis of data. They had employed particularly random sampling and systematic sampling techniques, machine tabulation, statistical analysis, comparisons, participant observation, personal interview and used secondary data as well as the well prepared and pre-tested schedules.

### *Social Survey in India*

Research studies based on survey method were increasingly undertaken in a number of developed, under developed, less developed and developing countries. For instance, in India a number of socio-economic surveys were initiated right from the end of the 18th century. Several economic problems were systematically studied by individual, institutions, the Government and the Reserve Bank of India. The important earliest surveys were (i) A sociological and statistical survey of some Madras villages by Sir Theodore Morison in 1931; (ii) Socio-economic survey of Madras and Bombay provinces by Dr. Gilbert Slater and Dr. Mann in 1918. In all these surveys, the schedule and interview techniques were chiefly used to obtain accurate data. In 1921, a systematic and detailed investigation into the supply of milk in Lahore was undertaken. To assess the economic changes in the villages, the Royal Commission on Indian Agriculture stressed the importance of surveys in 1928. Professor S. Kesava Iyengar, conducted an economic survey in Hyderabad in 1929. This survey concerned a sample of 4 districts and 12 villages. Personal interview techniques was chiefly employed. Data was also collected from the records of the village office. In 1936-37, Professor P.J. Thomas undertook a socio-economic survey in Madras state. This survey used improved techniques of investigation and statistical analysis. In the following year (1937-38) another urban survey was taken up by Professor Dr.Gadgil in Poona.

Prior to Independence, the survey studies initiated in the country were limited and in most of the studies advanced research techniques were not employed. After independence, that too during the planning era survey research began to receive greater importance. A number of research bodies and institutions were set up. They have contributed much to the development of social surveys in the country. The Gokhale Institute of Politics and Economics and the Indian Statistical Institute had been conducting a number of enquiries on socio-economic problems of the society. For example, the Gokhale Institute of Politics and Economics engaged in a large number of studies between 1945 and 1952. The important studies conducted by the Indian Statistical Institute were survey related to consumer preference in Calcutta, Bengal Handloom survey, the survey of Rural Indebtedness, Agricultural Labour and the National Sample Survey. The National Sample Survey was started in 1950, which is conducting the biggest sampling survey in India. Another outstanding survey conducted in the country was the RBI's All India Rural Credit Survey headed by A.D. Gorwala in 1951. This was an economic survey aimed at the study of the patterns of agricultural credit in different parts of the country. This survey covered a sample of 1,27,343 families in 600 villages, selected in 75 districts all over the country. The random sampling technique was used for the selection of the units of study. Techniques like interviews, case studies and tools like schedules, questionnaires and records of different types were used in this study. This was one of the extensive studies, which provided innumerable statistical data relating to the agricultural credit. A survey on the Levels of Living in India was initiated by B.N. Ganguli and D.B. Gupta in 1954. This survey included 15 major states in the country. This study covered various aspects like economic, social, nutrition, housing, medical care, education, clothing, leisure, security, environment and consumption pattern.

An outstanding development in the country was the setting up the National Council of Applied Economic Research at New Delhi which is an important research body in the country. The NCAER has initiated a series of national and regional studies covering several facts of human life. Some of the important socio-economic surveys were: (i) The Urban Savings Survey in Delhi(1959); (ii) The All India Saving Survey in (1960); (iii) The Attitudes Towards and Motivation for Savings (1963); (iv) A study on Contractual Saving in Urban India (1963); (v) The All India Household Survey of Income, Saving and Consumption Expenditure (1972). In all these surveys improved research techniques were employed. The sample, random sampling, stratified random sampling and probability sampling techniques and tools like schedules, questionnaires etc. were used. Statistical analysis and comparisons were also made. Besides these surveys, the NCAER has conducted some techno-economic surveys. The Techno-Economic Survey of West Bengal (1959-60), Gujarat (1959) and U.P. (1962) were some of the important such surveys conducted at the requests of the Governments concerned.

The RBI has also recently conducted the All India Debt and Investment Survey in 1961-62 and 1971-72. The former one was conducted to estimate the debt, investment and other related characteristics of rural households not only for the country as a whole but also for major individual states. The second All India Debt and Investment Survey was a countrywide investigation on household indebtedness and investments. This survey was confined to the entire rural and urban areas of the country. A two stage stratified random sample design with villages as first stage unit, and household as second stage unit was adopted for the survey. The total sample size was 12,452. Schedules were chiefly used to obtain data from the households.

Survey method is exhaustive in nature and covers wider population and geographical area. It has immense use for a social researcher and is a method of research widely used by social researchers. It is a process under which data are collected systematically from the population or a section of the population. For a social researcher, the use of survey research has abundant value and is a popular method of research that is often used.

## Definition

Wells defines survey as "a fact finding study dealing chiefly with working class poverty and with the nature and problems of the community."

P.V. Young – "In search of information which could be obtained easily from large, representative but diverse and widely scattered group of population, researchers have resorted to the sample surveys,"

### *Features of Surveys*

*1. Surveys Collect Primary Information*

Information or data needed for a survey research or problem are collected mainly through primary information. Collecting information at the very source is the basic strength of a survey.

*2. Surveys Vary in their Scope, Objective, Content and Approach*

As different types of surveys are conducted to study different socio-economic problems, they vary in their scope, objective, content and approach. Moser and Kalton say that, "the coverage of a survey can range from a few case studies to a complete enumeration, from carefully selected samples to an arbitrary collection of volunteers."

*3. Wider Coverage*

Surveys cover a wider area. Universal problems like poverty, unemployment, etc. could be studied covering wider population. Any length a breadth of a country can be covered by surveys. Surveys conducted by world bodies like UNC, FAO, UNESCO cover many countries.

*4. Problems of Deeper Nature*

Acute social, economic, educational or administrative problems could be studied deeply applying survey method. Current problem which need immediate solution could also be dealt with surveys.

*5. Entire Life of a Problem studied*

The genesis of a problem from the inception is studied in a survey. Dimension of a problem is studied from various angles so as to pinpoint the real force behind a problem.

*6. Survey is a Continuous Process*

Surveys are conducted continuously focusing on a particular problem. Problem of long standing nature like unemployment need continuous study and monitoring. We have permanent bodies like National Sample Survey to provide information on various national issues.

*7. Use of Sampling*

This is the most distinctive nature of a survey. Hence, surveys are usually called as 'Sample Surveys'. Using the representatives of the population to collect data is a significant nature of a survey.

*8. Pre-Test and Pilot Study*

Before a tool is used it is pre-tested in a survey. Likewise pilot study, which is a miniature study is conducted to find out the course of the main study.

***Purpose of Surveys***

According to Moser and Kalton, the expert team on social surveys, the purpose of surveys are as follows:

(a) The purpose of surveys, is to provide someone with information. Here the researcher needs the aid of surveys to get information on varied aspects.

(b) "Surveys have their usefulness both in leading to the formulation of hypotheses and at a more advanced stage, in putting them to the test. Their function in given research depends on how much is already known about the subject and on the purpose for which the information is required."

***Subject Matter of Surveys***

According to Moser and Kalton surveys have four types of subject matter. They are as follows:

*1. The Democratic Characteristics of a Set of People*

They are concerned with matters such as family or household composition, marital status, fertility, age and so on. These are certainly useful for social research as they mainly deal with human behavior.

*2. Their Social Environment*

Their social environment is taken to cover all the social and economic factors to which people are subject, including occupation and income as well as housing conditions and social amenities. These are subjects which cover, in the widest sense, the question "How do people live?" Surveys on these conditions are essential for social research to find out the standard of living of the population and their purchasing power.

*3.Their Activities*

"By this is not meant occupation (which forms part of social environment) but, for instance, use of leisure, traveling habits, expenditure pattern, television viewing, radio-listening and newspaper reading. Much of the work of the government social survey lies in this field, and so does a good deal of social research." This approach of survey has enormous use for social research.

*4. Their Opinions and Attitudes*

"Opinion polls as the name suggests deal mainly with these, in many other surveys they are of marginal importance," For social research measurement of opinions and attitudes is necessary to know the tastes of the consumers, their liking for a product, size colour, packing of a product. To improve the quality of a product of a product and to introduce a new product opinions of consumers' must be necessary. Sometimes, even consumers may suggest a new product or would like to give a new brand name.

***Advantage of Surveys***

1. Its main purpose is to provide someone with information. It may be an individual researcher, an institution or even government. They need information to implement new schemes. "To a social scientist, a survey may equally have a purely descriptive purpose, as a way of studying social conditions, relationships and behavior."

2. It is to explain the relationship between a number of variables Any problem will have the influence of variables, independent variables or dependent variable which have more influence over the other or over the problem could be clearly found out in a survey.
3. To make policies—government and institutions need lot of information to frame policies. Surveys are useful in such contexts.
4. Finding solutions to problems—Any research study is geared to find solutions to problems. Surveys are very purposeful in finding solutions to problem.
5. To evaluate programmes—when huge money is spent by government or institution on various projects it is necessary to evaluate such programmes. Through such evaluations we can come to know the success or failure of such programmes. Community development schemes, family planning programmes are such examples.
6. To assess the benefits from a project—when projects or schemes are introduced it is necessary to know whether the project benefits have reached the people to whom it was intended. The type of benefits and the degree of benefits can also be measured by surveys.
7. To study problems—every problem in the working of an institution could be studied.
8. Consumer surveys—Through consumer surveys we can know the opinions and attitudes of consumers. Their reactions to new products, their quality and price could be measured. The strength and weaknesses of the competitors can also be measured by surveys.

### *Kinds of Surveys*

1. *General or specific surveys*—collecting general information about any population without any specific objective is called as general survey. If it is collected for specific purpose, then it becomes a specific survey.
2. *Regular and ad-hoc surveys*—when surveys are conducted at regular intervals it is called as Regular survey. Surveys on price level form part of such surveys. Ad-hoc surveys are conducted to supplement missing information.
3. *Preliminary and final surveys*—pilot study is equal to that

of a preliminary survey. Final survey is undertaken after the pilot study.

4. *Census and sample surveys*—under census survey entire population is covered and contacted to collect information. In sample surveys only a small part is taken as representative of the whole.
5. *Social surveys*—social surveys deal with current social problems of the society. Surveys on poverty, unemployment, housing, etc, from part of such surveys.
6. *School surveys*—Through school surveys, problems of education are studied.
7. *Public opinion surveys*— very often public opinion surveys are conducted to know the opinion of the population on certain issues or problems. Before elections, such surveys are conducted to know the party preference of voters.
8. *Market surveys*—such surveys are undertaken by industries and business community. When a new product is introduced the liking for such product, market share for such product, type of competition, etc. could be analyzed by market surveys.
9. *Community surveys*—For the development of a community such surveys are conducted. It helps the planning of schemes and the future development.
10. *Observational surveys*—It is to observe 'what people do?'

### *Steps in Conducting Surveys*

#### *1. Initial Preparation*

Initial preparation is relating to the coverage of population, type of information to be collected, how to collect data? Etc. Time and cost involved must also be planned.

#### *2. Objectives and Resources*

The objectives of the survey must be clearly laid down. The initial statement should explain why the survey is being done, exactly what questions it means to cover, and what kind of results are expected. Most important, especially if the survey is being done for a client, the statement needs to discuss how the information is to be used and what degree of accuracy is required."

*3. Coverage*

Coverage denotes the coverage of population to be studied. Hence, the population must be defined in terms of its geographical, demographic and other boundaries. This must be decided properly in order to decide the size and type of sampling.

*4. Collection of Data*

The researcher must also decide the tools to be used to collect data. Mailed questionnaire, interview and observation are the important tools used in survey to collect data. While questionnaire is used it must be pre-tested and training for the interviewer must be given if it is administered through interview.

*5. Processing of Data*

Equal care must be shown for processing the data. The questionnaire must be scrutinized for errors, omission and overlapping before ready for tabulation. The type of statistical tool used must also be decided.

*6. Report*

The report must be written by the researcher himself. Viewing the topic and objectives of the study the report must be schemed.

***Limitations of Surveys***

James Black and Dean Champion point out the following limitations of surveys:

1. Surveys are superficial reflections of population sentiments. As opinion of sample respondents are not deep they seldom represent the sentiments of the population.
2. Surveys, particularly political surveys, are unstable collections of population characteristics. "A study of opinion of a sample of individuals one week may be quite different from a similar survey of the same individuals a week or two late."
3. The researcher has little or no control over individual responses— " Those responding differ from those who do not respond. The potential bias resulting from such surveys significantly limit the generalizability of one's

findings to total populations from which the original samples were obtained."

4. Statements about populations from which samples are obtained are tentative—"The researcher manipulates the data obtained by tabular and statistical analyses and arrives at tentative conclusions related to some notions held about the targets population." Such conclusions may not represent the views of entire population.

### *Experimental Research*

Experimental research has ample use in physical science researchers and it has limited use in marketing or social science research. It is a method of research where two groups are selected and compared. These comparisons may be relating to their behaviour, expression, feeling or emotions. Theses two groups are called as "Control group" and "Experimental group." Control group is an element not exposed to an experiment. Its behaviour is natural. On the other hand an experimental group is one that is exposed to an experimental variable. Individual could be changed from control group to experimental group in order to find out the changes in behaviour of the individual under both circumstances. In physical or chemical science substances or agents are changed.

Experimental research is defined by Black and Champion as, "all such designs that seek to control conditions within which persons are observed and analysed may be called experimental designs."

Lack and others have defined experimental research as, "the actual trial of a proposed course of a proposed course of action or other hypotheses under consideration, so conducted that its effects can be observed (measured) objectively and distinguished from the effects of extraneous variables. When the effects on the pay off can be reliably isolated, the experimental design can be applied."

A term that is very often used here is the 'variable'. Variable is a factor or phenomenon which can influence change. Variables are classified into two namely dependent variables and independent variables. Independent variables. Independent variables will influence changes over the other whereas dependent variables would be influenced by independent variables. Variables are tested in control and experimental conditions. The influences of the variables could be measured by statistical tools in social research.

### *Preparations in Experimental Research*

Luck and others suggest the following preparations in experimental research:

1. Determining the number and identifying the variables to be tested. The answers to this basic determination may not be at all evident and may require a very good preliminary study.
2. Selecting the range of values within which these variables would occur and being sensitive to the supposed casual factors. It would be sheer waste to exert or measure factors within ranges that would provide no information towards the problem solution.
3. Determining the character and inter-relations of the data and their method of measurement, which tend to be even more crucial than determination of the experimental techniques. Time and effort in planning should be carefully gauged to put due emphasis on the decision.
4. Determining the point at which internal validity may be increased only at the cost of lower external validity. In seeking to gain the former, the experimental model may become too unlike the real would or the subjects in the test may become biased, which would spoil the external validity. A proper balance between theses qualities may be a nice question.

### *Types of Experimental Research*

There are three major types of experimental designs namely:

1. Classical experimental design
2. After-only experimental design
3. Before-after experimental design

#### *1. Classical Experimental Design*

Goode and Hatt have explained this method intensively. They define it giving an example: "If there are two are more cases, and in one of them observation Z can be made, while in the other it cannot; and if factor C occurs when observation Z is made, and does not occur when observation Z is not made: then it can be asserted that there is a casual relationship between C and Z."

So in classical design two series of observations and situations are necessary. This type of research has greater use in biological or medical experiements. In marketing pharamachical goods, this research method may be helpful for a marketing research.

The above authors have explained this method by quoting an example of malaria infection and application for atabrine to it; Atabrine is administered to one group, the experimental group and withheld from the other, the control group. If the experimental group recovers and the control group not, the conclusion is that Atrbrine and malaria systems are related. If all recover in both groups, then it can be concluded that Atabrine does not affect malaria.

2. *After Only Experimental Design*

This method assumes that prior to the introduction of the experimental factor, the control and experimental groups were identical and the nature are same.

3. *Before-after Experimental Research*

In this method, the group is observed prior to its exposure to the experimental variable. That means to have a preliminary observational period so as to measure control behaviour and introduce a 'stimulus':

By means of using stimulus we can study the effect of previously identified experimental stimulus on experimental group and the effect of lack of stimulus on the control group.

# 10

# Methods or Types for Business Research

Business research has labored hard to invent various methods and techniques of research in social sciences, out of which we are able to get guidelines to proceed in our research activities. The popular methods of research are historical method survey, case study, descriptive method and experimental research. The last said method is used in a very limited way in business research.

## Historical Method and Business Research

Through historical method we can study the past and theories or facts relating to the past could be verified and the authenticity of the past could be analyzed and verified. Historical method of Research has immense value for Business Research. Studying the past, past performance of companies and the history of the corporate movement during a particular phase, period or year have become inevitable to private sector. Corporate sector has changed a lot after Second World War. Since the economic liberalization, started from 1991, lot of changes are taking place in the business world. Globalisation has its own impact on business. Such changes could be studies through Business Research. Unlike other methods of research, historical method needs greater orientation and familiarization of verification of data, documentation, etc.

## Survey Method and Business Research

Survey method has been popularly used in Business research. Wider coverage of population and macro approach facilitate the fuller utilization of this method by the Business researchers. Through surveys we can study the growth, development and current trends in the corporate sector. Competition as a factor of business could be studied very deeply and accurately through surveys.

## Case Study and Business Research

Another important method of research, which provides helping hand to Business researchers, is the case study. Case study though a method of research, is very often used as a tool of research. Case study can be useful to study a individual company's performance as well as its achievements. The success factors can be emulated by other companies also.

### *Unique Features of Case Study for Business*

1. *Study of a single unit*—In the context of business institutions single unit for case study purpose may be the working performance of a company or a specific factor connected with the functions of the selected companies.
2. *Complete study*—Case study is an approach, which use any social unit as a whole. For example, total working aspect of a particularcompany, operational efficiency of a factory in the functional management, marketing efficiency of firms, etc.
3. *Intensive study*—Case study is a method, which is penetrating, inclusive, and intensive study of an individual unit. It implies systematic collection of all information about a company to facilitate any one to understand how the corporates functions.
4. *Qualitative study*—The materials related to the history, growth, management, etc of a corporate are used for case writing is bound to be qualitative in nature. To ensure quality, the researcher should depend on his own objective observations and logic.
5. *Inter-relationship of causal factors*—In case study, an effort can also be made to establish cause and effect relationship between variables.

6. *Flexible method*—The case problems can be approached from any angle of the unit. For example, the services rendered by a sugar factory to the farmers can be studied from the company angle or farmers angle or both angles.

Other methods of research like descriptive research and experimental research are of less importance to Business Research.

# 11

# Research Gap and Study of Related Literature in Social Research

## Research Gap

Research Gap is in important area of research, which a researcher should not forget to recognize its merits. Hell of confusions could be avoided if this concept is understood in proper perspective by researchers.

'Research gap' in social sciences is referred to the 'unexplored area of research or areas of research which has not been touched by others so far. In other words research gap points out the following significances in a research area/programme:

1. It induces the involvement of the researcher in the task of mastering the areas/topics where research has been already undertaken.
2. Scope for creativity is created on the part of the researcher to refer all sources of publication and exhaust the review of literature."

### *Importance of Research Gap*

Research gap tells a researcher 'what to do' and 'what not to do'. It needs tremendous labour and meticulous observation of past work done by various researchers. More library reference will not do justification. Using of reference/bibliography cards and sources cards would be of immense help to them. This must be preceded by listing of books and journals in the field. If a particular book or journal is not available all other important libraries must be searched. Spending time and effort on such endeavor is not a waste compared to resting on others' efforts of copying another bibliography.

Consultation with experts in the field is another way of locating a 'research gap'. A honest and right thinking expert will definitely guide you in the areas to be searched. Referring foreign journals and foreign experts and additional sources, but they are time consuming and laborious job. A researcher has to come out of his 'shell' and have a open and frank mind of locating 'new vistas of knowledge' rather that beating round the bush.

Locating the research gap has multifaceted advantages to the researcher. One basis advantage is it avoids the wastage of resources. Availability of time is a crucial factor for a scholar and saving time is equal to that of saving money. Past experience in the field of social research has shown that rarely scholars complete their work in time. One of the stumbling blocks for a scholar is spending enormous time in selecting the topic of research. Providing clarity, narrow downing the scope, conceptual clarifications, etc. have to be evenly justified by a scholar in the selection process. For such purpose a side support is provided by the research gap. Hence, time as a vital resource is served by the location of research gap.

Research gap avoids repetition of research problems, methodologies and even findings. Today's bane of social research is repetition of research area and the fallout is stereo typed research findings. These things must be avoided and innovative findings must come out. These are the days of 'action research', which warrants the need to do research which are socially relevant. Any amount of money and time spent on research must have practical utility to society. This practical utility of resources of social research can be gained out of locating research gap and finding new and fresh areas of research.

While locating the research gap a researcher gains a lot by means of expanding his creativity and thinking faculty. Creative thinking and probing nature will provide greater scope for locating new areas of research.

## Study of Related Literature

Study of related literature is an important part at the stage of selecting a research problem as well as at later stages of research process. While selecting a research problem the researcher has to familiarize with his area of riled of research. Wider knowledge about the field is essential to understand the very area of research.

**Need to Study Literature**

1. Going through relevant literature a researcher can gain theoretical knowledge.
2. Study of related literature helps to familiarize oneself with the existing knowledge, and various types of research studies undertaken in the field.
3. Innovations, latest developments, new tools of research can be identified by reviewing literature.
4. New concepts and variables can be located.
5. By reviewing relevant literature the 'Research gap' can be identified. Through this process the researcher can fill the gap and can avoid repetition.
6. To frame effective hypothesis review of literature is needed.
7. Once can differentiate one's research problem from others. Thereby you can establish the unique nature of your study.
8. Relevant methodology and tools of data collection can be decided.
9. Appropriate statistical tools can also be determined by going through relevant literatures.

***Definition of Literature***

A researcher has to go through various types of literature like books, journals, committee reports, institutional reports, etc. Any type of literature that is used, referred or abstracted forms part of literature. Review of literature is a section in a study where researchers discuss ideas obtained from various sources in relation to their research topic. According to Taylor " a literature review is an account of what has been published on a topic by accredited scholars and researchers." Similarly Creswell says the following "Researchers use the scholarly literature in a study to present the results of similar studies, to relate the present study to the on going dialogue in the literature and to provide a framework for comparing results of a study with other studies"

This section is the place where the researcher provides the reader with an explanation of the theoretical rationale of the problem being studied. A good review of literature does not merely describe previous research, on the other hand it should be analytical and evaluative. Because it is not needed just for the sake of reporting what other researchers have found out or said before.

### The Purpose of Review of Literature

This job of reviewing related literature provides a researcher an extended knowledge about the issue at hand and in assisting them in tackling the problem. Moreover this is the place where the appropriate method to be followed will be specified. Hitchcock and Hughes say that "a literature search will help to focus research more directly and sharpen and refine the research question. It makes the explicit impact of theory in every stage of the study from formulation of initial problem and selection of the population through data collection and analysis to interpretation." Leedy (1999) has mentioned the following purposes of review of literature:

1. It can reveal investigations germane to your own, and it can show you how the researcher handled these situations.
2. It can suggest a method or a technique of dealing with a problematic situation which may also suggest avenues of approach to the solution of similar difficulties you may be facing.
3. It can reveal to you sources of data which you may not have known.
4. It can introduce you to significant personalities of whose research efforts and collateral writings you may have had no knowledge.
5. it can help you to see your own study in historical and associational perspectives and relation to earlier attacks on the same problem.
6. It can provide you with new ideas and approaches which may not have occurred to you.
7. It can assist you in evaluating your own research efforts by comparing them with related efforts done by others.

### *Stages of Referring Literature*

1. The first stage is at which the researcher has to gain familiarity with the 'Area of Research'. It is to know, What is what?
2. Second stage is to identify the research problem as such. This process is undertaken after establishing the 'research gap' in the field. As far as possible the research problem must be defined suitably and its scope must be pinpointed.

3. Next state is the 'Operationalization of concepts'. This process helps to identify suitable concepts and variables needed for the study.
4. Framing of hypothesis is the next stage where on e has to refer previous research studies.
5. While preparing the 'Research design' or 'Research proposal' one has to go through various literature.
6. For the construction of tools of data collection and for deciding the right type of statistical tools review of literature is essential.
7. While writing the theoretical chapter or portions of the report, reference of various materials is a must.
8. After writing the final report bibliography has to be collected, which is possible through the preparation of 'Source Cards.'

### *Precautions to be Followed*

1. Make it a habit to go through literature from the beginning to the end of your research process.
2. Study the materials thoroughly. Glancing amounts to 'half baking'.
3. Keep source cards ready and note things then and there.
4. Record only materials needed for your study.
5. Must be able to distinguish 'needed sources' and 'unwanted sources'.
6. Any source taken may be acknowledged. Abrupt copying amounts to plagiarism.
7. Keep all the cards safer even after your research work is over.
8. Continue the habit of referring sources even after your research work is over as you are expected to become an authority in your area of research by means of publishing more research papers, undertaking independent research works, guiding scholars or writing books.

## How to Write a Good Review of Literature?

The following steps are to be followed in writing a good review of literature:

*Remember the purpose:* This will help the researcher not to forget the purpose of writing the review of literature, since the review is not merely to tell the researcher what others have done.

It should be remembered that it is there to explain the research from various perspectives. The aim should be to show why the particular research needs to be carried out , how the methodology or theories are to be opted to work with and how the specific work adds value to the already done studies.

*Reading with purpose:* This helps the researchers to identify and decide on ideas and information that are important to be included in the work. It should be noted that while reading, the researcher must be trying to define the problems to be dealt with in the study. In defining the problem, identifying the gaps , posing questions and adding new findings to the previous researches are given special considerations. Looking at these areas helps to see similarities and differences among the works formerly done and expected to be done now or in future.

*Writing with purpose:* Writing the review is not mere repetition of what others have already said. The aim of writing the review of literature should be to evaluate the relationship between the previous and present work. The researcher must come out with new interpretation of what others have said and what gaps exists and how these gaps will be filled by his own research.

## *Organising and Writing up the Review of Literature*

The way the researcher chooses to organize the materials needs care. The researcher should present theories and facts logically and in a coherent manner in order to catch the readers attention and convince them about the issue raised. Lecomte and Pressile (1993) consider the review as an argument between the investigator and the audience and suggest that it should be constructed in a tight manner. They further say that it helps in the following ways:

1. It will convince the reader of the relevance and interest of the questions, adequacy and appropriateness of the choice of the population and research design.
2. anticipate and justify the results, and
3. where possible support the interpretation of data and conclusions reached.

Leedy says the following precautions relating to review of related literature:

1. It should be worked towards the proper psychological orientation ie it should be like a discussion with a friend and very clear in conveying the thinking.

2. It must be organized in a plan: There should be an outline prepared starting from the broader perspective and narrows to the specific problem.
3. It must be organized in a way that reminds the reader constantly how the points the researcher is discussing, are related to the problem.
4. It must be checked that it is not a copy: The researcher should note that more important than what the study says is what he/she says about the study.

In a more detailed way Frey et al (1991) recommended patterns of organizing the review of literature as follows:

1. *Topical order:* Organise by main topics or issues and emphasise the relationship of the issues to the main problem.
2. *Chronological order:* Organise by historical progression in terms of time.
3. *General to specific order:* Examine broad based research first and then focus on specific studies that relate to the topic.
4. *Problem-cause-solution order:* organize the review so that it moves from the problem to the solution.
5. *Known to unknown order:* Examine current literature about the problem and then identify at the end what still is not known.
6. *Comparison and contrast order:* Show how research studies are similar to and different from each other.

Specific to general order : Try to make sense out of specific research studies so that conclusions can be drawn Interaction with Research Journals.

### *Interaction with Research Journals*

A literature may be taken to include all that is recorded and available in the manuscript or printed from – official and non-official. Such literatures may provide detailed information which may be basic, advanced and operational and which are available in libraries, offices and archives etc.

Consulting literature in research either extensively or intensively is called interaction with literature. Such interaction begins for identifying research problems and destines at the research reporting. Literatures are secondary sources, which from the first working base for outlining the problems and analysis. A recognized literature is a beacon for research in alleviating problems.

### *The Forms of Interaction*

Interaction with literature can be generally made through different channels. In the process of research, knowledge on the sources of information, collection and establishing contact are the various dimensions. The sources are:

#### *(i) Subject Catalogue*

The catalogue maintained in libraries—subject-wise open up new vistas. The researcher can have exhaustive collection of item of various books/journals concentrating on the main and sub-themes. This will facilitate access to vital documents too. In the case of inter-disciplinary research, consultation of related subject will contribute for the accomplishment of the desired objective.

#### *(ii) Documentation Support Service*

Catering to the special requirements of research, documentation support services are available. Under one roof, at a time, the scholars can have access to materials, which appeared in literatures. This source provides a long list of the journals/magazines/reports/publications available on different subjects of choice on payment basis. These services are also offered by specialized centers for the benefit of research scholars in varied disciplines.

#### *(iii) Journals*

Journals regional, national and international are the carriers of latest sources of information or research providing insider information to different places at a time. Conceptual changes, findings, innovations are disseminated largely through this source. Hence, interactions with journals is a sine-qua-non. Hence, journals form a core source of information.

#### *(iv) Government Reports*

Consultation with report of the Government, Enquiry Committee, Study Teams, Special Task Force on policy implications and execution form part of other elements in spectrum.

### *(v) Research Abstracts*

Access to research abstracts helps to know the work. An abstract provides pertinent, bibliographical details such as title, author, periodicity, publisher etc., besides providing a brief outline of the research, methodology adopted, findings of research.

### *(vi) Information Source on Research Already Done*

Interaction on the dissertation already available will throw new lights to researchers in eliminating the area already covered by others, identification of newer ones. Scope for further research in terms of quantitative and qualitative analysis can well be planned through this kind of interaction.

## Interaction with journals

Interaction with journals are periodicals carrying matters relating to current events in the fields of specialization. The journals provide narrative material, statistical data, methods of analysis and interpretations in capsule forms.This is helpful to researchers to select a right research problem.

Interaction with journals by researchers keep abreast of knowledge in the field. Further, annual numbers and back volumes become an invaluable asset for any time reference paying way for updating the knowledge. Hence, it enables relating the contemplated investigation of earlier efforts, thus preventing repetition of research projects. It would also facilitate hypothesis formulation and suggest new avenues of approach, induction to unknown field etc.

## Interaction with Journal through Internet

In the dynamic world there is an increasing opportunity to consult the journals far and near through Internet satellite computer links. A scholar in one place can have easy access for information available in any library/achieve anywhere in the world and can copies in no time. This result in saving time and avoiding communication distortion. The library/achieve which has a computer terminal can be a registered member of the Internet Channel available on payment basic. The member has to enter HTTP (Hyper Text Typed Protocol/World Wide Web) and then the matter will be displayed on the screen.

### *When to Consult a Research Journal?*

The most abridge and çapsule form of answer to this question is consultation at anytime. For selecting the area, identification of topic precisely, survey of literature, hypothesis formulation, preparing the interview schedule/mailed questionnaire, theory building, tabulation of data, interpretation and up to the stage of writing the thesis consultation is inevitable and imperative.

### Indexing the Content

Access to the journal will not serve any purpose unless the research scholar acquires the information/data and uses them at the appropriate time and place. Efforts can be made to keep the data for any time use through some kind of arrangement. An easy way to bring the content in the thesis is through preparation of card index of items interacted. Classification of information/data according to the objectives of the study and chapter arrangements, will unfailingly yield good result.

### *Interaction with the Experts*

Research is a very much pleasant and beautiful experience. It ought to be because, the person who is doing the research is going to be a contributor to the society in which he is existing. Realizing this fact a research scholar should be careful enough to adopt right methods and approaches in all disciplines of a research task.

This is one of the formal ways to select a right problem of research and get clarifications.

One of the disciplines of the research is the work of collection of data. It is nothing but the collection of facts for evolving the theory. Of course, this work has it momentum throughout the research period after the major work of selecting the topic. Sometimes, we may have to get some important data even after completing the research.

The scholar should prepare himself both mentally and physically for this endeavor. First it is important for the scholar to prepare himself mentally.

He has to keep few things in his mind.

1. This is an incomparably significant discipline, in spite of having chances for errors and bias in the information. The sharing of the experiences of the experts in person,

receiving the pieces of advice and the expert guidelines will help to proceed with the research in proper perspective.

2. The scholar must understand that a conversation is going to take place in the interactions, which is going to benefit him only. So he must give place for emotional split at any moment.
3. It is also important to keep in mind that the interview is to elicit the required information from the experts only and not to educate him. Hence, to make the work as the most successful one, the scholar must adopt certain formal interaction process, which are inevitable.

## The Formal Interaction Process

### *1. Accessibility*

The expert, who is interacted, is supposed to be enriched with the information about the field of the scholar and to provide the required information to the scholar.

But this may be affected on account of several reasons like below:

(i) They would have forgotten the required information on account of his physical problems like old age and weak memory and non-familiar with the specific area of the scholar at the moment.

(ii) The expert would have got some emotional stress, which may prevent him from revealing the information. During such kind of situations, the scholar should be careful in dealing with the experts. He has to study the mind of the experts very much carefully.

(iii) There is much possibility for rising up of certain situations that the experts are not willing to share their views, on account of having different ideas about the subject. At the time, the scholar should be very much careful in undertaking the interaction programmes with experts.

### *2. Cognition*

This process occupies the second place of the formal interview procedures. Cognition is nothing but the understanding of the role of the expert on the occasion of interview. This should be given by the scholar to the expert already in a proper manner. Before the interview the scholar should ensure it.

### 3. *Motivation*

This process is the most important process, which makes the whole attempt a successful one.

This scholar should give perfect motivation to the expert about the interview on three backgrounds.

1. Motivation for initial decision to co-operate: This motivation provides the idea in the mind of the expert to co-operate with scholar for making the attempt a successful one.
2. Subsequent decision to continue: While the interaction is carried on, the motivation should be given to the expert subsequently that he should give more information to the scholar in order to help him. He should give accurate, and sufficient information avoiding the distorted replies.

The scholar must have patience to prepare himself for the task by having enough training for himself. If he is able to prepare himself mentally, it is much possible for him to prepare himself physically.

Some of the ideas for the scholars for preparing himself physically:

1. Dressing up in impressive manner
2. Go with suitable equipments for the interviews
3. Avoid mannerisms
4. Tone or voice should be soft
5. Avoid distractions.

## *Developing Research Competencies Through Attending Relevant Seminars/Workshops*

Seminar/workshop is the gateway through which the research experts bring to light their research findings. It would enable the participants to understand the selection of a right problem for research, methodology employed and the results arrived at by the researchers. It would also enable the researchers to highlight the practical difficulties encountered and their perseverance and dedication to the research.

A research finding is said to be good, if it is acclaimed, appreciated and accepted by majority of the participants who are specialised in the similar field of research.

The participants of any seminar/workshop can be grouped

into (i) the young researchers, (ii) the resource person and (iii) the sponsoring agency.

Finding solution to the existing as well as the emerging problem the society should be the chief objective for conducting any seminar/workshop.

*No Agency to Co-ordinate the Seminar/Workshop*

There has been no co-ordination among the sponsoring agencies while conducting seminars/workshop though we have many sponsoring agencies at the national as well as regional level.

In these days, the environment of the people is getting changed rapidly and it affects the social, cultural, political and economic life of the people.

Accordingly we have research problem relating to social, cultural, political and economic activities. The complexities and dimensions of these problems are not uniform and equal.

For instance, in the field of economics, the research experts conduct research on various subjects viz., economics of institutions, employment and savings, production and market, budget and taxes, export and import and plethora of other economic activities. No mechanism has so far been found by any agency to determine the order of importance of these activities and which of them need immediate solution from the subject experts.

At times the field experts do conduct research on those problems which need less attention and fail to concentrate on some of the vital issues which need immediate research findings.

From this perspective, there is a need for some agencies to co-ordinate the research activities and highlight the problems of the society which need immediate attention.

The deterioration of the quality of research is due to the absence of any agency which controls, regulates and monitors research work. A well co-ordinated body comprising academics, business houses and Government should be constituted by the Government. They should plan out the broad subjects on which micro studies may be taken up. Regional studies are the need of the hour for the planning purpose.

Otherwise the very purpose of research will be defeated, whatever mazy be the objective of the study. Research is being done for the research sale. In these days the number of theses is getting increased. However the results that come out of them are not commensurate with the number of theses. Inadequate knowledge in research methodology dilute the quality of the research findings and the quality has come down to its lower ebb. How to employ appropriate research methodology is still a grey area which needs attention of the experts.

We are living in the age of computers. We avail the excellent services of computers for the data processing, tabulation and interpretation. Computers reduce the physical strain of the researchers. However they fail to concentrate on certain other activities viz., personal observation, in-depth review of literature, etc.

The success of any research depends upon the individual's aptitude in the research. There is no tool to measure the quantum of work to be done and the minimum and maximum work to be exerted for a given study. To what extent, the researchers have to spare time, the clarity they need, the depth of knowledge they gain, before they bring out research results need some sort of clarity.

Attending relevant seminar/workshop is the only remedy for the participants to find solution to the above listed problems. Keeping this in mind, an attempt has been made to discuss about the development of research competencies attending relevant seminars/workshops.

### *What is Seminar/Workshop?*

Seminar means a small group of researchers engaged in advanced study and original research under a member of the faculty meeting regularly to exchange information and hold discussions.

Workshop means a seminar, discussion group or the like which emphasizes exchange of ideas and the demonstration and application of techniques, skills etc.

Conference— we mean the art of conferring or consulting together, consultation especially on an important or serious matter.

### *The Participants*

The participants include the resource persons, the organisers, the sponsoring agency, the young researchers and the target audience. From the researchers' point of view the attendance of seminar/workshop depends upon the research experts. The experts are the pioneers in their respective field of study. The advancement of any subject purely depends upon the active involvement of experts. Young researchers must see who are the subject experts who present the papers in the seminar/workshops.

Experts focus the subjects from two angles viz., (i) the existing problems and finding solutions to it and (ii) the development of new techniques. The young scholars may attend those seminars/ workshops where the experts focus their attention to the problems.

The subjects experts highlight the grey areas which need the attention of the researchers at the micro level. For instance, there is a problem in the field of management due to globalisation. Hitherto the subject describes the management of people/ personnel of the respective nation. Now we need managers to know as how to understand the intricacies and complications to be involved in the managing of people of different nations, different language and different culture who come to work together. The subject experts of the Harvard University now direct attention towards the development of new strategy in this regard.

Thus, attending relevant seminars would enable the scholars to find not the experts but also a suitable guide/supervisor for their further study.

Present research work is aimless, haphazard and without any objectives. Isolated problems at the whims of the researchers/ supervisors are taken up for the study. They have no relevance to the national or regional priorities. They are unconnected and no continuation of the work is done already in that field. Attending relevant seminars would enable the scholars to choose the right guide.

## The Sponsoring Agencies

It is not easy task to organize a seminar/ workshop without sponsoring agencies. Attending relevant seminars depends upon the sponsoring agencies. Some agencies limit the programme to the academic community and some agencies limit the programme to the field experts only. Now-a-days government agencies like UGC and ICSSR liberally provide financial assistance for the conduct of seminar/workshop at regional, national and international level. Besides, we nave research institutions and autonomous institution like IIM, etc., who sponsor programmes.

At the state level there are plenty of organisations that come forward to sponsor seminar programmes. Now-a-days the commercial banks especially the private sector banks show keen interest in sponsoring the seminar programmes. In our country, the private sector business community is still reluctant to show interest in sponsoring programmes.

There has been no link between the academics and the business institutions at all levels, leave apart the technical institutions like REC, and IIT which are mostly engaged in the independent research activities.

While sponsoring the programmes, there has been a chance to bring together the academy and the business world. This would enable them to find out the practical problems and solutions. The participants should see therefore who are sponsoring agencies and for whom they sponsor so that they could find out whether there is any role for them to play.

We have the following agencies who sponsor and organize seminars/workshops at regular intervals:

**National Level**

1. The University Grants Commission
2. The Indian Council for Social Science Research
3. All Indian Management Association
4. All Indian Commerce Association
5. Indian Institute of finance
6. Institute of Company Secretaries of India
7. Institute of chartered Accounts of Indian
8. Institute of Human resource Development
9. Research Development Association
10. University
11. Indian economics Association
12. National Research Development Corporation
13. International Co-operative Alliance
14. National Co-operative Union of India
15. All India Association for Christian Higher Education

**State Level**

1. District Industries Centre
2. Small Industries Service Institute
3. Commercial Banks
4. Labour/Teachers Association
5. Small Industries Development Corporation
6. National Small Industries Corporation

7. Director of Industries and Commerce
8. Colleges
9. Voluntary Association
10. State Corporative Unions.

**Participants**

The participants of seminars/workshops mostly consist of aspiring young researchers. They expert to find research topics in the seminar for probing further. In these days scholars as well as supervisors who do not attend seminars/workshops at frequent intervals find difficulty of choosing the research topics. It is a ticklish issue. Those who attend seminars at regular intervals have a long list of topics which are amenable for research. In these days, the these presented in the universities are stereo-typed and examiners are reluctant to value them and simply return the same by saying that 'preoccupied with other engagements'. Those who attend seminars never feel dearth of research topics. The gist of research papers presented in the seminar throws more light on the new areas of research.

Instead of familiarizing with the existing review of literature and find out the gap for further research, it would be an alternate for the scholars to select topics which are declared as 'gap' in the seminars/workshops.

**Finance**

As how it is difficult to conduct a seminar, it is equally a tough job to attend the seminar. In these days, it is a costly affair. For attending a national seminar, one should spend a minimum of Rs.3,000, leave a part the delegation fee, boarding and lodging. He has to travel and undergo tedious journey. No organizers are ready to meet these especially for the young scholars. The shortage of funds not therefore mind in spending from their own pocket. However, they would get reward if they sincerely make an attempt to attend the seminars/workshops.

In these days, wise scholar not only attend the seminars, instead they go with research schedule and consult with the subject experts. They are scholars who attend the seminars/workshops. With a number of schedules and get them filled with the help of fellow participants. They go back with the filled schedule. It will be processed and they prepare papers out of it which will be worth for publication. The following shall be the chief objectives of the participants while attending the seminar.

1. It aspires young scholars to develop research bent kind of mind.
2. conceive new problems which are relevant to the present day of the society.
3. Enable scholars to apply new tools and methodology.
4. An occasion to share the practical difficulties with the fellow participants.
5. Contact learned scholars and keep in touch with them in the future days.
6. Enable the participants to became full-fledged researchers.

Ask the following questions to get clarified with regard to attending relevant seminar.

**1. Why do we Attend Seminars?**

1. To identify the areas to be researched.
2. To test your research findings.
3. To determine the level of acceptance and objectives.
4. To find out the objectives and hypotheses.
5. to decide the objectives and hypotheses.
6. To share your experience.
7. To share others experience.
8. To familiarize with the delegates.
9. To acquaint with the research experts.

**II. What Seminar do we Attend?**

1. seminar which deals with the subjects of national/regional importance.
2. Seminar to be conducted by the University/Colleges/Associations.
3. Seminar of your relevant subjects.
4. Seminar that is sponsored by the Government.
5. Seminar that identifies you as a delegate.
6. Seminar conducted by the institutions where you hold membership.

**III. When do You Attend?**

1. When you have aspiration for research.

2. When you seek research topics.
3. When you are in the midst of practical difficulties.
4. When you complete your research study.
5. When you want to specialize in a special field.
6. When you are invited to become a resource person.
7. When you need contract with the subject specialists.
8. When you findings give immediate solution.

## IV. Where do you Attend Seminars?

1. At places which are accessible to you.
2. At places where your topic will be discussed.
3. At the places where you meet your colleagues.
4. At the national level seminars organized by the university.
5. At the state level seminars organized by the Govt. Department.
6. At the regional level seminars organized by the institutions.

## V. Whom do we Contact for the Seminar/Workshop?

1. The organizing body.
2. The Seminar Director/Co-ordinator/Convener
3. The institutions where you are working.
4. The information centers for collecting secondary data.
5. The agencies for financial assistance.
6. Fellow researchers.

## VI. How to Attend the Seminar/Workshop?

1. Sending your delegate fee and get your name registered.
2. Obtain paper acceptance from the Chairman of the technical session.
3. Prepare an abstract of the paper.
4. Get the copies of the paper for distribution.
5. Move cordially with the fellow participants and give respect to all.
6. Do not think that you know everything.

# 12

# Selection of a Problem for Research—How to Find a Research Problem

## Introduction

Socio-economic life in modern times is beset with innumerable problems. The immediate environment of the researcher provides ample scope for identification of a research problem. The cognizance of and/or the existence of unsolved difficulties is the first symptom for locating a research problem. Coupled with this the felt need, constructive imagination and reflective thinking are the essential pre-requisities for identification of a research problem. The problem begins to appear when the need for explanation or solution is intense; or when it kindles the curiosity of the researcher due to the shrouded mystery or controversy of the subject. To those who are already engaged in the field of research, selecting a research problem won't be a difficult task. Through the continuity of his deep, devoted work a researcher may come across many problems. Hence, for an experienced researcher, selecting a research problem may not pose problems so much as to a new corner. Further a research study concluded leads to further research by extending the possible areas of research. The task is always onerous to a new corner. He is always anxious to snatch a problem. In that process he may loose his balance and in hurry he may land himself in difficulties. A research problem selected in haste more often leads to waste at later stages. John Best, an Educational Researcher cautions that, "the beginner is likely to selected a problem that is much too broad in scope. This may be due to his lack of understanding of the nature of research and systematic problem-solving activity. It may also be due to his enthusiastic, but naïve desire to solve an important problem quickly and immediately. Those who are more experience know that research is often tedious, painfully slow and rarely spectacular. They reaslise that the search for truth and the solution of important problems take a great deal of time and energy and to intensive application of logical thinking.

A research problem rightly and rationally selected solves half of the problem of research. The right selection of a topic has ultimate advantages and boosts the morale of the researcher. A right selection of a research problem helps the researcher to proceed in his work methodically and step by step. This paves the way to complete the project within the prescribed time limit and the cost can be rounded within the budgeted amount. A right selection also gives an enlightened picture of the problem at every stage, thereby avoiding as far as possible, unnecessary modification, omissions and additions. The seriousness of research will be kept alive throughout the period which ensures clarity of thinking, grasping of the concepts, logical analysis of data and justification of the title and objectives. In social science research when the project is at full steam, problems are bound to arise. Such problems could be reduced if the right topic, over which the researcher has mastery, is selected. Confusion at the selection level leads to confusion at every later stage, which ultimately result in the failure of the project.

This paves the way to complete the project within the prescribed time limit and the cost can be rounded within the budgeted amount. A right selection also gives an enlightened picture of the problem at every stage, thereby avoiding as far as possible, unnecessary modification, omissions and additions

### Precautions to be taken while Selecting a Research Problem

1. Select a topic in the field in which you have familiarity or in-depth understanding. "If the scholar is familiar with his field and knows what research has already been completed in it, he will also know something of the many problems that remain."
2. A research problem should be time bound and cost bound. Allowing scope for modifications in time and budget the

scholars must complete the study within the limited period and cost. The selection of the topic must be made accordingly. A beginner can afford to choose only a simple problem.

3. The capacity of the research problem should be within the physical resources available to a researcher. Hence, a budget always forms part of a "Research Design" or "Research Proposal".
4. The basis for selection of the topic itself should be as strong as the foundation of a building which requires enormous reading, reference and discussion.
5. A researcher need not be in a hurry in choosing a problem. Carefully considered and objectively selected problems will imbibe confidence in a researcher. Spending considerable time to select a topic won't be a waste at all. It could very well save enormous time at later stages, which otherwise could not be available to a topic chosen in haste.
6. While selecting a topic the researcher need not be over-enthusiastic. He must be balanced and must be ready to fact unexpected twist, unreasonable delay, incompletion of data and subsequent second visit to the field. He should not feel the selected problem either too soft or two hard to deal with.

Pauline Young suggests that following points to be kept in mind while choosing a research topic:

1. Ability to grasp and time to deal with its broad implication.
2. Resources to carry the study forward may be exceedingly limited if no basic research has been previously done by experienced scientists in the field. At time resources are available, but they are not open to research beginners or they are confidential.
3. Applicability of study techniques should be considered for the particular topic chosen.
4. We should also consider degree of accuracy or approximation essential for the demands of scientifically conducted project.

### *What is a Research Problem?*

As has been pointed out already, in social research, selection of problem must be given careful consideration and thorough scrutiny. The problem should have a purpose and worth appreciated in research terms. The problem must have intensity, must provide scope for deep analysis and must take smooth and orderly course of action. In other words, it must be a running stream and not a stagnant pool.

A problem can be called a research problem only when it satisfies the following conditions.

1. It must be worth studying. In other words, it must have viability or potentiality to stand as a research problem.
2. It must have social relevance. The study must be able to bring the attention of the experts, policy-makers; academicians etc, who are familiar with the subject.
3. There must be a 'felt need' for research over the problem. Such problem must be in need of further elaboration and exploration. As far as possible, it should be untouched by other researchers or even if touched must be in need of further research possibility.
4. A research problem must come out with pragmatic solutions to the issues.
5. As far as possible a social research problem must be up to date or relevant to the current social happenings; it should not be sterile.

Hillaway advocates the following rules to define a problem.

1. Be sure that the topic chosen is neither too vague nor too broad in scope.
2. To make the problem clearer and more understandable, state it as a question, which requires definite answer.
3. Carefully state that limits of the problem, eliminating all aspects and factors, which will not be considered in the study.
4. Define any special terms that must be used in the statement of your problem.

### *How to find a Research Problem?*

For a researcher who is already engaged in research, selection of a topic will be an easier task.. But in the case of a beginner, to select a problem itself is problematical and he has to spend acquaint with relevant channels of research. In the course of his academic pursuit a researcher may come across many research problems. But many researchers, especially newcomers are in search of a problem. For such people, "Curiosity" for a problem of research study or "Curiosity about the unknown" is the best guide in selecting a problem. Satisfaction of personal curiosity would seem, then, to be the most desirable incentive in the selection of a topic for study. This comes ordinarily, from having a thorough knowledge of one's field and of the gaps that exist in it."

A caution that is always given to a newcomer is not to select the problem in a hurry. It would be better if he spares more time in the selection than indulging in wasting time later on due to wrongful selection. If he spends some more time analyzing the viability of the topic, clarifying the thinking, achieving a sense of focus and reaching a stage from vagueness, to elucidation, he could proceed his research orderly putting an end to unnecessary waste of time and resources. Careful selection of a topic and ultimate successful completion will sustain the researcher's keenness to research throughout his career.

### *Sources of Problems*

The sources from which one may be able to identify research problems or develop problem awareness are:

*1. Reading*

When we critically study books and articles relating to subject of our interest, pertinent questions may arise in our mind. Similarly, areas of research may strike to our mind when we read research reports.

*2. Academic Experience*

Classroom lectures, class discussions, seminar discussions and out-of-class exchanges of ideas with fellow students and professors will suggest many stimulating problems to be studied.

*3. Daily Experience*

Life is dynamic. We learn new things and undergo new experiences every day. If we are alert, inquisitive and sensitive to life situation, we may hit upon/questions worth of investigation. "It is a mark of scientific genius to be sensitive to difficulties where less gifted people pass untroubled by doubt."

*4. Exposure to Field Situations*

Field visits, internship training and extension work provide exposure to practical problems, which call for study.

*5. Consultations*

Discussions with experts, teachers, administrators and business executives will help a researcher to identify meaningful problems for research.

*6. Brain Storming*

Intensified discussion within a group of interested persons may often be a means of identifying pertinent questions, and of developing new ideas about a problem.

*7. Research*

Research on one problem may suggest problems for further research.

*8. Intuition*

Sometimes new ideas may strike to one's mind like a flash. Reflective mind is a spring of knowledge

# 13

# Process of Identification of Research Problem

The process of identification of problem for academic research may consist of the following steps:

### *1. Selection of the Discipline*

The subject in which one proposes to do research may be selected, e.g., Economics, Commerce, Management, Technology, Psychology, rural development etc. The selection of the discipline is easy. One can select any subject, which one has studied thoroughly and which has interested him most. Where one has to do research in his field of specialization (e.g., Rural development ) One has to choose the subject of one's specialization.

### *2. Demarcating the Broad Area or a Particular Aspect of the Selected Subject*

The second step is to select a particular aspect of the selected subject. For example, if the selected subject is financial management, then one may select capital budgeting, financial leverage, working capital management or profit management as specific area of study.

### *3. Identifying Two or More Specific Topics in the Selected Broad Area*

This is the final step in identification of problems. This requires a grasp of the branch of the subject as a whole and awareness of work already done on it. A student cannot just select anyone of the identified problems for his research. He has to evaluate them for choosing the most appropriate one. How can this evaluation be done? Against what criteria?

### *Criteria of Selection*

The selection of one appropriate researchable problem out of the identified problems requires evaluation of those alternatives against certain criteria. These criteria may be grouped into:

(a) Internal (or personal) criteria or factors, and

(b) External criteria or factors.

Internal criteria consist of (i) researcher's interest, (ii) researcher's competence, and (iii) researcher's own resource: finance and time.

External factors include (i) researchability of the problem, (ii) its importance and urgency, (iii) novelty of the problem, (iv) feasibility, (v) facilities, (vi)usefulness and social relevance, and (vii) research personnel.

### *Researcher's Interest*

The problem should interest the researcher and be a challenge to him. Without interest and curiosity, he may not develop sustained perseverance. Even a small difficulty may become an excuse for discontinuing the study.

Interest in a problem depends upon the researcher's educational background, experience, outlook and sensitivity.

### *Researcher's Competence*

A mere interest in a problem will not do. The researcher must be competent to plan and carry out a study of the problem. He must have the ability to grasp and deal with it. He must possess adequate knowledge of the subject–matter, relevant methodology and statistical procedures.

### *Researcher's Own Resources*

In the case of a research to be done by a researcher on his own, consideration of his own financial resource is pertinent. Does the cost involved in conducting the study of the problem is within the means of the researcher? If it is beyond his means, he will not be able to complete the work, unless he gets some external financial support. Time resource is more important than finance.

### *Researchability*

The problem should be researchable, i.e., amenable for finding answers to the questions involved in it through scientific method. "Although every problem in science involves a question or a series of questions, not every question qualifies as a scientific problem." To be researchable a question must be one for which by observation or other data collection on the real world can provide the answer. Many questions cannot be answered on the basis of information alone. They may involve valve elements. E.g., what is merit for the purpose of employee promotion? What is 'fairness' to the workers? Some questions may not be reasonable because procedures or techniques are inadequate.

### *Importance and Urgency*

Problems requiring investigation are unlimited, but available research efforts are very much limited. Therefore in selecting problems for research, their relative importance and significance should be considered. An important and urgent problem should be given priority over an unimportant one.

### *Novelty or Originality*

The problem must have novelty. There is no use of wasting one's time and energy on a problem already studied thoroughly by others.

This does not mean that replication is always needless. In social sciences in some cases, it is appropriate to replicate (repeat) a study in order to verify the validity of its findings to a different situation.

### *Feasibility*

A problem may be a new one and also important, but if research on it is not feasible, it cannot be selected. Hence, feasibility is a very important consideration.

### *Facilities*

Research requires certain facilities such as well-equipped library facility, suitable and competent guidance, data analysis facility etc. Hence, the availability of the facilities relevant to the problem must be considered.

### *Usefulness and Social Relevance*

Above all, the study of the problem should make significant contribution to the concerned body of knowledge or to the solution of some significant practical problem. It should be socially relevant. This consideration is particularly important in the case of higher level academic research and sponsored research.

### *Research Personnel*

Research undertaken by professors and by research organizations require the services of investigators and research officers. But in developing countries, research has not yet become a prospective profession. Hence, talented persons are not attracted to research projects. Employment in research projects is just considered as a stopgap arrangement pending securing a regular placement. Therefore appropriate qualified and experience research personnel are not easily available for the study of some problems.

### *Resources Needed*

The following resources are imperative in finding a research problem:

1. Physical resources
2. Monetary resources
3. Library resources

#### *1. Physical Resources*

Physical resources include the personal comforts, travel facilities etc. The problem area may be far away from the place of residence of the researcher and he has to spend considerable time and energy for that. So a comfortable travel arrangement is necessary. Clerical assistant, office help, communication facilities and stationary resources play no small role. Time is the foremost factor in choosing problem.

#### *2. Monetary Resources*

Next to time, monetary resources decide the selection of a research problem. A researcher can individually prepare the schedules, collect the data, and then write the report. When studies cover wider area, investigators must be appointed for data collection. Project experts must be employed and formation of an expert committee to guide the project may also be needed. Such projects are costlier and time consuming. But they carry with them accuracy, reliability and other concerned merits. So, depending upon the monetary resources available, a problem can be selected to cover limited or broader area. Its scope can also be limited or extended.

*3. Library Resources*

The prerequisite for a social research is library books, journals, periodicals, research reports, research journals, professional journals, bibliographies and indexes constitute flesh and blood for social research. One of the useful sources of selecting a research problem is to visit National Institutes and Research Institutes engaged in the field of research in particular field. Going through the library and contracting the scholars and such institutes will definitely give confidence to the researcher in selecting a problem.

# 14

# Variables and Measurement

## 1. Variables

Social scientists operate at both theoretical and empirical levels. At the theoretical level, there is a preoccupation with identifying constructs and their relations to propositions and theory. At the empirical level where the propositions are converted to hypothesis and testing occurs, the researcher is likely to be dealing with variables .

In practice the term variable is used as a synonym for construct or the property being studied. In this context a variable is a symbol to which we assign numerals or values.

The numerical value assigned to a variable is based on the variable's properties. For example some variables , said to be dichotomous, have only two values, reflecting the presence or absence of a property: employed-unemployed or male-female have two values, generally 0 and 1. Variables also take on values representing added categories, such as the demographic variables of race or religion. All such variables that produce data that fit into categories are said to be discrete, since only certain values are possible. An automobile variable for example, where Cheverlot is assigned a 5 and Honda is assigned a 6, provides no option for a 5.5.

Income,age,or a test score are examples of continuous variables. These variables may take on values within a given range or in some cases, an infinite set.

Among the important variables, the two namely, independent variable and dependent variable are important.

## Independent Variable

If one variable depends upon or is a consequence of the other variable, it is termed as a dependent variable, and the variable that is antecedent to the dependent variable is termed as an independent variable. Researchers is interested in the relationship among variables.

For example, does a leadership style (independent variable) influence job satisfaction or performance (dependent variable) or can a superior's modeling of ethical behaviour influence the subordinate? Some terms or words are synonyms for independent as well as dependent variable. Below here find some comparative picture of these variables:

| *Independent variable* | *Dependent variable* |
|---|---|
| Presumed cause | Presumed effect |
| Stimulus | Response |
| Predicted from...... | Predicted to....... |
| Manipulated | Consequence |
| Predictor | Criterion |

In social research, the independent variables influence the dependent variable. The change in the dependent variable takes due to the independent variables. In other words, independent variables are the cause and the dependent variable is the effect. The degree of influence made by each independent variable over the dependent variable can be measured by means of statistical tools like correlation and regression. A dependent variable may be influenced by one independent variable or group of independent variables.

## Dependent Variable

As noted above, dependent variable is the most significant in a research problem and it is influenced by a single or number of independent variables .Most probably, in social research, the dependent variable may be the particular topic of research or number of issues relating to the topic of research. The following example can explain the things clearly:

*Topic of research:* A study on the socio-economic factors contributed to the adoption of improved agricultural practices.

In the above topic of research, the dependent variable is: adoption of improved agricultural practices

*The independent variables are:* Socio-economic factors. These socio-economic factors may be: Age, education, size of family. Size of land holding, income etc.

### Other Types of Minor Variables

There are other types of minor variables namely, moderating variables, extraneous variables and intervening variables.

*Moderating variables:* It is a second independent variable that is included because it is believed to have a significant contributory or contingent effect on the original independent and dependent variable relationships.

*Extraneous variable:* Independent variables that are not related to the study, but may affect the dependent variable, are termed as extraneous variables. A study must always be so designed that the effect upon the dependent variable is attributed entirely to the independent variables and not to some extraneous variables.

*Intervening variables:* This may be defined as "that factor which theoretically affects the observed phenomenon but can not be seen, measured, or manipulated , its effects must be inferred from the effects of the independent and moderator variables on the observed phenomenon"

### Measurement

In social science research the data instruments and the variables are to be measured. Such measurement is necessary to verify their truthfulness and the reliability. The measurement of social and psychological variables is a complex and difficult task.

Measurement is defined as (Stevens) "the assignment of numerals to objects or events according to rules." Torgerson defines it as "the assignment of numbers to objects to represent amounts or degrees of a property possessed by all of the objects." In dictionary sense, to measure is to discover the extent, dimensions, quantity or capacity of something, especially by comparison with a standard.

Measurements consists of assigning numbers to characteristics of objects or events in such a way as to reflect some aspect of reality. The goal then is to assign numbers so that the properties of the numbers are the same as the properties of the objects or events that we are measuring. This implies that we have different kinds of numbers

The assignment of numbers or numerals to objects is done according to a rule. A rule tells the way in which numerals or numbers are to be assigned. It is the most significant part of the measurement procedure, because it determines the quality of measurement. The range of its uses increases with the exactness of the measurement.

Concepts used in research consist of objects and properties (ie characteristics) of objects. A person's physical properties consists of height, weight,etc and his psychological properties include his attitude, intelligence, etc. In a research process we measure the properties of objects and not the objects themselves. Abstract properties like intelligence, motivation and attitude can not be directly observed: one must infer them from the observation.

When a researcher develops a theory, the theory is tested through the verification of hypothesis derived from it. A hypothesis can be verified statistically, only when the variables in it are measured. Thus the need for measurement arises.

Measurement in research consists of assigning numbers to empirical events in compliance with a set of rules. This implies that measurement is a three part process:

### 1. *Selecting Observable Empirical Events*

Variables being studied in research may be classified as objects or properties. Objects include things of ordinary experience such as, people, book, building etc. Objects also include that are not as concrete such as attitudes, pressures etc. Properties are the characteristics of the objects. A person's physical properties may be stated in terms of weight height etc. A person's psychological properties include attitude and intelligence. Social properties include leadership ability, status etc. These and many other properties of an individual can be measured in a research study.

### 2. *Developing a Set of Mapping Rules*

A scheme for assigning numbers or symbols to represent aspects of the event being measured. in measuring, one devises some mapping rule and then translates the observation of property indicants using this rule. For each concept or construct, several types of data are possible, the appropriate choice depends on what you assume about the mapping rules. Each type has its own set of underlying assumptions about how the numerical symbols correspond to real world observations Mapping rules have the following characteristics;

A. *Classification:* Numbers are used to group or sort responses. No order exists.
B. *Order:* Numbers are ordered. One number is greater than, less than or equal to another number.
C. *Distance:* Distance between numbers are ordered. The difference between any pair of numbers is greater than, less than or equal to the difference between any other pair of numbers.
D. *Origin:* The number series has a unique origin indicated by the number zero.

Combination of these characteristics of classification, order, distance, and origin provide four widely used classification of measurement scales: nominal, ordinal, interval and ratio.

## Scales of Measurement

There are four different types of numbers or scales of measurement, namely, nominal, ordinal, interval and ratio. The rules for assigning numbers constitute the essential criteria for defining each scale.

### *Nominal Measurement*

Nominal scales are comprised of numbers used to categorize objects or events. A nominally scaled number serves only as a label for a class or category. The objects in each class are viewed as equivalent with respect to the characteristic represented by the nominal number. The only rules involved are that all members involved in a class have the same number and that no two classes have the same number. A mean or median can not be calculated for nominal data. A mode can be used. The percentages of items falling within each category also can be determined. A chi-square test can be conducted to determine if differences between the numbers falling in the various categories is likely to be the result of chance or randomness.

### *Ordinal Measurement*

Ordinal scales represent numbers, letters or other symbols

used to rank items. Items can be classified not only as to whether they share some characteristic with another item but also whether they have more or less of this characteristic than some other object. Ordinal scaled numbers do not provide information on how much more or less of the characteristic various items posses. The descriptive statistics that can be used are a mode or median, but not a mean. A mean should not be calculated because the differences between ordinal scaled values are not necessarily the same. The percentages of the total appearing in each rank may be calculated and are meaningful. The branch of statistics that deals with ordinal and nominal measurements is called as nonparametric statistics.

### *Interval Measurements*

Interval scales represent numbers used to rank items such that numerically equal distances on the scale represent equal distance s in the property being measured. The most frequent form of interval measurement is index numbers. An index number is calculated by setting one number , such as scales for a particular year equal to 100. This is known as the base period or base value. Other numbers for subsequent years are then expressed as percentages of the base value. One common type of data generally treated as interval scale data is attitude measures. A Likert scale for, example, requires the respondents to state their degree of agreement or disagreement with a statement by selecting a response from a list such as the following:

1. Agree very strongly
2. Agree fairly strongly
3. Agree
4. Undecided
5. Disagree
6. Disagree fairly strongly
7. Disagree very strongly

It is doubtful that the interval between each of these items is exactly equal. However most researchers treat the data from such scales as if they were equal to interval in nature since the results of most standard statistical techniques are not affected greatly by small deviation from the interval requirement. Virtually the entire range of statistical analysis can be applied to internal scales. Such descriptive measures are mean, mode. median. range and standard deviation

*Ratio Measurement*

Ratio scales consist of numbers that rank items such that numerically equal distances on the scale represent equal distances in the property being measured and have a meaningful zero. Any descriptive measures and inferential techniques are applicable to ratio scaled data

**Types of Measurement Scales**

| *Scale* | *Basic empirical operations* | *Typical usage* | *Typical statistics* | |
|---|---|---|---|---|
| | | | *Descriptive* | *inferential* |
| Nominal | Determination of equality | Classification: Male-Female, Social class | %ages, mode | Chi-square, binomial test |
| Ordinal | Determination of greater or less | Rankings: Preference data, attitude measures, | Median | Mann-WhitneyU two way ANOVA rank order correlation |
| Interval | Determination of quality if intervals | Index numbers. attitude measures, | Mean, range, standard deviatic- | t-test, factor analysis, ANOVA |
| Ratio | Determination of equality of ratios | number of respondents, costs. | | Coeffici-ent of variation |

## Functions of Measurement

Measurement serves the following purposes:

1. It facilitates empirical description of social and psychological phenomena. For example, in a study of a tribal society the researcher has to classify the cultural patterns and behaviours he observes. Measuring devices assist him in the classification process.
2. Measurement renders the data amenable to statistical manipulation and treatment. The application of various statistical techniques for comparing groups, studying relationship between variables etc is possible, only when the data collected are amenable to quantification. Measurement devices make it possible to quantify variables.

3. Measurement facilitates testing of theories and hypothesis. Once the variables in hypothesis are quantified through measuring devices, the hypothesis can be tested easily.

## Characteristics of a Good Measurement Tool

A measurement tool must satisfy the following criteria:

A. *Unidimensionality:* This means the scale should measure one characteristics at a time . for example the ruler should measure length, not temperature also.

B. *Linearity:* This means that a scale should follow the straight line model. Some scoring system should be devised, preferably one based on interchangeable units.

C. *Validity:* This refers to the ability of a scale to measure what it is supposed to measure

D. *Reliability:* This is an attribute of consistency. A scale should give consistent results.

E. *Accuracy and precision:* A tool should give accurate and precise measure of what we want to measure

F. *Simplicity:* A scale should be as simple as possible; an elaborate, complicate and over refined scale may become costly or useless.

G. *Practicability:* A tool should be easily administrable, it should contain proper instructions , it should be easily understandable and conveniently arranged for easy completion.

## The Process of Constructing a Measurement Tool

This involves the following steps:

1. *Knowledge of the area:* The researcher should gain thorough knowledge about the field of research. He should gather prior information about the needs of the research.
2. *Concept development:* Each concept that comes across the research must be defined operationally.
3. *Concept specification:* From the concept, the researcher must develop aspects, components, dimensions or similar specifications.
4. *Indicator selection:* The next step is to develop indicators by which to measure each element or dimension of the concept. Indicators are specific questions, statements or

devices by which the respondent's knowledge. Opinions etc are measured.

## Criteria for Evaluating a Measurement Tool

There are two major criteria for evaluating a measurement tool, namely validity and reliability. Validity refers to the extent to which a test measures what we actually wish to measure. Reliability refers to the accuracy and precision of a measurement procedure.They are discussed in.detail in the Chapter Methods of data collection

# 15

# Need for Research Design

## Definition and Meaning

A research design is a logical and systematic plan prepared for directing a research study. It specifies the objectives of the study, the methodology and techniques to be adopted for achieving the objectives. It "constitutes the blue print for the collection, measurement and analysis of data.". According to Kerlinger, it is "the plan, structure and strategy of investigation conceived so as to obtain answer to research questions.... The plan is the overall scheme or programme of research."

"A research design is the programme that guides the investigator in the process of collecting, analyzing and interpreting observations." "It provides a systematic plan of procedure for the researcher to follow." Keeping in view of the above definitions, the overall research design may be split into the following parts.

1. The sampling design—This deals with the method of selecting items to be observed for the given study.
2. The observational design—This deals with the conditions under which the observations are to be made.
3. The statistical design—This concerns with the questions of how many items are to be observed and how the information and data gathered are to be analyzed.
4. The operational design—This deals with the techniques

by which the procedures specified in the sampling, statistical and observational designs can be carried out.

### Important Features of Research Design

1. It is a plan—It is a plan that specifies the sources and types of information relevant to the research problem. Only through a proper research plan or a research design, the researcher can prepare himself for the research and conduct the research successfully.
2. Continuity—Research design plans the research activity to be undertaken by each stage. The initial preparation, preparation of tools for data collection, data processing, analysis of data, writing the report, etc are all clearly planned through the research design.
3. Approaches—A research design provides guidelines to the researcher specifying which approach will be used for gathering and analyzing data.
4. Statistical tools—The type of statistical tools to be used in the research study is also mentioned in the research design. This avoids confusions, which may arise in future for the researcher.
5. Time and cost budget—One of the essential features of research design is the inclusion of time and cost budget. Through this process, a research work can be completed within the prescribed period and prescribed cost.
6. Blind search—A research design prevents blind search and indiscriminate gathering of data and guides the researcher to proceed on the right direction.
7. Boundaries—A research design prescribes the boundaries of research activities and enables the researcher to channel his energies in the right work.
8. To anticipate problems—A research design enables the researcher to anticipate potential problems that may arise in data collection, operationalization of concepts, data analysis, etc.

### Essentials of a Good Research Design

The essentials of a good research design are:

1. It is a plan that specifies the objectives of the study and the hypotheses to be tested.

2. It is an outline that specifies the sources and types of information relevant to the research questions.
3. It is a blue print specifying the methods to be adopted for gathering and analyzing the data.
4. It is a scheme defining "the domain of generalizability, i.e., whether the obtained information can be generalized to a larger population or to different situations.

A research design appropriate for a particular research problem usually involves the consideration of the following factors.

1. The means of obtaining information
2. The availability and skills of the researcher
3. The objectives of the problem to be studied
4. The nature of the problem to be studied
5. The availability of time and money for the research work.

## Nature of Research Design

A research design is indispensable for a research project. However, it is not a precise and specific plan like a building plan to be followed without deviations, but rather a series of guideposts to keep one going in the right direction. It is a tentative plan which undergoes modification, as circumstances demand, when the study progresses, new aspects, new conditions and new relationships come to light and insight into the study deepens. For example, the scope of a study may be narrowed down, when it is discovered that certain kinds of data are not available; the sampling method may be modified from 'random sampling' if a list of units of study with particulars of size is not readily available; and so on.

Besides, a research study cannot be as extensive and intensive as the researcher may like it to be. It has to be geared to the availability of data and the cooperation of the informants. It has also to be kept within the manageable limits. i.e., with the researcher's mental ability to grasp the implications, his competence and the amount of time and other resources available for the purpose. Thus, a research design "represents a compromise dictated by many practical considerations."

## Classification of Research Designs

There are a number of crucial research choices, Various writers advance different classification schemes, some of which are:

1. Experimental, historical and inferential designs (American Marketing Association)
2. Exploratory, descriptive and causal designs (Selltiz, Jahoda, Deutsch and Cook)
3. Experimental, and expost fact (Kerlinger)
4. Historical method, and case and clinical studies (Goode and Scates)
5. Sample surveys, field studies, experiments in field settings, and laboratory experiments (Festinger and Katz)
6. Exploratory, descriptive and experimental studies (Body and Westfall)
7. Exploratory, descriptive and causal (Green and Tull)
8. Experimental, 'quasi-experimental designs' (Nachmias and Nachmias)
9. True experimental, quasi-experimental and non-experimental designs (Smith)
10. Experimental, pre-experimental, quasi-experimental designs and Survey Research (Kidder and Judd).

These different categorizations exist, because 'research design' is a complex concept. In fact, there are different perspectives from which any given study can be viewed. They are:

1. The degree of formulation of the problem (the study may be exploratory or formalized)
2. The topical scope-breadth and depth-of the study (a case or a statistical study)
3. The research environment: field setting or laboratory (survey, laboratory experiment)
4. The time dimension (one-time or longitudinal)
5. The mode of data collection (observational or survey)
6. The manipulation of the variables under study (Experimental or expost facto)
7. The nature of the relationship among variables (descriptive or causal)

## Why to Prepare a Research Design

Preparing a Research Design is an important stage in the process of conducting a research. According to P.V. Young; "Research design is the logical and systematic planning and directing of a piece of research."

Research design is nothing but a scheme of work to be undertaken by a researcher at various stages. Systematic work of research and methodical conducting of various operations could be facilitated by a research design. It acts as a guide to achieve the decided goal of a researcher step by step.

## Initial Preparation

While preparing a Research Design, a researcher must give careful consideration to the following aspects:

1. The topic of the study must be chosen appropriately and the researcher must be thoroughly acquainted himself with the topic, issues and intricacies related to it.
2. It is also better for the researcher to verify other research designs prepared by different scholars.
3. As the cost and time are important aspects, the judgment and the rationality in deciding the above items must have the priority.
4. A design is susceptible to alterations. Hence, it is better to design it two or three times and perfect it after due consideration.
5. The researcher while pursuing various stages work must strictly follow the schedule mentioned in the design. Small modification without affecting the overall time schedule can be effected here and there.
6. As the sample is an important aspect of empirical research, once a method is decided, the researcher should stick on to it throughout the research.

*The following questions should be asked*

1. What the study is about?
2. Why is the study made?
3. What is its scope?
4. What are the objectives of the study?
5. What are propositions to be tested?
6. What are the major concepts to be defined operationally?
7. On the basis of what criteria or measurements, the operational definitions to be made?
8. When or in what place the study will be conducted?
9. What is the reference period of the study?
10. What is the typology of the design?

11. What kinds of data are needed?
12. What are the sources of data?
13. What is the universe from which the sample has to be drawn?
14. What is the sample size?
15. What sampling techniques can be used?
16. What methods are to be adopted for collecting data?
17. What tools are to be used for collecting data?
18. How the data are to be processed?
19. What techniques of analysis are to be adopted?
20. What is the significance of the study?
21. To what target audience the reporting of the findings is meant?
22. What is the type of report to be prepared?
23. What is the time period required for each stage of research work?
24. What is the time limit within which the whole work should be completed?
25. What is the cost involved?

When the study is completed and the report is ready, the original design can be modified in the light of the analysis of data and writing of the report. But care should be taken to avoid reshaping the original design. It may amount to distortion of the various process of the research study.

## Important Concepts Relating to Research Design

Before going through the contents of research design, it is better to understand important concepts relating to research design.

1. *Dependent and independent variables*—In a research problem, there are two variables namely dependent variable and independent variable, which activate a problem. A dependent variable is one, which is influenced by independent variables. Independent variables influence the dependent variable. For example, the causes for unemployment, in such a study, unemployment becomes dependent variable and various causes like poverty, illiteracy, etc will become independent variables.
2. *Control*—One important characteristic of a good research design is to minimize the influence of extraneous variables, which are called as control. In experimental researches, the term control is used to refer to experimental conditions.

3. *Research hypothesis*—When a prediction or a relationship is to be tested by scientific methods, it is termed as research hypothesis. A hypothesis is a predictive statement that relates an independent variable to a dependent variable.
4. *Experimental and control groups*—In an experimental hypothesis testing, when a group is exposed to usual conditions, it is termed as control group. But when the group is exposed to some special conditions, it is termed as experimental group.
5. *Treatments*—The different conditions under which experimental and control groups are put are usually referred to as treatments.
6. *Experiment*—The process of examining the truth of a statistical hypothesis relating to a research problem is known as experiment.

# 16

# Contents of a Research Design

A Research Design must contain the following aspects:

1. Introduction
2. Statement of the problem
3. Reference to previous studies made
4. Objectives of the study
5. Definition of concepts
6. Hypothesis
7. Limitations of the study
8. Methodology and techniques used in the study
9. Budget
10. Chapter Scheme.

### *1. Introduction*

In the introduction, the researcher has to introduce the subject and relevant information relating to the topic of research. The researcher can quote authentic research studies and authors to support his views. Introduction should not be too lengthy. Over enthusiastic young researchers write long introduction running into number of pages like theory chapter. This is unwanted and may not fit in the pattern of crisp research design. As the purpose of introduction is to introduce the subject it is in the fitness of things be brief. Statistical information if at all needed and found relevant can also find a place in the introduction.

### *2. Statement of the Problem*

The problem that has been chosen for researcher may have

many facets. A problem can be analyzed from various angles. The focus of attention of the researcher towards the problem chosen must be pinpointed. The researcher must also point out the reason or reasons for choosing this particular problem for the research study. Hence, a researcher must analyze the following aspects in the statement of the problem:

(i) The need to study the problem of research.

(ii) What connotation does the problem contain?

(iii) Why this particular topic has been chosen by the researcher? Or what type of interest has evinced the researcher to undertake this study?

### 3. *Reference of Previous Studies/Review of Literature*

Various research institutions and researchers bringing out research studies on similar topics. Referring such studies may be useful in many ways. It can impress upon the readers that the researcher has gone through the related studies. It can also help the researcher to locate a course of action for his study based on the earlier studies. It is enough if the important features of he studies and main findings are mentioned. Here also, researchers may be tempted to reproduce the original studies. This must be avoided. If possible, the researcher can give his own opinion about the previous studies. He can also explain the way in which he is going to improve his work upon the earlier studies. If new studies are made and if material is not available the researcher need not ponder over the previous studies, only research studies must be mentioned. In very many occasions we come across researchers referring to books and journals in the introduction, which could be conveniently listed under bibliography section.

### 4. *Objective of the Study*

While framing the objectives, it is better to limit the number of objectives to suit the needs of the topic. Framing of two many objectives may lead to confusion and the researcher may not be able to justify all of them.

The objective must be framed bearing in mind the topic of research. In other words, the objectives must elaborate the title and must indicate in its wordings the tings to be investigated further. The objectives must also help to decide the chapters and analysis of various issues in each chapter. In other words, there must be a close and intimate relationship between the topic of research, objectives framed, chapter scheme and analysis of research. Objectives are also important to choose the relevant methods of research and tools to be followed. Framing of clear objectives can help the preparation of schedules immensely.

Languages and the contents of the objectives are as important as deciding the topic of research. The language jugglery must be clear, precise and meaningful. It must do away with playing of words. The contents must be expressed within a sentence.

### 5. *Definition of Concepts*

The important concepts that appear frequently in the study must be explained. These concepts, may relate to the title of research or the objectives or with the analysis. If suitable and authentic definitions are not found, the researcher can give his own working definition.

### 6. *Hypothesis*

A researcher can include hypothesis in the study or he can omit hypothesis. The need or otherwise of having hypothesis in a research study is a subject of controversy. The researcher has to make his own judgment, based on the nature of the study about the desirability of the inclusion of hypothesis. But once hypothesis is included, it must be tested. Through this test, it can be proved or disproved. A different style of language must be used to frame hypothesis. Degrees of comparison are to be necessarily used. The objectives of the study will provide guideline for framing the hypothesis.

### 7. *Limitations of the Study*

A study as well as the researcher are subject to limitations of time, cost, sample etc. While interviewing respondents, he has to face many difficulties. Eliciting of response may be difficult. The researcher can point out such limitations in his report.

### 8. *Methodology and Sampling*

Under this heading the researcher has to state the method of research followed for his study and the tools and techniques of research used to collect data. The number of schedules prepared and the way in which data have been collected could also be explained.

The method of sample that has been followed for the study

at various stages must also be mentioned. The researcher can give the sampling frame mentioning how he has arrived at the number of samples at various stages.

### *9. Budget*

Though budget does not have a place in all research designs it must find a place in Research Projects aided by various sponsoring agencies. Time budget as well as const budget must find separate place in the budget. The budget aids the researcher to complete the project within the stipulated cost.

### *10. Chapter Scheme*

Last item of the Research Design is the Chapter Scheme. The number of chapters that the study contains and name of each chapter must be mentioned. The basis for the chapter scheme must include main findings prominently in independent chapters. The last chapter must always be the findings, conclusions and suggestions.

We have discussed the various components of research design. If scrupulously adhered to, these steps will ensure the success of a research project. The researcher design will also enable the optimum utilization of the time, energy, and sources at the disposal of the researcher. The scheduling of various steps and procedures are, nevertheless, tentative. A pragmatic research design can never be too rigid, and there must be provisions for small alternations based on the needs and circumstances.

# 17

# Importance of Objectives and Framing of Objectives

## Importance of Objectives

Objectives are the guiding posts for a researcher. They point out the directions to the researcher. The specific objectives of the study should be stated clearly. These refer to the questions to which the researcher proposes to seek answer through the study. Although there is no limit to the number of research objectives, it is desirable to limit the objectives to a reasonable number. What is reasonable depends upon the time limitation. Resource constraints, capability, etc. It is wise to pick objectives that are challenging but not impossible to achieve.

The objectives may be stated as under:

to study the extent of -------------
to identify the factors which influence-----------
to examine the nature of relations between ------------ and
to investigate the impact of -----------------
to identify the cause of -----------------

The statement of objectives should not be vague or nebulous like "to study industrial marketing inIndia", "to explore unemployment in India" and the like.

These statements are vague, as they fail to specify what exactly are aimed at. The statement should be specific and indicate the exact purpose of the study. Such precise statements give functional guidelines to the research process.

Following are the importance of formulating objectives:

1. Guiding point—Objectives are the guiding points or guiding post for a researcher. It gives the guidelines to the researcher as to what to do and when to do.
2. Framing hypothesis—Framing the hypothesis is decided by the objectives. Objectives provide proper guidelines for framing the objectives.
3. Preparation of tools—In preparing tools for data collection, objectives help the researcher a lot. Data collection tools are schedule, questionnaire, interview, observation, and scales.
4. Size of sample—In deciding the size of sample, the guiding point for the researcher is the objectives. If the objectives are broader, have a wider coverage, then a bigger size of sample would be needed.
5. Coverage—The coverage of the research report and the final outcome of the research report depends on the number of objectives fixed by the researcher.
6. Chapterization—The number of chapter to be included in a research report will also be guided by the objectives of the research study.

## Framing the Objectives

The objectives are derived from conceptual model. They state which elements in the conceptual model – which levels of, which kinds of cases, which properties, and which connections among properties—are to be investigated. But it is the conceptual model that defines, describes, and states the assumptions underlying these elements.

The objectives may aim at description or explanation or analysis of causal relationship between variables and indicate the expected results or outcome of the study.

The objectives may be specified in the form of either statements or questions.

Illustration—An example for framing the objective is given below.

The profitability of commercial banks has tended to decline year after year even though the volume of business (deposits and deployment of funds) has been increasing. How a researcher may formulate a problem when he views this situation?

1. *Title of the research problem*—An enquiry into the declining trend in the profitability of X commercial bank.
2. *Objectives of the study*—

   In a statement form:

   The objectives of the study are:

a. To identify the major factors affecting the banks profitability
b. To determine the major causes of the declining trend in its profitability, and
c. To develop a strategy for improving the bank's profitability.

The above objectives may be stated in question form as under:

The study aims at seeking answers to the following questions:

a. What are the major factors affecting the bank's profitability?
b. What are the major causes of the declining trend in its profitability?
c. What strategy can be adopted for improving the bank's profitability?

The successful research will provide answers to these questions.

## Setting Investigative Questions

Once the objectives of the research or the general research questions have been defined, the formulation moves to the next level, i.e., investigative questions. These sub-questions are setup for each of the major research objectives/questions. These specific questions guide the details of the research effort, including the development of concepts, operational definitions and measurement devices. There may be several sub levels of investigative questions, each being progressively narrower in scope.

Example: The investigative questions relating to the first objectives of the previous example (factors affecting a commercial bank's profitability) are:

### *a. What are the Factors Affecting Interest Earned on Advance?*

i. Has the proportion of the total earning assets to deposits tended to decline?
ii. What is the composition of earning assets?
iii. What is the rate of yield on each type of asset?

***b. What are the Factors Affecting Interest Paid on Deposits and Borrowings?***

i. Have the interest paying liabilities tended to increase?
ii. What is the composition of interest paying liabilities?
iii. What is the rate of interest on each component?

***c. What are the Factors Affecting Manpower Expenses?***

i. Has the number of employees tended to increase?
ii. What are the seniority and composition of employees?
iii. What is the salary structure?

**Factors to Be Considered in Framing the Objectives**

1. Objectives must be few in number; otherwise the number of chapter will also increase, as the chapterization depends on the nature of objectives.
2. Objectives must be based on the title of the research study. It must be expressive of the title in content and must be a further elaboration of the title of the study.
3. The terms that are used to frame objectives must be simple and words of double meaning and words of confusions must be avoided.
4. Objectives must help to find out the course of study and the depth needed for various aspects and emphasis on crux of the research study.
5. Objectives must be guideline for framing the chapters of the study.
6. If the objectives are few in number the chapters also be few in number.

# 18

# Definition, Needs and Characteristics of Sampling

## Definition of Sampling

Sampling may be defined as the selection of some part of an aggregate or totality on the basis of which a judgment or inference about the aggregate or totality is made. In other words, it is the process of obtaining information about an entire population by examining only a part of it. The items selected from the population is technically called as sample, their selection process is called sample design. Sample should be truly representative of population characteristics without any bias so that it may result in valid and reliable conclusions.

In all research studies, to select the respondents, sampling is used. As the population or the universe involved will be large, it is impossible to contract all of them. As human beings have certain homogeneous nature among themselves, it is enough if we meet few of them as they will have the representative nature for the population. Sampling as a technique has been widely used by marketing researchers, as they have to cover a population spread in wider geographical area.

The social scientist is confronted with the task of investigating vast population. Sampling is a method to make social investigation practicable and easy. According to Goode and Hatt: 'A sample is a smaller representation of the larger whole.'

Blalock and Blalock define a sample thus:

"It is a small piece of the population obtained by a probability process that mirrors, with known precision, the various patterns and sub-classes of the population."

Ya-Lun-Chou defines a sample, "as a collection of primary sampling units selected as a representative microcosm from which references about the population may be made."

The above definitions contain three important implications as listed out by ya-Lun-Chou

Firstly a sample may contain primary sampling units such as firms of an industry, even though its purpose is to observe the properties of the elementary units such as the workers in the industry. Second, a sample is not chunk or a slice of the population selected because of convenience and ready availability, but a microcosm, a small universe or a subject which is expected to be representative of the parent population. Third and last, the ultimate purpose of sampling is not merely to secure sample statistics but to make inferences concerning the population.

**Need for Sampling:**

Sampling is needed for the following reasons:

1. Sampling can save time and money, which are essential in a research project. A sampling study is usually less expensive than a census study and delivers results quickly.
2. Sampling may enable more accurate measurements for a sample study
3. Sampling remains the only way when population contains many members.
4. Sampling enables to estimate the sampling errors and thus assists in obtaining information concerning some characteristics of the population.

**Requirements/Characteristics of a Good Sample**

The main requirements of a good sample are:

1. *Representativeness:* Representative ness denotes the reflection of certain characteristics of the sample as that of the universe or population A sample must be representative of the population. It should represent the characteristics of the population from where it is chosen. When selecting a sample the researcher must have complete details of the population. Haphazard method

will lead to waste of time and resources.

2. *Adequacy:* A good sample size must be adequate in size in order to be reliable. The sample should be such size that the inferences drawn from the sample are accurate to a given level of confidence. According to Goode and Hatt, "a sample is adequate when it is of sufficient size to allow confidence in the stability of its characteristics." In other words it should not be too large than is necessary.
3. *Avoiding Bias:* According to Moser and Kalton bias in selection of sample can arise: If the sample is done by a non-random method which generally means that the selection is consciously or unconsciously influenced by human choice;(ii) If the sampling frame (list, index or other population record) which serves as the basis for selection does not cover the population adequately, completely or accurately.(iii) If some sections of the population are impossible to find or refuse to cooperate." The best method to avoid bias in sampling is to use random method of sampling.
4. *Accuracy:* Accuracy is designed as the degree to which bias is absent from the sample. An accurate sample is one which exactly represents the population. It is free from any influence that cause any difference between the sample value and population value.
5. *Precision:* The sample must yield precise estimate. Precision is measured by the standard error or standard deviation of the sample estimate. The smaller the standard error or estimate, the higher is the precision of the sample

## Advantages of Sampling

Sampling has certain obvious advantages. They are:

1. Sampling avoids the necessity of studying each and very member of the population and thus avoids necessary wastage of time and resources by collecting large quantities of data from large number of people
2. It ensures greater precision and contributes to the quality of data as it facilitates the collection of smaller amounts of data from fewer cases and their intensive analysis.
3. Sampling if properly drawn to represent a cross-section of the population, will give an accurate estimation of the

population. It is said that, appropriate sampling, gives greater accuracy than even the complete enumeration by census.

5. Sampling reduces the time and cost of a research project. Through sampling we can undertake research studies at any geographical level starting from village level to the global level.
6. Labour and human energy could saved by sampling. Smaller personnel is enough both for the field work and for the processing and analysing the data.
7. The quality of a research work will be better, if a study is undertaken using sampling. In each and every part of the research work precision can be achieved.
8. Sampling provides quicker results than by a census. The speed of execution minimizes the time between the recognition of a need for information and the availability of that information.

# 19

# Sample Design, Sampling Theory and Sample Size

A sample design is a definite plan for obtaining a sample from a given population. It refers to the technique or the procedure the researcher would adopt in selecting items for the sample. Sample design may as well lay down the number of items to be included in the sample the size of sample. Sample design is determined before data collection. There are many sample designs which a researcher can choose.

## Census Versus Sample

Some times in surveys the total population or the universe is taken for study. This is called census. A census is feasible when the population is small. Census is necessary when the elements are quite different from each other. In many times it is impossible to take the universe. A difference is made between universe and population. From statistical point of view, the term universe refers to the total of the items or units in any field of enquiry, whereas the term population refers to the total of items about which information is desired. The attributes that are the object of study are called characteristics and the units possessing them are called as elementary units. The aggregate of such units is generally called as population. Thus, all units in any field of enquiry constitute universe and all elementary units constitute population.. Quite often, we do not find any difference between population and universe, and as such the two terms are taken as inter changeable. However, a researcher must define these terms precisely. While choosing a census or sample, there are certain considerations, which decide this. They are noted below:

### *Cost and Cost Versus Sample*

Cost is one of the considerations to decide whether a censes should be taken. If enough money is available the researcher can go for the census method.

### *Time and Census Versus Sample*

If the time available to the researcher is abundant then there may not be any problem in taking a census. Bur in majority of social researches time is a constraint and the researchers go for sampling.

### *Accuracy and Census Versus Sample*

A study using a census contains no sampling error. A study using sample may involve sample error in addition to other types of errors. Therefore, other things being equal, census will provide more accurate data than a sample. Some times it is possible, given the same expenditure of time and money, to reduce the non-sampling error in a sample relative to those in a census to the point of at which the sum of the sampling and non-sampling error alone in the census. When this is the case, it is possible to obtain more accurate measurements from a sample than from a census.

## Steps in Sample Design

While developing a sample design, following steps is required:

1. *Type of universe:* The first step is to clearly define the set of objects to be studied, technically called as universe. The universe can be finite or infinite. In finite universe the number of items is certain, but in the case of infinite universe the number of items is infinite. We can not have any idea about the total number of items
2. *Sampling unit:* Before selecting a sample, the sample unit must be decided. Sampling unit may be a geographical one like region, district, village etc. the researcher has to select one or more of such units that he has to select for the study.

3. *Source list:* This also known as sampling frame, from which sample is to be drawn. It contains the name of all the items in the universe. Such list should be comprehensive, correct and reliable. It is important to note that the source list must as representative of the population as possible.
4. *Size of sample:* This refers to the number of items to be selected from the universe to constitute a sample. The size of sample should neither large nor too small, it should be optimum. an optimum size is one which fulfills the requirements of efficiency, representative ness, reliability and flexibility.
5. *Parameters of interest:* While determining the sample design, one must consider the question of the specific population parameters which are of interest. There may also be sub-groups in the population about whom we would like to make estimates.
6. *Budget:* Availability of sufficient funds is an important consideration for the sample size and to the type of sample.
7. *Sampling procedure:* The researcher must decide the technique to be used in selecting the items for the sample. There are several sample designs, from which the researcher can choose the needed one. He must select that design which for a given sample size and for a given cost, has a smaller sampling error.

## Characteristics of a Good Sample Design

Based on the above discussion , we can list out the following as the characteristics of a good sample design:

1. Sample design must result in a true representative sample.
2. A good sample design must result in a smaller sample error.
3. It must be viable in the context of funds available for the research work.
4. Sample design must be such that systematic bias must be controlled.
5. Sample should be such that the results of the sample study can be applied in general, for the universe with a reasonable level of confidence.

## Different Types of Sample Designs

The sample design can be based on two factors, namely, the

representation bias and the element of selection technique. On the representation basis the sample may be probability sampling or it may be non-probability sampling.

Probability sampling is based on the concept of random selection, where as non-probability sampling is based on non-random sampling. So the sample design can be classified into two types, namely probability sampling and non-probability sampling.

Non-probability sampling: Under non-probability sample the individual items are selected by own judgment. In other words, it is a process in which judgment element enters into the selection of the numbers of a universe included in the sample. On- probability sample is also called by different names like deliberate sampling, purposive sampling and judgment sampling. Here the researchers choice weighs supreme than other reasons. In other words in non-probability sampling, the researcher purposively choose the particular units of the universe for constituting a sample.

In such a design personal element has a great chance of entering into the selection of the sample. the researcher may select a sample which shall yield results favorable to his point of view and if that happens, the entire enquiry may get spoiled. So, there is always the fear of bias entering into this type of sampling technique. Further in such sampling there is no assurance that every element has some specific chance of being included. Sample error in this type of samples can not be estimated and the element of bias is always there.

***Some of the Non-Probability Samples are:***

1. Convenience sampling
2. Judgment sampling
3. Quota sampling
4. Purposive sampling
5. Accidental sampling
6. Snow ball sampling

**Probability Sampling**

In probability sampling, individual items are chosen by a process of random selection , where by each member of the universe has a known chance of being selected for the sample. This sampling is also known by other names like, random sampling or chance sampling. Under this sampling, every item of the universe has an equal chance of inclusion in the sample

The following are some of the probability samples:

1. Simple random
2. Systematic sampling
3. Stratified sampling
4. Cluster sampling
5. Multi stage sampling

## The Choice Between Probability and Non-Probability Sampling

The choice between probability and non-probability sample is based on the cost versus value principle. We want to take whichever kind of sample yields the greatest margin of value over cost.

The following factors are to be considered in estimating the relative value:

1. What kind of information is needed- We have to specify this.
2. What kind of error tolerance does the problem allow?- Does the problem require highly accurate estimates of population values/
3. How large are the non-sampling errors likely to be? How sizable are the population specification, frame, selection, non-response, and experimental errors likely to be/
4. How homogeneous is the population with respect to the variables we want to measure? Is the variation likely to be low among the sampling units or will it be high?
5. What is the expected cost of errors in the sample information? What is the cost if the average proportion obtained from the data and are they above the error tolerance on the high side or the low side?

Generally, the need for projectable totals, low allowable errors, high population heterogeneity, small non-sampling errors and high expected costs of errors favor the use of probability sampling. Small non-sampling errors likewise favor probability samples, the sampling error becomes relatively more important the smaller the other errors are..

## Sample Size and its Determination.

The sample size should be optimum to meet the needs of a research proposal. Technically, the sample size should be large enough to give a confidence interval of desired width and as such the size of the sample must be chosen by some logical process before sample is taken from the universe. The following points must be considered:

1. *Nature of the Universe:* Universe must be either homogeneous or heterogeneous in nature. If the items in the universe are homogeneous, a small sample can serve the needs of the researcher. If the items are heterogeneous, a large sample size is required.
2. *Number of Classes Proposed:* If many class groups are to be formed, a large sample would be required, because a small sample may not be able to give a reasonable number of items in each class group
3. *Nature of study:* If items are to be studied intensively, the sample should be small. For bigger surveys the size of sample should be large.
4. *Type of Sampling:* Sampling technique play an important role in determining the size of sample. A small random sample is enough for simple studies.
5. *Funds:* In practice the size of sample depends on the availability of funds for the research project. A larger sample size may tell upon the cost of the project..

The principles that influence the sample size:

1. The greater the dispersion or variance within the population, the larger the sample must be to provide estimation precision.
2. The greater the desired precision of the estimate, the larger the sample must be.
3. The narrower the interval range, the larger the sample size.
4. The higher the confidence level in the estimate, the larger the sample must be.
5. The greater the number of sub-groups of interest within a sample, the greater the sample size must be, as each sub-group must meet minimum sample size requirements.
6. If the calculated sample size exceeds 5 percent of the population, the sample size may be reduced without sacrificing precision.

Since researchers can never be 100 percent certain a sample reflects its population, they must decide how much precision they need. Precision is measured by (A) the interval in which they would expect to find the parameter estimate, and (B) the degree of confidence they wish to have in that estimate.

## Sampling Theory

Sampling theory is a study of the relationships that exists between a population and samples drawn from the population. Sampling theory is applicable only to random samples. For this purpose the population or a universe may be defined as an aggregate of items about which knowledge is sought. the theory of sample studies the relationship between the universe and the sample drawn from it.

The main problem of sampling theory is the problem of relationship between a parameter and a statistic. The theory of sampling is concerned with estimating the properties of the population from those of the sample and also with verifying the precision of the estimate. This sort of movement from particular sample towards the general universe is what is known as statistical induction or statistical inference. in more clear terms "from the sample we attempt to draw inference concerning the universe. In order to be able to follow this inductive method, we first follow a deductive argument which is that we imagine a population or universe and investigate the behaviour of the samples drawn from this universe applying the law of probability". This methodology is called as sampling theory. The objectives of sampling theory are as follows:

A. *Statistical Estimation:* Sampling theory helps in estimating unknown population parameters from a knowledge of statistical measures based on sample studies. In other words, to obtain an estimate of parameter from statistic is the estimate or it may be an interval estimate.

B. *Testing of Hypotheses:* Sampling theory enables to decide whether to accept or reject hypotheses ; the sampling theory helps in determining whether observed differences are actually due to change or whether they are really significant

C. *Statistical Inference:* Sampling theory helps in making generalizations about the population from the studies based on samples drawn from it. it also helps in deciding the accuracy of such generalizations.

# 20

# Types of Samples

## Introduction

As noted earlier, samples can be grouped under the two broad categories, namely probability samples and non-probability samples. Here below find various types of samples and their merits and limitations.

### *1. Simple Random Sampling*

According to Parten: "Random sampling is the term applied when the method of selection assures each individual element in the universe an equal chance of being selected."

Thus, the unit in the population under simple random sampling is provided an equal chance of being selected. As Moser aptly puts it: "Equity not be misunderstood as a haphazard, unprincipled selection. It is a methodical selection.

### Features of Simple Random Sampling

1. Items in the sample are selected completely independent of each other, which means that the selection of one unit does not influence the selection of others, positively or negatively.
2. It is a probability sample. Each item has the same chance of being selected. As stated by Goode & Hatt: "The units of the universe is so arranged that the selection process

gives equiprobability of selection to every unit in that universe."

3. It is purely a chance selection but it is not haphazard or hit and miss selection. Deliberate methods are used to ensure chance selection.
4. There is absolutely no room for bias of any kind in the selection of sample units. There cannot be any conscious selection.

## Principles of Simple Random Sampling

Parten in her famous book "Surveys, Polls and Samples" lays down some important principles to be followed in adopting simple random sampling. They are:

1. Population and the units must be clearly defined.
2. The units must consist of large number of small units.
3. The universe must consist of large number of small units.
4. Units must be independent of each other.
5. List of the universe must be got ready.
6. Methods of selection should be completely independent of the characteristics to be examined.
7. Units drawn should be accessible for investigation.
8. Once selected the unit cannot be discarded.

Procedure of Selection: While selecting the sample units following are the procedures adopted.

First of all serial numbers are allotted to each member of the universe. Secondly, selecting the serial number of units on either of the following modes:

1. Random number tables, which will be available in any book on statistics.
2. Drawing by lot numbered slips of paper from container, either with or without replacement. It is always preferable to make selection with replacement to ensure probability and independence of selection.

## Advantages

This method has several advantages. They are:

1. No advance knowledge of the characteristics of the population is necessary.
2. Assessment of the accuracy of the results is possible by sample error estimation.

3. It is representative of the universe.
4. Bias due to human preferences and influences is estimated.
5. It is a simple and easily practicable procedure if the population is not large.
6. It is less expensive.

## Limitations

Simple random sampling has got certain practical difficulties and inherent limitations, which are as follows:

1. Definition of the universe in many times is inadequate.
2. The ready lists of universe are not always available, serializing the large population is also difficult.
3. Sampling is likely to be biased at the survey state due to non-response or non-availability of the sample units.

## 2. *Stratified Random Sampling*

It is a sampling plan which attempts to design a more efficient sample. It retains the random element, at the same time, it is more representative of the population. It is a method used for increasing the precision of sampling. According to this method, first the population is divided into homogeneous groups or strata and sample is drawn from each stratum. Ya-Lum-Chun defines stratified random sampling thus: "The Process of stratification requires that the population is divided into groups or classes called strata. Then a sample is taken from each stratum by simple random method and the resulting samples is called a stratified sample." The basis of classification is anything such as sex, education, income, land holding etc., which is known as stratification factor. The stratification factor is selected in correlation with the problem under study, which becomes a logical basis of stratification. For instance, if adoption of improved agricultural practices is studied, then naturally size of simple is taken. Disproportionate sampling includes equal number of samples from each stratum. A proportional stratification yield a sample that represents the universe in the same proportion in which each stratum is represented in the population.

### *Principles of Stratification*

The stratified random sample has to observe certain basic principles, particularly at the time of stratification. They are:

1. There must be as much uniformity as possible within each stratum i.e., homogeneity.
2. There should be as great differences as possible among various stratum i.e. heterogeneity or variability.

*Advantages*

1. Stratified sampling is more representation of the population.
2. It is more precise and to a great extent avoids bias.
3. It saves time and cost of data collection since the sample size can be less in this method.
4. It is geographically concentrated and renders data collection convenient.

*Disadvantages*

1. It requires the knowledge of the traits of the population.
2. Classification or stratification becomes sometimes difficult and still difficult in the assignment of each unit of the population to a particular stratum.
3. The results sometimes have to be weighted according to the size of strata, which is a difficult task.
4. Preparing a stratified list is a task as the lists may not be readily available.

### 3. Systematic Sampling

Systematic sampling is a frequently used sampling plan. According to this method, sample is taken from a list prepared on a systematic arrangement either on the basis of alphabetic order, or on house number or any other method. Strictly speaking it is not a random sampling, though it includes an element of random selection. Therefore it is sometimes called quasi-random sampling. If simple random sampling cannot be adopted for some reason, systematic sampling is an alternative method, since it is reasonably accepted as equivalent to random sampling.

*Steps in Systematic Sampling*

1. First of all the population is given serial number from I to N.
2. The sampling interval is determined by dividing the population by the size of the sample i.e., N=K
3. Any number is selected at random from the first sampling

intervals.

4. The subsequent samples are selected at equal and regular intervals.

For example, let the size of the population be, 1000: and the sample size be 100. this is 100 samples are to be drawn from the population numbering 1000. the sample interval is 10. Suppose the first sample selected at random from the first interval is 6, then the subsequent samples are 16, 26, 36, 46, 56 and so on. Thus, in the systematic sampling the initial start is made on random basis which determines the subsequent samples. The randomness is retained at only one stage.

*Advantages*

1. It is a simple design and easy to execute.
2. Randomness and probability features are present which make the sample representative.

*Disadvantages*

1. As in simple random, the population has to be serialized in this sample also, which become a difficult task when the population is huge.
2. Any hidden periodicity in the list will adversely affect the representativeness of the sample.
3. There is always a temptation to reselect or restart while making selection.

### 4. Cluster Sampling

Cluster sampling refers to the procedure of dividing the population into groups called clusters and drawing a sample of clusters to represent the population. A cluster may consist of either the primary sample units or elementary secondary sample units. In a selected cluster either all the sample units are elected or a few of them are chosen on any sampling method. For instance, if a study has to be made on the industrial workers of a district, the industrial units are the primary sample units. If the primary sample units clustering in one particular locality is selected then it forms the first stage cluster; and when workers employed in one or two firms are selected that forms the second stage cluster. A plan to make selection of clusters within clusters is called multi-stage cluster sampling. Thus, one significant factor that differentiates the cluster sampling from other methods of sampling is that unlike in other types of samples in which each element in the population is separately selected, in the cluster sampling, groups are selected. A cluster may be anything, a school, municipal ward, an industry or a cooperative society.

*Principles of Cluster Sampling*

The participles that are basis to the cluster sampling method is just opposite to those governing the stratified sampling. These principles are essential to ensure maximum efficiency in sampling.

1. The differences or variability within a cluster should be as large as possible i.e., heterogeneity.
2. The variability among or between groups or clusters should be as small as possible i.e., homogeneity.

*Advantages*

1. This method provides significant cost gain.
2. It is easy and more practical method, which facilitates the field work.
3. Because of the geographical contiguity of the sample more units can be included.

*Disadvantages*

1. Probability and representative ness of the sample is sometimes affected.
2. The results are likely to be less precise and accurate.

***5. Sampling with Varying Probabilities***

1. It is also known as the sampling with probability proportionate to size. This is an important sampling plan applied in multi-stage selection. It ensures that the probability of selection of any sample is proportionate to the size of the group. That means, we have more chance of selecting samples from larger groups than from small groups. After assigning appropriate sample size, proportionate to the size of the cluster, a systematic selection is made at the second stage. For example, if the members of cooperative societies are our secondary sample units, the respective cooperative societies with varying size of membership are the primary sample units or first stage cluster

*Advantages*

1. It is helpful in giving the group with large number of units, greater probability of selection and thereby making the sample more representative.
2. It is an appropriate sampling plan in finding out the variability of groups.

*Limitations*

1. Listing and totaling of sampling involves elaborate work.
2. This sample is more appropriate in two-stage or multi-stage sampling plan.

### *6. Area Sampling*

Area sampling is very similar to the multi-stage cluster sampling. One special feature of area sampling is that the basis of selection is the map rather than the list of population. The basic technique in area sampling is to divide the primary sampling units such as district, development block, revenue village, municipal ward etc. For example from a city map one or two wards are selected where from a compete enumeration of households is made or a sample of households are studied. Likewise from a district map one or two development blocks are chosen and from each block, one or two revenue village segments may be enumerated completely or a sample household may be studied.

*Steps*

1. Stratification of the primary sampling units on the basis of geographical area.
2. Selection of primary sampling units from each stratum.
3. Sub-sampling of small units within each stratum.
4. Enumeration of household.

*Advantages*

1. Survey work can be conducted with considerable speed.
2. It is reliable and satisfactory as complete enumeration is involved.

*Disadvantages*

1. It is fairly expensive.

2. It also involves considerable amount of listing of areas and sub-areas, though complete listing of households or individuals is not necessary.

### 7. Quota Sampling

Quota sampling is one of the commonly used methods of sampling in market surveys and opinion polls. Though basically it is a non-random sampling, this method combines the aspects of probability sampling and purposive selection. Following are the three basic steps in quota sampling:

1. First the population is stratified on some basis, preferably on the basis of the characteristics of the population pertaining to the study.
2. Determination of the proportion of the population falling in each stratum.
3. The quota of sample units is decided and assigned for each stratum.

*Advantages*

1. It is a practical as well as a convenient method.
2. It is economical.
3. It is the only useful method when no sample frame is available.

*Disadvantages*

1. It is unreliable and prone to bias.
2. It is not a representative sample.
3. It is not possible to estimate the standard error.
4. Control of field work is difficult.

### 8. Purposive Sampling

Due to certain practical difficulties, it may not be always possible to follow probability sampling. In that case the researcher will look for an alternative sampling plan which will ensure representative sampling. When he decides to select a sub-group which is a 'barometer' or representative of the whole population, it is called a purposive selection. Thus, the selection of the sample units are left to the choice or discretion of the researcher. But it is ensured that the selected units are the representative of the universe. As defined by Jensen: "purposive selection denotes the method of selecting a number or groups of units in such a way that the selected groups together yield as nearly as possible the same average or proportion as the totality with respect to the characteristics which are already a matter of statistical knowledge." In short the selected units must be typical.

*Advantages*

1. It is a practical method when randomization is not possible.
2. Enumeration is quick and economical.

*Disadvantages*

1. Considerable prior knowledge of the population is necessary.
2. Estimation of sampling error is not possible.

# 21

# Data Collection and Types of Data

## Data Collection

The gathering of data in social research may range from simple observation to a mammoth survey. The method selected will determine how the data are collected. Schedule, questionnaire, interview, observation etc. are some of the tools used for data collection.

Data may be defined as the facts presented to the researcher from the study's environment. Data may be further characterized by their abstractness, verifiability, elusiveness and closeness to the phenomenon. As abstractions, data are more metaphorical than real.

For example, the growth in GNP cannot be observed directly, only the effects of it may be recorded. Second, data are processed by our senses, often limited in comparison to the senses of other living organisms. When sensory experiences produce the same results, our data are said to be trustworthy because they may be verified. Thirdly, capturing data is elusive, complicated by the speed at which events occur and the time-bound nature of observation. Finally, data reflect their truthfulness by closeness to the phenomena.

Data are edited to ensure consistency across respondents and to locate omissions. In the case of survey method, editing reduces errors in the recording, improves legibility and clarifies unclear and inappropriate responses. Edited data are then put into a form that makes analysis possible. Because it is impractical tom place raw data into a report, codes are used to reduce the responses to a more manageable system of storage and future processing. The codes follow various decision rules that the researcher has devised to assist with sorting, tabulating and analyzing.

Data analysis involves reducing collected data to a manageable size, developing summaries and applying statistical tools. The researcher has to interpret these findings in the light of the research questions or determine if the results are consistent with their hypothesis and theories. Finally, the researcher has to make meaningful and pragmatic suggestions based on their interpretation of data.

## Types of Data

The data needed in social research may be classified into the following categories:

*Data on individual characteristics:* The demographic and socio-economic characteristics of individuals fall under this category. Variables like age, education, sex, marital status, income, occupation etc will come under this category.

*Data on behavioral variables:* Data relating to attitude, opinions, knowledge etc will come under this category.

*Organizational data:* Informations relating to an organization's origin, growth, resources, performance, employees etc will come under this category.

*Territorial data:* These are data relating to the geographical character. Such data are on resources, population, occupation, infrastructure etc..

*Importance of data:* The primary and secondary data collected by the researcher serve as the bases or raw material for the analysis. Without an analysis of data, no inferences can be drawn on the questions under study. The relevance, adequacy and reliability of data determine the quality of the findings and the ultimate quality of the research work. Data also form the basis for testing the hypotheses formulated for the study. Data also provide the facts and figures required for constructing measurement scales and tables, which are analysed with statistical techniques. Inference on the results of statistical analysis and tests of significance provide the answers to research questions. Thus the scientific process of measurement, analysis, testing and inferences depends on the availability of relevant and adequate data.

## Sources of Data

The sources of data may be classified into Primary data and Secondary data. Social research can be done using either primary data or secondary data or having both primary data and secondary data.

## Primary Data or Primary Sources

Primary sources are the original sources from which the researcher directly collects data. Primary data can be collected directly by the researcher in the case of small projects or case studies. Some times he may employ trained investigators and can collect data. Primary data can be collected through the tools like schedule, questionnaire, observation, interview etc.

***Choice of the Methods of data collection:***

While choosing the right method of data collection, the following factors must be considered:

1. *The nature of the study:* If it is a study of opinions or preferences, questionnaire or interview may be followed. A study which needs data from the respondents whose language is not known, observation as a method of data collection may be useful.
2. *Availability of funds:* Availability of funds determines to a larger extent the method to be employed for data collection. If enough funds are available larger surveys can be done through trained enumerators using interview method.
3. *The unit of enquiry:* The unit of enquiry may be an individual, an institution or community. To collect data from individuals interview with schedule is preferable. If it is an institution mailed questionnaire can be used. Studies for communities call for the method observation.
4. *Time factor:* If time available for the research project is short methods like mailed questionnaire can be used. If the time availability is not a problem then interview can be used.
5. *The size of the sample:* If the sample size is small interview may be effective for data collection. If the sample size is large and the area to be covered is wider mailed

questionnaire is appropriate.

6. *Scale of the study:* If the study is of a larger nature, the survey can be done by trained enumerators applying interview.
7. *Educational level of the respondents:* If the educational level of the respondents is high mailed questionnaire can be applied. On the other hand if the respondents have poor educational level interview can be used.
8. Depth of information to be collected: If the study needs detailed informations to be collected it is better to apply schedule with interview, on the other hand, if the study needs only basic data other methods can be followed.
9. *Availability of trained manpower:* If trained manpower is available large surveys can be done. If the manpower is poor it is better to use other methods.
10. *The rate of accuracy and probing:* If the study needs accurate data and to be mixed with probing interview is the best suited method.

Even various methods of data collection have their own merits and limitations. Schedule as a method or tool of data collection has to be combined with one more tool of data collection, namely interview, which leads to higher cost. But it has the chief merit of collecting accurate data and avoids refusals. Probing is also possible in this method, for which we can not find this merit in other methods. Questionnaire can cover a wider geographical area and can save lot of money and time. But this method has the major drawback of non-contact and large number of refusals to questions. Observation is a very useful tool when we apply this tool to communities and population to which we could not talk or communicate. But this method has the drawback of timeliness, continuity of incidences etc.

## Secondary Data or Secondary Source

Secondary data are the informations which have already been collected by some other agencies and which have already been processed. Generally speaking, secondary data have been collected by some agency for its own purpose but can be allowed to be used by others. Such secondary data have been collected by government and non-governmental agencies.

Such agencies may be from local level to international level.

At international level agencies like UNO, FAO, WHO, UNESCO etc will come under this category.

Secondary sources contain not only published reports but also unpublished reports.

### *Types of Secondary Data*

The following types of secondary data are useful to the researchers:

1. Population data.
2. Employment data.
3. Income data.
4. Sales data.
5. Occupation data.
6. Industry data.

### *Sources of Secondary Data*

Following are the sources of secondary data

1. Books and journals
2. Government source
3. Media source.
4. Census reports.
5. Commercial sources..

### *Advantages of Secondary Data*

The central advantage of secondary data is the saving of time and cost. A researcher may not get all the required data from secondary sources, but they can aid in the formulation of decision problem, suggest methods and types of data for meeting the information needs and serve as a source of comparative data by which primary data can be interpreted and evaluated.

### *Secondary Data Have the Following Advantages:*

1. *Economy and time:* Secondary data provide economy in time and cost. Primary data collection is costly and consumes lot of time to gather data. Secondary data could be collected easily through library or by direct contact of the concerned source. Through this process lot of time and money could be saved.
2. *Easy availability:* The secondary data are collected by various agencies for certain purposes of their own. They

may allow others to use such data freely or for a payment. Government and international agencies, mostly allow others to use their data freely. Private agencies, in very many cases make the data available for a price.

3. *Quicker and cheaper:* Secondary data if available can be secured quickly and cheaply. Once their sources are located, collection of data is a matter of time. Even the tediousness of copying the source has been simplified by websites and e-mail systems.
4. *Coverage:* Secondary data can cover wider geographical area and longer reference period. Thus it extends the researchers space and time reach. International agencies like FAO,ILO,etc provide vast data covering countries and continents, which have become very useful to social science researchers.
5. *Verification:* The sources of data help the researcher to verify the data relating to the authenticity and reliability, which are very important in research. The researcher need not wait for the time to supplement them with additional primary data

### *Objectives of Secondary Data Research*

There are two major objectives of secondary data research, noted below:

1. *Fact finding:* The very purpose of research is fact finding and to find out the truth in a problem. In business organisations, secondary data help to compare the position of one organisation with its competitors. Financial and other business performances can be compared and efforts can be made to improve the position in future.
2. *Model building:* Model building is one of the routine works of scholars and secondary data are very helpful to them. Model building involves specifying relationship between two or more variables. Models developed help the present future researchers. Fore casting models help government organisations and private firms in number of ways.
3. *Exploring market potential:* Business researchers regularly explore the market potential for various commodities and the market for specific companies. When primary data are not available, using secondary data from various sources the market potential can be identified.

4. *Reference material:* Secondary data, kept in storages act as the best reference material for researchers and organisations. Reference of materials need to be undertakes very oftèn to verify facts, sources and reliability.
5. *Bench marking:* Secondary data may be used as bench marks against which the findings of a research may be tested.
6. *As a sole source of information:* Secondary data may be used as sole data for very many research and business purposes. market behavior, consumer behavior , farmers behavior etc can be identified through this process.

*Characteristics of Secondary Data*

Before using secondary data, the researcher must see that they posses the following characterizes:

A. *Data pertinary:* The first consideration in using secondary data is to examine the pertinary of the available secondary data to the research problem under study. The following questions must be considered:
   1. What are the definitions and classification employed?
   2. What are the measurements of variables used? What is the degree to which they conform to the requirements of our research?
   3. What is the coverage of the secondary data in terms of topic and time.

B. *Data quality:* The quality of the secondary data is an important consideration in any research activity. The quality of data refers to their accuracy, reliability, and completeness. By means of verifying the data with other similar sources we can arrive at the quality also.

C. *Reliability of the data:* The reliability can be tested by finding out by finding out th following infomations:
   1. Who collected the data?
   2. What were the sources of data?
   3. Were they collected by using proper methods?
   4. At what time they were collected?
   5. Was there any bias on the part of the compiler?
   6. What level of accuracy was desired and had it been achieved?

D. *Suitability of data:* The data that are suitable for one enquiry may not be suitable for another enquiry. If the available data are unsuitable they should not be used. In this context the researcher must carefully scrutinize the definition of various terms and units of collection used at that time of collecting data. Similarly, the object, scope and nature of the original data enquiry must also be studied.

E. Adequacy of data: If the level of accuracy in data is found inadequate, they will be considered as inadequate and should not be used by the researcher. The data will also be considered to be inadequate if they are related to an area which may be narrower or wider than the area of the present study.

The researcher must be careful in using secondary data based on the above observations. At times there may be wealth of unusable information in the already available data which may be used by an intelligent researcher with due precaution.

### *Disadvantages of Secondary Data*

The following are some of the disadvantages of secondary data:

1. *Data fit problem*: One of major problems of secondary data is the available data may not fit our needs, some times. The definitions adopted by those who collected them may be different, units of measurement may not match our needs The degree of fit ranges from completely inadequate to very close. The degree of fit is influenced by the following factors:
   A. *Units of measurement*— Many times secondary data are expressed in units different from those required by the project.
   B. *Definition of classes*. Improper definition may lead to confusion
   C. *Publication currency*. This the recency of the data. Up-date data may not be available. Some sources have long time gap between the data collection and publication.
2. *Accuracy problem:* They must make sure that the secondary data are accurate enough for the purpose of the research project in hand. There may be number of sources errors in secondary data like the sampling, data collection, analysis and report, which may influence the accuracy

of data. The following criteria can be used in the difficult task of assessing the accuracy of secondary data:

A. *Source*—secondary data may be secured from an original source or an acquired source. An original source is the source that originated the data, while an acquired data is one that procured the data from an original source. The original source is more detailed and accurate than the acquired source. Errors in transcription and failure to reproduce footnotes and other comments can seriously influence the accuracy of the data.

B. *Evidence concerning the quality:* This is to asses the general evidence of quality of data. If the primary data do not disclose the details of research design, one can be cautious. When the details of the research design is disclosed, the researcher should evaluate the areas such as, sampling plan, data collection procedure, quality of field training, and data analysis procedures A section discussing the limitations of the research design and data should be included.

3. *Updatedness of the data:* The data available through secondary sources may not be updated to meet the current needs of the researcher. The time lag between the data collection period and the publication period may be very long, in which case the data may become obsolete.

4. *Data conversion:* When secondary data are reported in a format that does not suit the researchers needs, data conversion may be necessary. (or data transformation) This is the process of changing the original form of data to a format suitable to achieve the research objective.

5. *Bias:* The research conducted by other people may be biased to suit their needs and might have vested interests. The researchers using such secondary data must be cautious in this respect.

6. *Cross checks:* Researchers must verify the secondary data before they start using them. Cross checks of data from multiple sources should be made to determine the similarity of independent projects. When the data are not consistent the researcher, should attempt to identify the reasons for the differences or to determine what data are most likely to be correct.

7. *Sufficiency:* Some times, secondary data may be available, relevant and accurate, but may not be sufficient to meet the requirements of the study. This may warrant the researcher to go for primary data, which may lead to cost escalation.

6.4.6 Based on the above discussions, the following precautions must be taken before using the secondary data, in the form of answering the following questions by the researcher:

1. When were the data generated?
2. What was the source for the data and what is the general reputation of the source?
3. Do the data have any stated limitations about their use?
4. What were the stated assumptions concerning conclusions drawn from the data?
5. Are the methods used for collecting, tabulating and analyzing the data stated? If not, can they be ascertained?
6. Are the methods still reliable or have subsequent practices indicated certain weakness?
7. Are those who took part in generating the data still available for consultation?
8. What methods were used to collect the data? Did the researchers use observations, physical measurements, analysis of other secondary data or interviews by the researchers or by paid enumerators?
9. Did the basis for collecting the data changed during period for which the data are required and if no, how does this affect estimates of trends?
10. Do the data contain gaps that could cause statistical errors in their use?

## Validity

Validity means the effectiveness of an instrument in measuring the specific properties which it intends to measure.

The measurement of physical properties like height, weight and length. Because it is direct and standardised measurement devices are available. But measurement of abstract properties like attitude, morale, motivation etc, is indirect and pose the problem of validity. Validity can be classified into internal validity and external validity. Internal validity is limited to the ability of a research instrument to measure what is expected to measure. When the effects of extraneous variables are eliminated and the observed effects on dependent variable can be ascribed to the effect of experimented dependent variables, then the experiment has internal validity. This is generally achieved in laboratory experiment because in it extraneous variables are controlled. On the other hand external validity refers to the data's ability to be generalized across persons, settings, and time.

## Types of Validity

Validity is classified into content validity, predictive validity and construct validity. Each of these types use either logic, statistical verification or both for determining the degree of validity and has special value under certain conditions.

### *Content Validity*

There are two forms of content validity, namely, face validity and sampling validity. Face validity is a logical type resting on the investigator's subjective evaluation as to the validity of a measuring instrument. Face validity is a poor way of determining validity, it is often a matter of opinion.

### *Sampling Validity*

This refers to the representative character of the content of the instrument. Sampling validity can be determined by comparing the instrument items with the universe of items that could theoretically be included.

### *Predictive Validity*

This refers to the empirically measured association between the results produced by the instrument and the subsequent actual out come.

### *Construct Validity*

This refers to the measure or infer the presence of abstract characteristics for which no empirical validation seems possible. Attitude scales and personality tests fall under this in this category. To evaluate construct validity both the theory and the measuring instruments are used.

### *Threats to validity*

Combell and Stanley list the following twelve threats to validity:

1. *Maturation:* This means the effects of time. Between the pre-test and post-test of the data sources, the subjects undergo various changes such as fatigue, boredom etc which may influence their performance and so the difference between the pre-test and post-test performance cannot be ascribed to the effects of experimental variables only.
2. *History:* Some events like political, economical or cultural may affect the course of the study. The influence of this source of invalidity is greater in a field experiment than in laboratory experiment.
3. *Testing:* It is possible that the experience gained in the pre-test may result in an increase in the post-test performance. This testing effect is confounded wirh the effect of experimental variable.
4. *Instrumentation:* If the tests of instruments used for measurement are not accurate or consistent the results will be vitiated.
5. *Statistical regression:* Those who scored highest on a pre-test are likely to score relatively lower on a pre-test, where as subjects who scored lowest in the pre-test are likely to score higher on a re-test. Thus their average score in re-test may be closer to the overall population average. This is merely a statistical artifact. Failure to recognise this fact may lead the researcher to arrive at wrong conclusions on the results.
6. *Differential selection:* Selection bias arises when the experimental and control groups are not identical.
7. *Experimental mortality:* This refers to the loss of subject due to dropout, migration etc. The remedy is to omit the pre-test scores of subjects who did not take the post-test.
8. Selection maturation, selection history or selection-testing interactions. These interactions between selection and other factors arise when the effect of the other factors differs between the groups selected.
9. *Reactive effect of testing:* The pre-test may affect the responsiveness of the experimental group to the treatment.
10. *Reactive effect of experimental arrangement:* The knowledge of participation in an experimental group may introduce bias in favour of the experimental group. This effect is

popularly known as Hawthrone Effect.

11. *Multiple treatment interference:* In experiments like medical experiments several experiments are conducted, at this stage , the residual effect of the previous treatment would interact with the effect of the next one.
12. *Contamination:* This is a type of bias that arises when the researcher has some previous knowledge about the subjects involved in an experiment. This may affect the objectivity of his judgment.

## Reliability

Reliability means the ability of a measuring instrument to give accurate and consistent result.

For example a weighing scale is reliable, if it gives the same reading when the same object is weighed several times. A measure is reliable to the degree that it supplies consistent results. Reliability is a necessary contributor to validity but is not a sufficient condition for validity. Reliability is concerned with estimates of the degree to which a measurement is free of random or unstable error.

Reliability has two aspects, namely, stability and non-variability or equivalence. An intrument is stable if it gives consistent results with repeated measurements of the same object. While stability is concerned with personal and situational fluctuations from one time to another, non-variability or equivalence is concerned with variations at one point in time among investigators and sample items.

### *Methods of Estimating Reliability*

There are three methods of estimating reliability, as noted below:

1. *Test-retest method:* A measuring instrument is administered to the same group of persons at different times. The coefficient of correlation between the two sets of scores is computed. The obtained coefficient is a measure of reliability. Higher the coefficient, higher the degree of reliability.
2. *Parallel forms technique:* One way of overcoming the limitations of the test-retest method is the use of two parallel forms of the same tool, containing different but relevant items. The two forms are administered to the

same group of persons, and the two sets of scores are correlated to obtain an estimate of reliability.

3. *Split-half method:* This method is designed to split the instrument into two sets- say odd numbered items as one half and the even-numbered items as second half. Each half is used as a separate instrument and the scores of both halves are correlated.

# 22

# Schedule and Questionnaire

## Primary and Secondary Sources of Data

In social research, the information/data needed for the researcher can be collected from two sources, namely primary source and secondary source.

## Primary Source

Primary sources of data are collected directly by the researcher. Such methods of data collection are through schedule, questionnaire, mailed questionnaire, interview, observation, and scaling. Primary data are providing firsthand information to the researcher and they have reliability and validity of data.

The following are several tools of primary data.

### *Schedule and Questionnaire*

The term "Schedules" and "Questionnaires" are used synonymously by most of the researchers. There is a very thin line of distinction between these terms. It is based on technical distinction. The schedules are those used in personal interviews whereas questionnaires are the forms distributed through mail. This distinction does not seem to have significant bearing on the principle, method and important considerations in preparing the research tools. The methods adopted for preparation of schedules and questionnaires are commonly discussed in this chapter. The questionnaires/schedule is an indispensable tool in social sciences research. So it has to be scientifically designed. Various steps involved in the preparation of questionnaires (hereafter questionnaire will be used to denote both questionnaires and schedules) are discussed below.

### *Design of the Questionnaire*

Following are the steps in designing the questionnaire:

1. Define the problems to be tackled by the survey so as to decide on what questions to ask. The temptation is always to cover too much to ask everything that might turn out to be interesting. This must be resisted. Lengthy sampling questionnaires are as demoralizing for the interviewer as for the respondent. The questionnaire should not be longer than is absolutely necessary for the purpose.
2. The survey planning must rigorously examine every question and exclude any that are not strictly relevant to the objectives of the survey. In this respect the pilot survey is the most helpful tool. All the marginal questions can be tested out and dummy tabulations made from the results. Questions likely to prove to be of small importance in the final analysis can be spotted and those which turn out to be not worth asking be excluded.
3. In setting the scope of the questionnaire the questions should be practicable. This needs emphasis, even though no amount of text book admonition can take the place, of common sense.

### *Steps Which are Necessary at the Planning Stage:*

1. The researcher must learn as much as possible about his subject matter before he begins to formulate questions.
2. The researcher should layout tentatively the logical implications of his problems and then draw upon his own experience and the literature for questions which are relevant to those logical implications. At this point the researcher should consult colleagues to get their thinking on the problem.
3. While the formulation of a list of areas and questions the researcher should submit this list to experts both in the field of the problem and in related fields. With each consultation some changes occur: (i) the list of possible questions grows (ii) the number of areas which are of

interest increases (iii) the number of areas which the researcher can cover must be decreased (iv) ambiguities, biases, poor phrasing etc. are corrected gradually and (v) a closer logical relationship developed between the parts of the schedule.

4. Any questionnaire must be limited in its length and scope. In general, in the absence of special motivations for the respondent, an interview should not extend much beyond half an hour and even this length is difficult to sustain without fatiguing the informant.

Hence, in planning a questionnaire a researcher must get himself thorough with the subject he has chosen for research. Then he has to decide the areas to be covered by the study and must frame the objectives. The questionnaire areas will ensure the collection of adequate and relevant data. Consultation with experts in the field will also help to prepare an ideal questionnaire.

### *Unification of Areas*

After proper planning is made, major areas of the questionnaire must be arranged in an order to ascertain unification of the areas of the questionnaire. Goode and Hatt say that such unification is necessary in order to make the respondent:

(a) drawn into the interview by awakening his interest
(b) easily brought along from items which are simple to answer to those which are complex.
(c) Not affronted by an early and sudden request for personal information.
(d) Never asked to give an answer which could be embarrassing without being an opportunity to explain, and
(e) Brought as smoothly as possible from one frame of reference to another rather than made to jump back and forth.[3]

### *Principles to be Adopted in Organizing the Questions*

As for the introductory item of the questionnaire, it should catch the attention of the respondent throughout the interview and should not result in refusals. It is better to avoid controversial items at the beginning. Generally questions are devised in such a way that they have the power to evoke interest and to involve the respondent in the interview without arousing a strong controversial response.

Secondly, simpler items should be introduced in the first and items which require thinking or scratching of the brain or crucial issues must come in the body of the questionnaire. Such questions should not be taken to the end since the interview might have got tired or he might have got interview fatigue. Likewise questions involving too much personal information or delicate questions should not be brought at the beginning.

It is important that sources of embarrassment should be removed from the questionnaire. Questions which are too personal and controversial should be avoided as far as possible.

With regard to the last aspect of moving smoothly from one item to the other, questions pertaining to the same area be placed together so as to have subject sequence. It will also aid the respondent to answer easily.

### *Question Content*

While preparing the questions for the questionnaire the respondent's knowledge of the subject, ability, willingness, etc., must be weighted properly. If we are preparing a questionnaire for educated people we can ask questions with standards or with rich content or what are known as loaded questions. On the other hand, if it is for the uneducated the subject content must be minimum.

### *Question Wording or Language*

While framing the question the language used must be simple. It must be easily understandable by all the sample respondents. As uniformity in answers are very important for the later stage of processing, the questions must be worded in simple language to give the same meaning to the respondents.

*Following are the Principles of Question Making:*

*1. Use Simple and Familiar Language*

Vocabulary used in the questionnaire should be simple which is used in the daily life. It should be within the comprehension of the least intelligent of the group studied. Phrases and expressions known only in certain regions of the country should be avoided.

*2. Make the Questions Concise*

A question should be as concise as possible, long involved sentences with conditional clauses require extended concentration on the part of the respondent. Such questions confuse the informants and will result in wrong answers. Concise wording and clear arrangement will condense the wide range of information in a small schedule.

*3. Avoid Leading Questions*

Questions and statements of a leading character should be guarded against. According to Moser "a leading is one which by its content, structure of wording, leads the respondent in the direction of a certain answer."5 For the question: Do you read 'The Hindu Daily? The respondents tend to answer 'Yes". Instead the question may be phrased thus: what newspaper do you read daily? Presenting a choice to the respondent is acceptable, provided that more than one choice is offered.

*4. Be Specific and Explicit*

The question should be made explicit so that the interviewer is able to get the kind of interpretation desired. For example "What kind of radio you own?" may mean anything the model, type of brand. Make the question pin-pointed and specific by giving different alternatives; (a) transistor (b) trade model; or (a) single band (b) 2 band (c) 3 band; or (a) Philips (b) Murphy (c) Bush (d) other (specify).

*5. Make the Question Self Explanatory*

The question should be self explanatory as far as possible, so that the desired information is gathered and tabulation becomes easy. Questions like where is your birthplace? How often do you go to movies? Lack clarity. They should be made more explicit and specific. So also units of enumeration such as birr, cents, weights in terms of kg, and quintals should be clearly defined in the schedule.

*6. Avoid Ambiguous Questions*

In the question wording ambiguity should be avoided at all costs. Ambiguous question will mean different things to different people. It is confusing and beyond the comprehension of respondents. For example the question: Have you paid back the loan you obtained from the bank? if asked irrespective of the fact whether one obtained the loan or not will be understood differently. A "no" for such question will either mean that one has not obtained loan or one as not paid back the loan. Such ambiguous questions are the result of vague phrasing or unwarranted assumptions.

*7. Avoid Vague Questions*

Vagueness creeps in the question when the descriptive adjectives and adverbs like good, bad, fair or frequently, occasionally, rarely, are used. Such wording do not have agreed or generally, accepted meaning. Similarly phrases like kind of, 'generally' 'on the whole' etc., should be avoided. For instance; What kind of house be specific such as : What is the type of roofing in your house? (a) Terrace (b) tiled (c) thatched?

*8. Allow Maximum Alternatives*

Questions should be phrased in such a way that all possible alternatives are provided. For instance a question regarding material status of a person should include all the following alternatives: (a) single (b) married (c) widowed (d) divorced (e) separated. For questions which have infinite answers, besides, other known answers, 'others-specify' category should be included.

*9. Avoid Double-Barreled Questions*

Each question should cover only one issue. Double-barreled and multiple meaning questions should be split up into two or more questions. Example: Do you think that all the commercial banks in the country should be nationalized and more funds diverted to priority sector?

*10. Avoid Presuming Questions*

Questions should not presume anything about the respondent. For example the question to which party have you voted in the late election? Such question is relevant only after asking a filter question: Did you vote in last election?

*11. Avoid Hypothetical Questions*

Such questions are based on assumptions and predictions. Answers to hypothetical situation will not be realistic, as the respondent never experienced such a situation.

*12. Avoid Questions which Involve the Prestige*

If an answer to a question is likely to affect the prestige either positively or negatively, such questions will not receive correct answers. People generally want to project a good image of themselves as generous, progressive and intelligent. A question like do you favor a socialistic a socialistic society, will receive affirmative answer, which may not reflect the inner wishes of the respondent.

*13. Avoid Advance Categorization*

It is always better to classify the response yourself rather then allowing the respondent to choose the categories. While asking occupation of a respondent advance categorization like, professional, skilled labor, clerks, farmer etc., will affect accuracy. Simply ask, what is your occupation?

***Framing of Effective Questions***

As pointed out earlier the questions must use simple language and they should be short in nature. Questions can be broken into pieces wherever necessary. Herbert Hyman gives the following criteria in constructing effective questions.

1. Complex questions that require the respondent to go through several steps of reasoning before answering are undesirable and have often resulted in misleading information.
2. Questions on controversial issues should be broken down into components so that the tester can determine the respondents' feeling about many aspects of the problem including those which he refuses to comment upon. A series of specific questions is needed, sometimes referred to as filter-questions in order to gather adequately the reactions to all sides of the issue.
3. When questions feel to assess the degrees of intensity of feeling or conviction, it is often necessary to find out to what extent the respondents' attitude have been crystallized towards the subject. It is well to include a series of "Why" "When" and "How" questions, the answers to which are analyzed in relation to answers to other specific questions.
4. The required answers should be within the informational

scope of the respondent.

5. The length of the questions and statement used should be governed by an estimate of the respondents' comprehension level. If a question appears too long, the best way of slitting it should be investigated.6

*Question Order*

Following order should be observed in organizing the questions:

1. Questions asked at the start of the interview should be such that they are easy to answer. Such "stage setting" questions will help to built rapport. They may be factual questions like name, age, occupation or those which appeal to human interest such as fashion, film, etc. It should be ensured that such interest-catching questions are not sensitive and controversial. Advice-seeking questions will also encourage the respondents.
2. Questions should be arranged sequentially according to the subject matter or on the basis of periods. Questions pertaining to one subject or one reference period should be grouped together in order to avoid mental exertion to the respondent.
3. Questions must be arranged logically and must move from one topic to another. The progression of questions should be natural and spontaneous.
4. The transition from one topic to another must be easy and smooth. The questions should not jump abruptly from innocent to embarrassing subjects. While proceeding from one set of questions to another it is better to explain the break and the relevance of a new set of question in one or two sentences.
5. Questions which may embarrass the informant must be placed at the middle of the questionnaire, so that they do not create any misgiving at the close of he interview.
6. Questions which will affect the answer for later questions should not be arranged at the interview.
7. Highly sensitive questions, which may lead to the termination of interview owing to the respondent's refusal to continue the interview, should be placed at the end. If any such refusal is met, the loss of information will be relatively small.

### *Questions that Need Carefulness*

There are certain question which can be omitted and there are certain questions which need caution while using. Such questions are as follows:

*(a) Insufficiently Specific Questions*

Questions must be specific to get the expected response. For example, Are you satisfied or dissatisfied with your canteen, is unspecific. It must be like this, Are you satisfied or dissatisfied with the prices of meals of your canteen?

*(b) Ambiguous Questions*

Ambiguous questions are not clear in comprehension. They fall into categories like incomplete references (How well does your mind work over this issue) or indefinite comparisons, of times, place or persons (How often do you go to cinema) Hence, ambiguous questions must be avoided. Vague words and phrases like "fairly" "generally" "many" should be avoided.

*(c) Leading Questions*

Moser defines a leading question thus: "It is one which by its content, structure or wording, leads the respondent in the direction of a certain answer". For example a question like "Do you read a newspaper like Hindu?" a leading question must also be avoided.

*(d) Presuming Questions*

Questions should not presume anything about the respondent. It should not imply that he possess that knowledge or have a particular habit. For example ask question "are you a smoker?" Only after putting certain filter questions for knowing first he is a smoker.

*(e) Hypothetical Questions*

Such questions which always attempt to give affirmative answers-would you like an increase in salary? If the response I s 'no' there is something wrong. Moser says "If he did (i.e., said no) it could only be because he has taken into account some hidden factors of his own, or because he has failed to".

*(f) Personalized Questions*

Such questions are those involving too much of personal nature. For example, asking a question on family planning if a question is asked like, "have you undergone Vasectomy?" the answer can be 'no' even from a respondent who had undergone such operation.

*(g) Embarrassing Questions*

Such questions are those which people do not like to discuss in public. For example questions on family planning for women. To get response to such questions which are very essential female interview can elicit response from a women respondent easily.

*(h) Questions on Periodical Behavior*

It is about a particular habit like going to cinema, purchases etc. How often do you go to cinema? When did you lat go to cinema? Such questions must be asked in a specific and tactful way to get correct response.

*(i) Questions Involving Memory*

These are questions involving the respondent in recollecting information – when did you last go to cinema? What was the price paid for paddy in 1976?

*(j) Questions Which are too Sensitive*

Questions on burning issues such as religion, politics, tradition, superstition etc, should be avoided as far as possible.

*(h) Labored Questions*

Lengthy questions may involve longer memory of a respondent and to such questions the respondent ma get bored or exhausted. For example: some people say walking is good for health some people say cycling is good for health some people say horse riding or swimming is good for health. Which method do you think is good?

***Pre-test***

By pre-testing the questionnaire errors can be eliminated, unwanted questions can be removed, language or the wordings can be corrected.

Goode and Hatt in their book 'Methods in Social Research', give the following advantages of pre-test.

*(a) Lack of Order in the Answer*

Lack of order in questions may arise if questions do not tap same experience in each respondent. This may be due to the use of difficult words, or questions which attempt to obtain too much data at one time or the other, but whatever the reason may be, totally unordered answers should always lead to critical re-examination of the questions.

*(b) "All-or-None Responses"*

Such stereo typed responses being answered by all or none must be avoided and the questions much be re-arranged or worded properly.

*(c) A High Proportion 'Don't Know' or Don't Understand Answers'*

This is an indication that the questions are improperly drawn or that, a bad sample design has been used. Large percentage of 'don't know' responses suggests that (i) questions are vague, or (ii) that they are too complex, or (iii) that they involve difficult answers on which the respondent needs expert interviewing help, or (iv) that the respondent simply is not in a position to answer the questions.

*(d) A Great Number of Qualifications or Irrelevant Comments*

Qualifications are the conditions put in answers, i.e., the respondent adds conditions like, 'if' and 'but'. If many of these are offered by the respondents the questions need to be changed or re-arranged.

*(e) A High Proportion of Refusals to Answers*

During the course of the interview some questions may be unanswered. If the refusal order is above 10 percent, questions need revision. Refusals may be due to the inclusion of a taboo subject without any warning, or a question which is out of context. Refusal may take place if the interviewer asks person questions which the respondent thinks that he cannot assure anonymity.

***Mailed Questionnaire***

A questionnaire is a tool to collect data from diverse, large and widely scattered social group. Questionnaires are prepared in advance by the interviewer and are generally mailed to the informants. Sometimes questionnaires are also administered to groups.

One important factor that differentiates questionnaires and other means of data collection such as interview schedules and interview guides is that the questionnaire is self-administered. The questionnaire will prove to be an effective tool, if used in appropriate research designs and situations.

The appropriateness of the mailed questionnaires will depend on: (i) the types of information required (ii) the type of respondent reached (iii) the accessibility of respondents and (iv) the precision of the hypothesis.

### *Advantages of Mailed Questionnaire*

Mailed questionnaire, compared to interview has enormous advantages. It is cheaper and consumers less time, it allows the respondent to express freely. The following are the important advantages of mailed questionnaire.

#### *1. Cheaper in Cost*

Mailed questionnaire is cheaper to administer as it involves only postal expenses. Expenses relating to travel by the interviewer are avoided. The problem of supervision is also dispensed with.

#### *2. Covers Larger Area*

Mailed questionnaire is very useful to cover a large size of sample. When a study needs to cover the population extending a state or the whole of the country, mailed questionnaire can reach the sample respondents who are far away from the study center.

#### *3. Saving in Time*

The use of mailed questionnaire saves the time of respondent as well as that of the researcher. In the absence of the interviewer time taken for unnecessary conversations is saved. Deviations from the main purpose of interview is quite common and such wastage of time is avoided under mailed questionnaire. Moser views that: "It takes little time to send out or to get the bulk of the eventual returns to follow-up attempts. It can be reasonably expected that the mailed questionnaires will be returned within three weeks."

*4. Free-flow of Responses*

In the absence of a second party a respondent is allowed to give his responses. He is allowed to take his own time for thinking and to consult and verify information. This can assure free flow of responses.

*5. Validity, Reliability and Accuracy*

As the respondent is remote from the study center and the absence of personal proximity and association can assure validity of responses. As anonymity is maintained it can safeguard the reliability of the responses.

*6. Problems of Non-Contracts*

When a questionnaire is to be administered through interview several respondents may not be available. In villages or rural areas respondents may not be available during the daytime, as they might have gone to the fields. In cities or urban areas they might have gone to offices. Either early mornings or late evenings must be fixed as the right time for interview. This handicap could be avoided by the mailed questionnaire.

**Limitations of Mailed Questionnaire**

Mailed questionnaire has the following limitations:

***1. It Needs Higher Rate of Literacy***

Mailed questionnaire can be used in countries where the rate of literacy is high. Even in countries where the literacy rate is higher, the respondents must have enough knowledge of the subject and implication of research studies

***2. Probing not Possible***

An interviewer can clarity the responses and can supplement the questions to get clarity in responses by means of a thorough probing. This is not possible with mailed questionnaire. The responses given by the respondent is final. Vague questions, emotional questions, etc., may not be answered well when compared to the interview method.

### *3. Response will not be Independent*

As the respondent is allowed to go through the questionnaire he happens to see all the questions before he answers them. This may set a situation to bias answers. Hence, we are not sure that independent answers have been given each question.

### *4. Answer by Right Person*

Another limitation with regard to mailed questionnaire is that one is not sure whether the right person fills the questionnaire, in spite of clear instruction

### *5. Poor Response*

Further the rate of response over mailed questionnaire would be poor. Hence, its usefulness for deep studies has been questioned. In countries like India, where the rate of literacy is low and research consciousness even among educated population is at a low level, the usefulness of mailed questionnaire as a tool of data collection raises doubts.

### *6. Bias*

The poor response will lead to sampling bias. The persons who can answer the questions or are willing to answer the questions may be those who are interested in the subject matter, or those who have higher education or higher socio-economic status. This is a source of bias, which will distort the results.

# 23

# Interview, Observation and Scales

## Interview

Interview is one of the important tools of social research. Interview must be combined with schedule. In other words interview is a technique used to administer the schedule. The person who is interviewing is called as interviewer. An interviewee is called as respondent also. Only through interview, varied types of data can be gathered intensively and extensively. Besides, interview is a means for assessing the personality of the respondent.

Young defines interview as "an effective informal verbal and non- verbal conversation, initiated for specific purposes and focused on certain planned areas."

## Objectives of Interview

The main purpose of interview as a research is tool to gather data extensively and intensively. It also helps to measure the personality of the respondent. It provides an opportunity for the interviewer to move freely with the respondents and to study their reaction to particular questions

The objectives of interview are:

1. To exchanges ideas and experiences
2. To elicit information

## Advantages of Interview

As a tool collection, the interview has certain specific advantages. They are as follows:

### *1. Measuring Personality*

To assess the personality of the respondents it is a very useful tool. Emotions, opinions, reactions etc. are measured by means of taking the respondent to various issues. Such measurement of personality is not possible in tools like questionnaire.

### *2. Full Information Collected*

By means of an interview, all information and data needed for the study are collected. Interview leads to probing an interviewee, which further gives full scope to elicit detailed information. The interviewer can ask additional questions not enumerated in the schedule. By this process, clarity and continuity of responses are attained. The interviewer has also the freedom to clarify the questions. It is through this manual process, smooth responses are achieved.

### *3. Delay due to Non-Response Avoided*

In the other methods, especially in the mailed questionnaire method lot of time is consumed to complete the process of data collection. The rate of response will also be sometimes poor. These limitations are all avoided by interview method because proper rapport is created before starting the interview.

### *4. Accuracy of Responses*

The interviewer can eliminate unwanted responses. Thus, he can record only the needed responses. Accuracy of responses is arrived at by means of asking questions under conductive climate, by means of probing and by means of asking additions and clarifying the questions of the respondent.

## *Qualities of an Interviewer*

Eminent research authorities all agree on the following qualities needed for an interviewer.

### *1. Honesty*

Honesty denotes the straight forwardness and truthfulness

to the duty of data collection. Even without meeting the respondents one may be tempted to fill up the schedule, based on previous interviews. It is said that, "Honesty and integrity are not characteristics that can be easily assessed at the selection stage, but interviewer who are later found deficient on these scores can and should be quickly dismissed."

*2. Interest*

The interviewer must have enough aptitude for this type of job. He should not consider it as an unattractive job or a stop-gap arrangement to further his career. Moser stresses that, "errors and poor quality of work are much more likely if the interview is bored and regards the work as valueless. The quality of most interviewer's work deteriorates after a time an important consideration to remember when they are being engaged for a lengthy period."

*3: Accuracy*

Interviewers should be accurate in their recording of answers. They should scrupulously follow instructions, and faithfully carry out their administrative duties.

*4. Adaptability*

The interview must adapt himself to different types of surveys, respondents, places, and time. He should not have any bias and prejudice against certain groups of the population.

*5. Personality and Temperament*

An interviewer must avoid 'over-rapport, with the respondent. He should not involve himself emotionally with the respondent. "Interviewing on most surveys is a fairly straight forward job, not one calling for exceptional industry charm or tact. What one asks is that the interviewer's personality should be neither over-aggressive nor over-sociable Pleasantness and a business-like manner is the ideal combination."

*6. Intelligence and Education*

The interviewer must have sufficient education and intelligence to follow the instructions given to him to conduct the interview.

### *Limitations of Interview*

Interview has the following limitations:

#### *1. Interviewer Bias*

"An interviewer may have bias relating to the socio-economic activities. He may have leaning towards certain ideologies. The interviewer may approach the respondent with a set of beliefs and pre-conceived notions. Such biases may be reflected while interviewing as well as in recording the responses.

#### *2. Forgetfulness*

Sometimes the interviewer may forget to record the data or he may record irrelevant facts omitting the relevant. He has to grasp the response carefully and must record the needed responses. This he may fail due to faulty memory, or lack of insight.

#### *3. Meeting of Minds*

In very many circumstances the interviewer and the respondent will never come to a common place of thinking. It is possible that each one will be emphasizing his own position forgetting the course of interview. It is not uncommon for the interviewer to drag the respondent on certain issues or controversies.

#### *4. Subjectivity*

Lack of objectivity in approaching the interviewee is a common drawback of interviewer. The interviewee sidesteps his experiences and may focus his attention towards issues not relevant to the subject. The same thing may be repeated by the interviewer.

#### *5. Impact of Emotions*

Interviewer as well as the interviewee are human beings and they are susceptible to the impact of emotions like any other human beings. At the time of interview the respondent or the interviewer might have heard shocking information or might be facing family problems or had travel weariness. Such circumstances may certainly influence the normal response or normal interview.

### *Steps Involved in the Interview*

Before starting an interview the interviewer as well as the research authorities must prepare all arrangements to conduct the interview and to bring out the positive effects. Rapport is an important aspect of interview and before starting the interview the interviewer must familiarize to the respondent. The other steps involved in the interview are as follows:

*1. Planning and Preparation*

Careful planning and meticulous preparations are necessary to make an interview successful. In the case of structured interview, interview guide must be at the disposal of the interviewer.

While planning an interview, it is necessary to take proper introduction letters. Young advices, that the introduction should if at all possible, be personal or by one who in a sense sponsors the interviewer. This will not only make the respondent trust the interviewer but also make him willingly cooperate with the interviewer.

It is often advised by experts that the interviewer must contact the leaders of the village or community to get the co-operation of the respondents. Introduction of the interviewer by such leaders will be more effective than direct contact of the respondents.

*2. Starting the Interview*

After careful initial planning and meeting the leaders or heads of households, the interviewer can approach the respondent for the interview. Before starting the interview as such or coming to the business he must inform the interviewer of his purpose of conducting the interview. Such aspect is called as rapport

While doing so, the interviewer should be honest and avoid exaggerating the benefits expected of the survey; nor should he give false promises. Besides he should be polite and ask for the information pleasantly. Such a human relation approach will induce the people to co-operate even when they are not convinced about the utility of the survey.

It is also necessary to inform the respondent of the confidential nature of the data collected. They should be assured that their name will not be revealed at any time and the data collected are used purely for research purpose and without any ulterior motives. These things can ensure a bond between the interviewer and interviewees. The interviewer should not stop with mere creating the rapport. He must come to his business slowly.

Creating rapport is only an element which paves way for beginning the interview in a conducive atmosphere and it is not an end by itself. The interview is far from being a mere personal friendly conversation. It is a conversation with a purpose. The interviewer should slowly come to his business and maintain professional competence

*3. Asking the Questions*

Unless the interview is of non-structured type, the interviewer must ask each question exactly as it is worded. Each question must be carefully pre-tested, to express the precise meaning desired in as simple a manner as possible. Even a slight reordering of a questions other than those specifically authorized in the instructions should be carefully avoided. Such an explanation may change the frame of reference and bias the response.

The question should also be asked in the same order as they appear on the schedule. Each questions sets up a frame of reference for succeeding questions and if the order is changed responses may not be in order as required.

The interviewer must ask all questions on the schedule unless there are instructions to skip over certain questions. In certain cases a question to be asked might have been answered previously as a side comment on an earlier question. Such a question should be repeated in order to get direct answer or an entirely different answer, then the earlier answer.

Goode and Hatt in their book, "Methods in Social Research", broadly suggests the following instructions while asking questions:-

1. The interviewer cannot be a passive listener. He must be a critical and intelligent questioner.
2. The interviewer must use his ingenuity to avoid losing the interview. He must probe more deeply to avoid the clichés which are used to cover motivations.
3. The interviewer cannot be satisfied with merely writing down the answer. He must be certain that he understands the answer and that is actually an answer to question. Often this will require further questioning, an attempt to probe more deeply into the meaning of the response given.
4. When the respondent does not have the information, a probe will be of no use, except to be certain that the respondent really does not know.
5. If there is a large percentage of 'don't know' answers to a given question, it means that the question itself is not

properly phrased. In such cases, it is necessary to discover the communication problem and to rephrase the question in the draft of the schedule so as to elicit a greater proportion of answers.

*4. Eliciting Complete Response*

Obtaining clear and complete response to questions is an important, at the same time a difficult aspect of interview. People may simple respond: 'Don't know' to questions, in order to avoid thinking or to evade real answers. Interviewers may misinterpret the question and may give a wrong answer; sometimes he may contradict himself. The interviewer should be alert of all such situations and must elicit complete and correct responses. Simple repetition may sometimes help to get a complete answer.

There are five principal symptoms of inadequate response. They are:

(a) *Partial response:* In which the respondent gives a relevant but incomplete answer.

(b) *Non-response:* When the respondent remains silent or refuses to answer the question.

(c) *Irrelevant response:* In which the respondent does not answer the question asked.

(d) *Inaccurate response:* When the question is answered by a reply, which is biased or distorted.

(e) *Verbalized response problem:* When the respondent explains why he cannot answer the questions, perhaps because he fails to understand it, because he lacks in the information necessary for answering it, or because he thinks it is irrelevant or inappropriate.

In order to elicit full information the interviewer should explain the question to make sure that the respondent understands it fully. If the answer is found inadequate, the interviewer can stimulate the respondent for further explanation. However the interviewer should ensure that such explanations do not affect the standardization of the questions.

*5. Recording the Interview*

Recording the interview is one of the important functions of an interviewer. This is a difficult task and the fruits of labour lie with proper recording of responses. The answers of the respondent are to be recorded differently in the case of pre-coded questions and open ended questions. In the pre-coded questions it is enough if the interviewer makes tick over the relevant answer. In the case of open-ended questions he has to use his skill, rationality and expertise. In this case while recording the answers the meaning of the response should not be misrepresented by wrong recording. As far as possible the exact words of the respondents must be recorded.

Errors may arise in both type of questions, due to the following factors:

(a) weariness due to travel and walk before reaching the respondent,

(b) repetitively administering lengthy questionnaires to several respondents,

(c) psychological upset caused by ill-tempered, non co-operative respondents,

(d) simultaneous operation of asking questions, recording, verifying the correctness and preparing for asking next question.

In the course of the interesting conversation, there is always a possibility that the interviewer may forget, to record the responses. He might even be thinking that he has recorded the responses. To avoid such error, the interviewer himself can check the completeness of data collected.

*6. Closing the Interview*

While closing the interview, the interviewer must check whether he has collected all the information needed, completeness of data attained, clarifications properly recorded and has not omitted to ask a question or forgotten to code an answer. Closing an interview is as important as the starting an interview. It must be natural and it should not be closed in a hurry. The interviewer after closing the interview can engage in a conversation other than the interview subject. But he must be careful in not leading the respondent to a controversy. The time at his disposal is short and he must indicate his position to leave the respondent and to proceed to his work further.

While taking leave the interviewer should do well to express thanks in recognition of the respondent's co-operation. Generally the parting should be pleasant and mutually satisfying.

*Observation*

Observation is a primary tool of scientific enquiry. It is increasingly employed in social science research as in physical or natural science researchers. The observation technique is perhaps the only logical approach available for the study of complex social problems. Observation gives an opportunity for direct first hand knowledge and authentic picture about the social phenomena. But it must be clearly understood that it is supplementary to other methods and techniques of scientific enquiries as it is sometimes only through direct observation certain types of data/ information can be obtained.

***What is Observation?***

Observation means acquiring knowledge through the use of sense organs. In the strict sense, it implies the use of eyes rather than the ears and the voice. Observation is not merely seeing things or activities or situations. It is watching minutely, slowly and systematically the occurrences with a purpose in a given situation with a view to deriving the results.

The Oxford Concise Dictionary defines observations as, accurate watching and noting of phenomena as they occur in nature with regard to cause and effect or mutual relations

Observation has three important components namely (a) sensation (b) attention and (c) perception.

(a) Sensation gained through the sense organs. Man has six senses, i.e., sight, hearing, touch, smell, taste and rationality. Some of these senses work in combination and our response may be a result of this combination. The eye is a very specialized organ through which we see and understand what happens around us

(b) The second element in observation is attention. By attention we mean the process by which a certain small area of the conscious field is focused on. In other words, it implies the researcher's ability to concentrate on the subject under study. Interest, motivation, novelty, inner drives, will power, adequate training and adequate experience etc., are the contributing factors for concentration.

(c) The third ingredient, perception means interpretation of the sensory reports. It is a complex of sensory and imaginary elements. "Perception is always a built-up complex experience out of sense impressions, characteristics and qualities supplied by mental activities."

### *Characteristics of Observation*

The general characteristics of observation are discussed below:

1. Observation is a physical as well as mental activity. In every act of scientific observation the sense faculties are involved. Observation has three distinguishable components namely sensation, attention and perception.
2. Observation is always specific and selective. It is not just seeing any thing and everything. It is carefully defining things and the act of observation is narrowed down.
3. Observation is purposive and not random. It is guided by distinct motives or gainful purposes. It may be done to study the complex social problems or measurement of personality or characteristics or studying the complex behavior of people.
4. Observation is systematic and scientific. What to observe, how to observe, when to observe, whom to observe and where to observe etc. are clearly defined and carefully planned. Intelligent planning, expert execution adequate recording and scientific interpretation are various steps involved in a scientific and systematic observation.
5. Observation is exert, that is done by a specially well-trained person for a distinct purpose. To make the observation efficient and more accurate the investigator should be thoroughly conversant with the problem under investigation.
6. A record is made of the observation as promptly as possible. All occurrences have to be carefully noted either at the time of observation or immediately after the observation. The social investigator uses recording devices such as check lists, rating scales, score cards, sealed specimens and blank forms for tallying frequencies. The use of well-constructed proforma of the above listed, helps in summarizing and quantifying of the data collected by observation.
7. The results of all systematic observation are subjected to checks and verification. The results are checked and substantiated by comparing the results of different

observers or by repeating the study to ascertain reliability and validity.

### *Choice of Observational Technique*

In social science, the choice of observational technique is a very important aspect to be considered. The choice naturally depends on the nature and purpose of the study. Whatever may be the purpose of the study, the observer must be sure about the following points: (a) What should be observed? (b) How observations should be conducted? (c) What are the aids to be used? (d) How should observations be recorded? (e) How to ensure reliability of data? (f) What relationship should exist between the observer and the observed and how can such a relationship be established?

The scientific observation may be classified as follows:

1. Participant and non-participant observation
2. Controlled and uncontrolled observation
3. Structured and unstructured.

#### *1(a). Participant Observation*

Observation may be (a) participant or (b) non-participant. These concepts were first introduced in social science by Prof. Edward C. Lindeman. He suggested that if one was interested to know what the subject was really doing, one should watch him and not ask him. The French social reformer by name Frederick Le Play and the English reformer Charles Booth, used this technique in their famous social surveys in 1886. Prof. Le Play who used the participant observation technique in his study entitled European Working Class Families, stated that the investigators lived as members of the family as participants in community activities, taking part in games and dances and in study but did not disclose that their purpose was to gather facts.

A participant observer is interested to gain greater insight into the activities. His intimate and active participation helps to penetrate into the thoughts, emotions and actions of the group. His closer contract with the field situation avoids misleading meaningless questions and provides him with a variety of useful information which cannot otherwise be gathered but only through formal methods of investigation. Participant observation also facilitates the sensing and the learning of the social atmosphere the inter-relations between members and the group.

It is very important that the observer should not associate too closely with one particular group in the community he is studying. He should enter into the life of a community at several different levels different levels so as to get a complete or a whole picture. Sometimes his closeness may be instrumental in affecting changes in the group behavior. Therefore, one should be careful in his total immersion.

The success of the participant observation ultimately depends on his skill, personality, how he introduces himself to the community/group and how good a relationship builds up with its members. That it is rightly observed "that participant observation is a highly individual technique."

*1(b). Non-participant Observation*

Non-participant observation takes place when some activity is in progress and the observer keeps himself outside that activity and records what is going on. Observation may be of a non-participant type, when observing and recording conditions in a classroom, in a superintendent's or principal's office, in slums, factories, retail stores, banks, strikes, ceremonies and rituals, police station, judicial courts or mayor's office..

The non-participant observation has the merit of maintaining objectivity and scientific outlook. The observer can be unattached and impartial which enable him to command the respect and co-operation from everyone in the group. The group may also be willing to disclose even their weakness or delicate matters to the observer since he has more opportunities to conduct formal interviews with the members. It is also claimed that non-participant observation can be easily checked, verified or repeated by another person.

*2(a). Non-controlled Observation*

In social science research, most of the data that we derive are from non-controlled observation, whether participant or non-participant. We learn the social behavior from the situations which we have witnessed or participated. The life situations are such as can hardly provide the chance of laboratory method of study. Therefore, they have to be observed in natural surroundings where they occur.

Non-controlled observation provides us valuable preliminary

data, while helping in the development of mere precise observations which should occupy a later phases of investigation.

*2(b). Controlled Observation*

Controlled observation is not very uncommon in social science research. This technique has been introduced in social science to rectify the defects that are noticed in uncontrolled observation. Not only that, as our ideas, in-depth and sharpness, but also we wish to rely on much less uncontrolled observation.

In recent years controlled observation has become a useful method for studying small groups. Controlled observation can be applied to describe the behavior of conference leaders, behavior of children in a variety of situation, the administrative efficiency of a social institution, the record of personal behavior or the characteristics of social groups in a community etc. Similarly, studies can also be conducted to find out the effect of lighting upon production in factories.

***Ways of Control***

Controlled observation may take place in natural and laboratory situations. We can exercise control in two ways: (i) control over the phenomena and (ii) control over the observer. The phenomena may be put to laboratory test under guided controlled conditions. In laboratory situations, the controls are applied to bother observed. But, it is difficult for a social science researcher to control the object under study, however he can very well control himself.

***Planning and Execution of Observation***

All scientific observations need to be planned and executed systematically. While planning for observations the following important aspects have to be considered:

1. The individual who develops observational study must have a sound background of theory and knowledge in the area of his study. As pointed by Walter R. Borg, "Without this theoretical foundation and an extensive background of knowledge, the observational study often yields inconclusive information that is difficult to express in quantitative terms."[16]
2. Carefully select and define clearly and preciously the activities to be observed. This will save time and help

the observer to concentrate on relevant facts only. In defining the activities, the purpose is to include those activities truly representative of the general category under study. The validity of results to a large extent depends on how well the investigator selects his activities and defines them.

3. The next important aspect to be considered is formulation of testable hypotheses. It is essential to develop specific hypotheses relating to the observable behavior to the variable being studied. The hypotheses may be refined in course of the research.
4. Decide the size of units to be observed. Observation being a time consuming and expensive technique, one cannot observe and record all the behavior that takes place in a given situation, but only a fragment of the population. Therefore, steps should be taken to obtain representative sample of the behavior to be observed. Decide the type of observation technique to be used. The observation may be carried on in natural surroundings on non-controlled basis or on a laboratory type experimental basis. The choice of observational technique, of course, depends on the nature and purpose of he study. In all cases, proper arrangements must be made for objective observation.
5. Determine the period to be observed which involves the length of each period, number of periods and interval between periods. The process of observation may be of short duration or may be for a long period. Generally, the length of period of observation is related to the type of activity under study. Sometimes period of a minute or two are suitable for some situations where a time period of an hour or even more may prove as more useful for other activities or aspects of behavior.
6. Select appropriate aids and mechanical devices to be employed to obtain adequate data and to achieve greater objectivity. There are a number of devices which are used as aids in field observation such as detailed field notes, schedules and questionnaires, maps, photographs, socio-metric scales, motion pictures, tape recorders, films etc.
7. Decide the number of observers needed. The observation may be done by the researcher himself or by a team of observers depends on the nature of the study. As the

reliability of observation depends on the quality of the observer, he should possess a number of qualities. These personal qualities are the most important. He should be physically fit, intellectually sharp and alert. He must have genuine interest and aptitude for research. He should be quite adjustable, courteous and also be very cautions in asking questions pertaining to sentiments or secret matters. He should deal very cautiously with illiterates as his questions may react adversely with his understanding.

8. Arrange for expert training to the observers. Efficiency and objectivity can be attained through training of observers. If observers are not properly trained his observation may lead to inaccuracy
9. Arrange for preliminary observation. A preliminary observation may be conducted to perfect the observation form. It also helps in the efficient conduct of the main study and provides guidance to overcome several practical problems.
10. Arrange for proper recording of data. Once entered into the field and decided to have the type of relationship with the subject, the observer should focus on the recording of the observation.
11. After data have been collected, the researcher has to pay full attention to their analysis and interpretation. By means of organizing, analyzing and interpreting the data their salient features, inter-relationship and cause and relationship are brought out. Information collected through observation should be interpreted scientifically.

### *Advantages of Observation*

Observation has some distinct advantages which are listed below:

1. Observation is one of the simplest and non-technical methods. Observational studies can be conducted by person through proper training.
2. It is one of the common methods used in all sciences and therefore it is systematized.
3. It is one of the main sources of formulating hypotheses.
4. Observation helps to study the subject in-depth.

5. It helps in the free flow of information as the situation is nor disturbed.
6. It is possible to record behavior as it occurs.
7. It is a very useful technique of studying various activities and characteristics of infants and children.
8. The researcher is able to record natural behaviors of the group.
9. The researcher can collect a wide range of information.
10. The data collected through observation is more reliable and valid then otherwise.
11. It is a useful method of doing research in delicate areas.
12. This method involves less expense.

### *Limitations*

Though observation is a widely used technique, it has its own limitations. They are discussed below:

1. All occurrences may not be open to observation. For instance, the personal activities are not open to actual observation by an outsider.
2. Personal bias of the observe at times distorts the observation.
3. Observation of a phenomena has to be made where it actually takes place. Most of the occurrences are quite uncertain in nature. Their place and time cannot be predetermined. Therefore, systematic and preplanned observation is very difficult.
4. Sometimes, natural factors, such as weather conditions, side attractions and the like may affect the observational task.
5. There are difficulties in sampling. Sometimes, it is not possible to ensure that participants represent a cross-section of the population.
6. It may be impossible for the researcher to collect all the necessary information if the events spread over a period of years or the events occur simultaneously in different geographic locations

### *Scaling Technique*

In recent days greater emphasis is laid on the measuring

instruments in social sciences research. Scaling is a technique used for measurement of some aspect of human behavior by means of a precise scale. In its simplest form measurement consists of substituting symbol or name of a real object. According to Barnard S. Phillip, "Scaling is a procedure for assignment of numbers (or their symbols) to a property or object in order to impart some of the characteristics of numbers to the properly in question."

Scaling techniques are useful in measuring the social behavior and personality of individuals. It is also used to measure certain aspects of cultural and social environment.

Scaling serves the following specific purposes in social sciences research:

1. Scales help to reduce the complexity of data and present a single score that represents several variables.
2. It helps to test hypotheses by means of quantifying different dimensions of a single underlying concept.
3. It aims at reducing the error in measurement and increasing the reliability of analysis.

The scales may be broadly classified into following types:

(i) Nominal
(ii) Ordinal
(iii) Rating and
(iv) Ratio
(v) Attitude scales

*(i) Nominal Scale*

When the measurement is made with help of an arbitrary number or symbol it is called Nominal scale. It is generally used to distinguish one property or objectives from other properties. It helps to determine whether the object belongs to the same class or not. For example, we may classify the individuals as athletes, politicians, students etc. The nominal scale has the following characteristics:

- Nominal scales are used to classify the objects,
- The classifications do not overlap,
- Nominal scales are discrete, and
- Nominal scales result in measurement process.

Although nominal scales may look like a simple technique, the measurement becomes more complex when a given property or variable becomes complex. For example a nominal scale for the classification of societies into 'scared' and 'secular' ones cannot be easily evolved. Besides, the normal scale implies the division of objects categorically. There may be border-line cases which may be difficult to judge as to which category they belong. There is also an element of arbitrariness in nominal scale. The scale is not sensitive to various gradation within a given category.

*(ii) Ordinal Scale*

The ordinal scale is used when there is some kind of relationship between two or more classes of objects. It incorporates order relationship manifested by numbers, the number indicating rank in this context. "

However, the social science researcher comes across several social phenomena which cannot be simply rank ordered, as the property of a phenomenon may not be unitary in character. Another limitation of the ordinal scale is that it permits only a limited statistical application. While constructing the ordinal scale, the researcher is presented with two tasks.

1. To order the objects with respect to a given property through the assignment of ranks, and
2. To determine whether the actual phenomena posses the order characteristics of number.

*(iii) Rating Scale/Interval Scale*

A rating scale ascertains in the degree, intensity or frequency of a variable. It not only places entities in a clearly defined order, but also utilizes some means of attaining equidistant intervals of measurement. This scale permits one to say that the distance between A and B equals the distance of B and C but it does not permit to say that A with the score of 15 is thrice as good as C and B with the score of 10 is twice as good as C.

The rating scale is amenable for statistical calculations like Mean, Standard Deviation, Product Moment Correlation etc. In this type of scale the zero point is arbitrary and just a matter of convenience. Different types of Rating/Interval scale are used to judge the persons or objects. The more common types among them are explained below.

### A. Graphic Rating Scale

This is perhaps the most widely used scale. In this method the researcher indicates his rating by simply placing a check at the appropriate point on a line that consists of brief statements indicating one extreme of the phenomenon to the other extreme. Scale points may also be indicated along the line. The scale serves as a guide in locating the rating rather than to provide distinct categories. This type of scale is relatively easy to use. For example, the following graphic rating scale may be used to enable the student to rate the instructor.

### B. Itemized Rating Scale

This type of scale consisted of a number of statements that are ordered in respect of their scale positions. The rater selects, one or two of the categories. Though the number of categories or scale positions vary depending on the research problem, normally five or seven categories are used. The verbal statements used to identify the scale positions may vary from brief statements indicating only degree of attributes to more elaborate descriptions and illustrations. The more clearly defined the categories are, the more reliable the ratings are likely to be.

### C. Comparative Rating Scale

Comparative Rating Scale is used for relative judgment. The position of individual in the rating scale is judged with reference to the position of other individuals or groups with which the individual may be compared.

#### (iv) Ratio Scale

It is the highest type of scale. It possesses all the characteristics of an interval scale. In addition to that, it is characterized by an absolute zero, which offers a consistent starting point for measurement. With such a scale, one can speak of relative amounts as well as difference in the amount and property or characteristic. It also determines the equality of rations.

#### (v) Attitude Scale

Fundamentally scale in methodology is same to all fields. Differences do exist in content, emphasis and purpose-for which scales are used. In the social sciences like sociology, psychology and in many other interdisciplinary researches, the most frequently used scaling technique is Attitude Scale. Therefore, it is of very great significance to social scientists. Different types of attitude scales are in vogue. They differ from each other in method of construction, method of response and basis of interpreting the scale. The important types of attitude scales are discussed in this section.

*1. Differential Scale*

This technique of Equal Appearing Interval method was evolved by L.L. Thurston has become the widely applied scale. In this scale the items from a gradation of such a nature that the individual is likely to agree with one or two statements, which correspond to his position in the dimension being measured. He is likely to disagree with statements on either side of the position he has selected. Thurston type of scale consists of a series of statements, usually about twenty. The position of each statement on a scale of favorable/unfavorable attitude towards the object has been determined by the judges' classification. In selecting the items for the scale and assigning values to them, following procedure is adopted.

1. The researcher gathers several hundred statements conceived to be related to attitude being investigated.
2. A large no. of judges – usually from fifty to three hundred-working independently, classify these statements into eleven groups. In the first pile, each judge places the statements considered most favorable to the object in the second, those considered next most favorable, and the eleventh pile, most unfavorable. The 6th or 'neutral' position is defined, as the point at which there is neither favorableness nor unfavorableness.
3. The scale value of the statement is computed as the median position (or pile) to which it is assigned by the group of judges. Statements that have too broad a scatter are discarded as ambiguous or irrelevant.
4. A final selection is made taking such items that are spread out evenly along the scale from one extreme position to the other.

The scale value are not shown on the questionnaire. Items are arranged in random order rather than in the order of their scale value. The individual's position in the scale is judged by the mean for the scale value.

*2. Summated Scale*

Summated scale, like differential scale, consists of a set of statements to which the subject is asked to react. The number of statements affecting a phenomenon are listed and values given to each. Respondents are asked to indicate their agreement or disagreement with each item. Each response is given a numerical score indicating its favourableness. For example, to understand one's attitude towards co-operative, the attitude scale may consist of the following statements:

The score given individual items are summed up. The most frequently used summated scale is the Likert type of scale. Rensis Likert has developed an elaborate technique of constructing a summated scale, a outlined below.

1. The score includes five categories of responses; strongly agree, agree, undecided, disagree and strongly disagree.
2. Statements are classified into those, which are favorable, and those which are unfavorable.
3. For favorable statements weight given to strongly agree, agree, undecided, disagree, strongly disagree are 5,4,3,2,1, respectively; and for unfavorable statements, the weights given are 1,2,3,4, and 5 respectively. Thus, agreement wit favorable statements and disagreement with unfavorable statements are treated as equals.
4. A large number of statements are administered to a group of respondents who are representative of those for whom the questionnaire is being constructed.
5. The responses are analyzed to determine which items discriminate between the high scoring individuals and low scoring individuals. Thus, for example items to which high scorers and low scorers respond similarly are eliminated. This is known as item analysis procedure.

*3. Cumulative Scale*

Cumulative Scales, like differential and summated scales are made up a series of items with which the respondents indicate agreement or disagreement. In cumulative scale, items are arranged in such a way that they are related to one another. They are arranged logically that an individual who replies favorably to item 2 also replies favorably to item 1; and one who replies favorably to item 1 and 2. an individual who has given favorable response to more number of items in the scale will be higher total score. The individual's score is computed by counting the number of items one answers favorably. The items are arranged in the order of favourableness. The Social Distance Scale developed by Bogardus was a cumulative type of attitude scale.

Guttman and his colleagues developed a scale analysis of "Scalogram", which is referred to by Guttman as the 'Cornell' technique. The steps involved in 'scalogram' analysis is given below7:

1. The area of content is first defined with reference to the problem on hand.
2. Ten or twelve statements are selected which are assumed to be representative of the selected area.
3. The statements are usually arranged in the form of a three or five point scale, so that subjects can indicate their intensity of their attitude for each item.
4. Ten or twelve items are submitted to a sample of 100 or more respondents' who will check the items. The step is designed to determine the scalability of the item.
5. After the total score is obtained for each person by adding up the weights of the categories checked, the questionnaires are arranged in the rank order from high to low according to the total score.
6. A table or 'scalogram' is prepared from the data of the questionnaires, by recording separately the responses of each person to each category, by providing a column for each person and a row for each category.
7. The reproducibility of each item is determined on the basis that no person with a lower total score ranks higher in any item than any person with a higher total score. By this method the error in reproducibility is minimized.

### *Principles of Scale Construction*

A researcher is performing one of the most important tasks when selecting and constructing a scale with a view to evaluating it. The evaluation is done on the following criteria.

### *Validity*

A test is valid when it measures what it purports to measure. This is the most significant criterion in the use of scale. A scale is valid when the following two conditions are met:

1. The attribute being measured where relatively 'objective' so that their meaning would be uniformly understood by the raters using the scale.
2. The ratings themselves were obtained under optimal conditions, including the carefully constructed scales, trained judges and specified common frames of references.

Validity of test also varies with the circumstances. A test may be highly valid for use in the situation but invalid if used in another situation. Therefore, validity must be appraised with reference to specific situation.

### *Reliability*

"A test or scale is reliable if it consistently yields the same result when repeated measurements are taken of the same subject under the same conditions."8 Reliability suggests consistency and accuracy from one time to another. The errors of measurement should be reduced to the minimum and the measuring instrument should possess a degree of precision. Reliability can be increased by the following measures:

- Careful training of the rater
- Attention given in the construction of scale
- Clear specification of the reference group
- Inclusion of concrete illustration of the question response, types of behavior and proper communication.

### *Objectivity*

An objective test or scale is one that produces the same score regardless of who makes it. The scoring should be independent of personal judgment of the selector. In order to improve the objective specific directions or scoring keys should be furnished to the scorer, that allows no room for subjective judgment.

### *Simplicity*

Simplicity enables their use to many. Ease of administration, scoring and interpretation is an important factor in selecting a test, particularly when expert personnel and adequate budget are not available.

### *Suitability*

When selecting a scale one must determine whether the instrument is suitable for the purpose. The researcher has to examine whether it can obtain the data needed or suited to the type of subjects studied. A prudent researcher must carefully examine the appropriateness of the testing instruments. Even a best instrument may fail to yield reliable data, if it is improperly administered, under inappropriate conditions and inaccurately interpreted.

### *Economy*

Tests should save time involved. The expense in administration is often a significant factor, particularly if the testing programme is operated on a limited budget.

# 24

# Use of Library in Research

## Introduction

Man's knowledge lies silently in his libraries. The knowledge of all time is to be found in these store houses of black marks on white paper. A library has been recognized as in important aid in self education. The concepts of library and library services have acquired new dimensions in recent years. With the advancement of education and research in different fields in post independence period, the national and state Governments had been taking various steps to improve the library system in the country. The function of library is to provide informations and authentic reference on various subjects to users. As Rabindranath Tagore said at All India Library Conference in 1928," Most libraries are possessed with the passion for accumulation. The facilities offered for their (books) use that should have been its (a library's) glory, and not deemed necessary for its pride." Thus, the primary purpose of a library is not only to lend boks, journals and other materials but also to encourage the formation of a life long habit of reading library resources by making necessary facilities to the users.

All types of researches involve the use of books, reports, journals magazines, news papers and other documentary materials in libraries. A research student has to tap various sources of data may be grouped differently: (i) available material and original data; (ii) primary and secondary data; and (iii) bibliographical and field data. But the most commonly used classification is primary, secondary and tertiary sources. Dr. P.V. Young has defined primary sources, as those data gathered at first hand, the responsibility of their compilation and promulgation remaining, under the same authority that originally gathered them.3 According to Walter R. Borg primary sources is direct description of occurrence by an individual who actually observed or witnessed the occurrence.4 Secondary data are those compiled from original sources and of which the promulgating authority is different from that which controlled the collection of data at first hand.5 In other words, secondary materials include any publications written by an author who was not a direct observer or participant in the events described. For example, for statistical and factual data on baking problems, bank records are primary sources, the Reserve Bank of India's statistics secondary source and books, written on banking are tertiary sources.

Writers like Dr. P.V. Young has classified the sources of data into field and documentary sources, "Field sources include living person who have a fund knowledge about or have been in intimate contact with social conditions and changes over a considerable period of time."6 Observation interview, questionnaire and other devices are used to gather adequate informations from the field. Documentary sources include published and unpublished documents, reports, statistics, letters and diaries.

A researcher should make the maximum use of the library sources as there is a wealth of informations and materials in the academic libraries. The researcher is warned not to hurry into the field without first consulting the necessary books, journals, past and present investigations of relevance, official reports and statistics, records of institutions etc.

## Use of Library for the Researcher

Consulting available library material will be useful to a researcher in several ways:

1. Library sources provides the necessary background knowledge of the problem to be investigated and develops the insight of the investigator.
2. It helps the researcher to review the literature to find out the research gap which is the basis of most of the research projects in social sciences;
3. It also provides orientation to the problem and eliminates the possibility of unnecessary duplication of effort:

4. The use of documentary source facilitates in the formulation of research hypotheses;
5. Library literature provides an opportunity of understanding the method, techniques measures and approaches employed by other research workers and thus lead to significant improvement of his design;
6. Secondary sources of data gathered from library serve as base for analysis and comparative study;
7. The available documents may also be used to supplement or to check informations gathered by the researcher in his investigations;
8. Where research consists more in interpretation than in the discovery of new facts, secondary sources would be more than adequate;
9. Authors of research articles may cite specific research topics for further research, which would be of great use to young researchers;
10. The knowledge secured from library reading will also help a researcher to understand the writing style and interpretation of findings.

### *The Essentials*

The researcher must be capable of (i) locating the necessary sources, (ii) deciding what is to be extracted from each source and (iii) taking relevant notes needed.

All libraries have a system of subject classification, a card catalogue and certain bibliographic and reference materials. A researcher must have knowledge of the card catalogue, the indexes and the reference shelves to locate easily the needed secondary sources.

Card catalogue is an index which lists all the publications in the library collection by author, by subject, and by title. This is perhaps the first source to find materials in a library. It is arranged like a dictionary with the cards filed alphabetically according toe the first word on the card. The name of the author, the subject heading or the title of the publication may be the first word. The researcher may seek the help of the librarian to use card catalogue.

The card catalogue may not always index all the materials that are available in the library. Further, the card catalogue lists every periodical available in bound volumes but it does not analyse the contents. There are periodical articles, pamphlets, magazines and government documents which form important segments of published materials may be organized and maintained separately in certain libraries. Therefore, a researcher must use the indexes kept in the reference shelves as guided for finding out materials. Indexes may be general or specialized. Thus, indexes supplement the card catalogue.

There are also encyclopedias, special dictionaries, year books, directories, abstracts etc. in a library. These reference materials may not be indexed in the card catalogue or in indexes and bibliographies because of their general character. As these serve a useful purpose, a researcher must have a knowledge of the above sources which are kept in the reference shelves.

## Library Sources

Some of the important such sources are listed and described briefly in the following section.

### *I. Bibliographies*

Bibliographic tool is commonly used in finding materials in libraries. A bibliography covers information regarding books, articles etc. published in a specific period in a particular subject. Each book or article is listed by author, title, place of publication. The important bibliographies are listed below;

#### 1. *Internal Bibliography of Social Sciences*

It is published by UNESCO since 1952. It is published annually in four parts—Economics, Political Science, Sociology and Anthropology. The important publications in four subjects are included in this bibliography.

#### 2. *Indian National Bibliography*

This is an authoritative record of current publications in the 15 major languages of India, received by the National Library, Calcutta.

#### 3. *Asia Social Science Bibliography*

This is the publication of the Institute of the Economic Growth, New Delhi. It covers subjects like Economics, Sociology, Anthropology, Political Science, Education and Communication and other social data.

*4. Bibliography of Research Studies in Education*

This is published by US office of Education since 1941. This is organized by subject areas.

*5. Bibliography of Doctoral Thesis in Arts and Science*

This is a valuable guide published by the Inter University Board of India. Theses accepted by the Indian Universities are listed under University, with subject sub-headings.

*6. ICA Research Register*

The research register is an ICA project within the frame work of the co-operative development decade. It has been published by the Cooperative Research Institute, Hungary in collaboration with the ICA. Information about the recently published books, articles and research works are reported author-wise and subject-wise. It is a very good reference to those who do research in the areas of co-operation.

***II. Indexes***

As started earlier indexes serve as useful tool to locate informations in recent journals, magazines etc. They also summarize the contents of the articles and cite the reference cited by author in a particular article while it was written. Generally, the indexed items include the name of the author title of the article, name of the journal, its volume number, periodicity, month and year of publication and pagination of a particular article. A social science researcher can make use of the following indexes:

*1. Social Sciences Index*

This is published in two parts: (1) Social Science Index and (2) Humanities Index. It is published by H.W. Wilson and Co, New York.

*2. Social Science Citation Index*

It is published by the Institute of Scientific Information, 325 Chestnut Street, Philadelphia, U.S.A. It is a multi-dimentional index to social science. This international publication indexes about 70,000 articles and important editorial from over 1,000 of the world's standard social sciences journals, belong to 26 disciplines.

*3. Cord Index*

It is published by the National Institute of Rural Development, Hyderabad. It is a systematic listing of the rural development literature published in over six hundred journals and thirteen news papers received in the card library. Particular requirements of the research scholars in socio-economic development are kept in mind while indexing the articles. This index includes subject like agriculture and allied areas, education and training, energy, health and nutrition, industry, manpower, political science and rural and tribal development.

*4. A Manual of Sources of Data on the Tamil Nadu Economy*

It is one of the publications of the Madras Institute of Development Studies, Madras. This index aims to fill the information gap relating to the Tamil Nadu Economy. It is the work of its kind listing in a systematic manner data sources on the T. N. Economy that researchers can have access to. The information contained in index shows that an impressive body of official and semi-official data pertaining to T.N. economy is available to researchers.

*5. Index India*

The Rajasthan University has been publishing this index since 1967. It is a quarterly publication indexes book reviews, index to theses articles published in Indian and foreign journals and Indian news papers.

***III. Dictionaries***

There are dictionaries that serve special purpose and interest. They define basic concepts used in different social science subjects. They include the following:

*1. A Dictionary of the Social Sciences*

Edited by Julius Gould William L. Kolb compiled under the auspices of the United Nations Educational Scientific and Cultural Organisation. It is designed to describe and define one thousand basic concepts used in the Social Sciences.

*2. Dictionary of Modern Economics*

By Douglas Green wald Associates (1973) published by

McGraw Hill Book Company, New York. It provides a simple definition of modern economic terms.

*3. Dictionary of Baking*

By Rev. Jones. It is a concised encyclopedia of Banking Law Practice. It provides in one volume the informations about any subject connected with the business of baking.

*4. A Modern Dictionary of Sociology*

By George A. Theodorson and Achillies G. Theordson. It defindes modern sociological terms used in popular books, magazines news papers, on the radio and on television. As many concepts as possible as included.

*5. Dictionary of Psychology*

Edited by Howard C. Warran, George Allen and Unwin Ltd, London; 1934. This book is designed to explain the meaning and technical terms which the reader will meet in psychological literature or which the scholar in the field of psychology wishes to use in his writings.

*6. Dictionary of Philosophy*

Edited by Dagobert D. Runes, Little Field Adam and Co, New Jersey; 1964. This aims at providing researchers interested in philosophy with clear, concise and correct definitions and descriptions of the philosophic terms throughout the range of philosophic though.

*7. The New Dictionary of Thoughts*

By Tryon Edwards, Standard Book Co, New York: 1953. It was first published in 1877. It is a very useful condensed dictionary which describes the striking thoughts of the world's best thinkers on important and interesting subjects arranged in alphabetical order of topic for ready reference.

*8. Dictionary of Education*

Edited by Carter V. Goode and published by Mcgraw Hill book Co. in 1959. It is concerned with technical and professional terms and concepts in the entire area of education.

### *IV. Encyclopedias*

Encyclopedia are huge or multi-volume work containing articles of both biographical and general character. They are the standard works done by experts in the various fields of social science. The articles in the encyclopedias are arranged alphabetically. An article in an encyclopedia can be useful for quick orientation to a subject and for specific items of information.

*1. Encyclopedia Britannica*

By William Beton, Chicago. A new survey of universal knowledge alphabetically and systematically arranged. Today the Britannica consisted of 23 volumes. It is a modern informational instrument in a changing and complex world. It is the work of 9000 authorities from most of the countries of the world. A very good reference containing informations on every essential subject.

*2. Encyclopedia of Social Science*

It is published in 15 volumes. It combines the characteristics of both a dictionary and hand book. It is arranged so flexible as to contain not only short articles but also long articles. A carefully worked out system of cross references are given to meet the special interest of scholars. It also includes biographies of deceased persons whose work has been significant in social sciences. A scholar can find factual and methodical information of value and also inter-relationship between tow social sciences.

*3. Encyclopedia of Parliament*

By Norman Wilding and Philip Landy, Cassell and Co, London: 1958. This attempts to present wide range of parliamentary informations in the form of an encyclopedia. It is a valuable work of reference to researchers in political science and public information.

### *V. Year-books and Directories*

The researchers can find current informations and latest data on different subjects in the yearbook and directories. Some of the important yearbooks and directories are listed below:

*1. Yearbook of International Organisation*

It is the publication of the Union of International Associations, Brussels. It was published since 1948. Informations about international organizations are included in the book.

*2. Yearbook of Agricultural Cooperation*

This yearbook had been published by the Plunkett Foundation for Cooperative Studies since 1927. The purpose is to provide a continuous review of agricultural cooperative development throughout the world, from a wide range of view points by publishing articles on countries at regular intervals and on particular aspect of cooperation which are innovatory or on topical interest. It is a useful source for researchers in cooperation.

*3. Cooperative Yearbook*

It is a compact book published by the Tamil Nadu Cooperative Union, which gives al that we want to know about cooperatives in Tamil Nadu. The progress of the cooperative movement in general and the constitution and working of individual cooperatives are presented in this work.

*4. Indian Poultry Industry Yearbook*

It is a comprehensive single volume of reference data on various aspect of poultry industry in India. It was first published by Shakuntala P. Guptha on behalf of the Government of India in 1973.

*5. India-A Reference Annual*

It is published by the Research and Reference Division, Ministry of Information and Broadcasting, Government of India. It is an established and popular world reference, seek to provide authentic information on the diverse aspects of our life, administration and economy. The data furnished in this volume include subject like agriculture, education, industry community, development, communication, irrigation and power, housing, commerce, planning, health, social welfare, scientific research, defence etc.

*6. Tamil Nadu-An Economic Appraisal*

This is the publication of Finance Department, Government of Tamil Nadu, it provides data regarding diverse of Tamil Nadu Economy.

*7. Asian Business Directory*

An exhaustive in-depth reference manual for business, trade and industry in Asia and Pacific published by Kothari and Sons for the Asian Chambers of Commerce and Industry. It gives not only facts and figures, about each country but also laws affecting investment, foreign trade and the like.

*8. Directory and Year book (1980-81)*

Edited by Girilal Jain and published by the Times of India press, Mumbai. It contains a wide range of informations about the country, natural resources, agro-based industries, education and science, welfare programmes demography, trade and industry, finance, communication, administrative and diplomatic matters, elections and legislatures.

*9. Directory of Scientific Research in Indian Universities*

It was published by the Council of Scientific and Industrial Research, New Delhi since 1974. The directory covers current research projects in field of agriculture, transport, industry and management carried out in the universities and other educational institutions in India

*10. Directory of Indian Women Today (1976)*

Edited by Ajeet Cour and published by India International Publications. The material in this directory gives us a microscopic estimate of the women power in India, it is very useful and purposeful publication for researchers.

*11. Directory of Educational Research Institutions in the Asian Region*

It was published by UNESCO regional office for Education in Asia, Bangkok since 1967. It gives informations about 107 institutions engaged in the research in the field of education including government agencies, universities and autonomous institutions in 18 countries.

***VI. Abstracts***

Abstracts is another type of reference guide useful to a researcher. It is a systematized list of reference source. It also gives a brief summary of the contents of articles ore research studies listed.

*1. World Agricultural Economics and Rural Sociology Abstracts*

It is published by North Holland Publishing Company, Amsterdam. It is a quarterly international abstract which covers subjects like agriculture, farm labour, marketing, agricultural economics and rural sociology.

*2. ICSSR Research Abstracts*

It is a quarterly and commenced publication in October 1971. The major findings of the research projects financed by the council are published in this journal.

*3. ICSSR Abstracts*

There are such journals for the subjects sociology and social anthropology, economics, geography, political science. In these half-yearly journals, abstracts of select articles and reviews of selected books are published.

*4. Indian Dissertation Abstract*

It is a quarterly published under the joint auspices of the ICSSR and the Association of Indian Universities. This publishes synopsis of Ph.D. thesis in social sciences submitted to Indian Universities.

*5. Student Research Abstracts in Social Work*

It was published by the Association of schools of Social Work in India since 1968. This is an abstract of research works. The topics studied by the students include the major aspects of family and child welfare, medical and psychiatric social work, labour welfare, industrial relations and personnel management, urban, rural and tribal community organisations, social defense, social welfare administration etc. This abstract will serve as a useful guide to future researcher. The analysis of these abstracts would help identifying gaps in information and at the same time discourage scholars from undertaking the projects already done.

*6. Indian Behavioural Science Abstracts*

This contains abstracts of behavioural science literature produced in India and abroad. Behavioural Science Centre, Delhi, publishes it. It is a quarterly publication covers disciplines like psychology, sociology, social anthropology, education, management, political science, extension education, human geography, economics etc.

*7. CORD Abstracts*

It is a monthly bulletin of abstracts of selected development literature published by the National Institute of Rural Development, Hyderabad. It provides information abstracts for the reports, articles based on the empirical studies relating to rural India.

Abstracts aim to bring out the salient features of these studies, keeping in view of the needs of researchers. It is arranged alphabetically subject-wise.

### *VII. Statistical Sources*

There are a large number of statistical statements relating to socio-economic problems which are published by governments, cooperatives and private agencies. These statements are very useful for social science researchers.

#### *1. Demographic Yearbook*

It is being published since 1948 by the United Nations Department of Economic and Social Affairs, New York. It is one of the coordinated and inter-related set of periodic publications issued by the United Nations and the specialised agencies, designed to supply basic statistical data for social scientists and scholars. Official demographic statistics from almost 250 geographic entities of the world are included in the issue.

#### *2. United Nations Statistical Yearbook*

The U.N. Department of Economic and Social Affairs, New York, publishes the yearbook annually. This contains country-wise statistics on population, national income, agriculture, energy, external trade, transport and industrial production.

#### *3. Census of India*

This volume is bring published once in ten years by the Government of India in different series. This is the largest single source of data. Data presented in this volume relate to diverse aspects of population in the country.

#### *4. Statistical Abstracts of India*

This is published by the Central Statistical Organisation, Department of Statistics,

Ministry of Planning, Government of India. This incorporates the latest available date under important heads of economic and social development. It gives national aggregates for 1950-51, 1955-56, 1960-61, 1965-66, 1970-71 and for the subsequent year upto 1977-78. This serves as an important source material for authentic data on different sectors of the Indian economy.

*5. Statistical Statements – Khadi and Village Industries Commission*

It is a useful statistical supplement that aims at projecting a detailed picture of the state-wise, and industry-wise performance in selected indicators of progress such as extension of finance, production, sales, employment and earnings, besides a broad summary of achievements.

*6. Indian Labour Statistics*

It is published annually by the Labour Bureau, Ministry of Labour, Government of India. It contains statistics relating to labour in India Covering population census, economic data, employment in factories, mines, railways, plantations etc., employment exchanges, training centers, wages and earnings in different sectors, levels of living, industrial disputes, trade unions and such other matters relating to labour in India.

*7. Statistical Tables Relating to Banks in India*

It is one of the annual publications of the RBI. This presents an alphabetical list of bank offices. Offices of Indian banks abroad and such other informations relevant to the geographic aspects of the bank's operation.

*8. Indian Agriculture in Brief*

This is annually published by the Union Ministry of Agriculture and Irrigation. It contains to Indian Agriculture.

*9. Hand-Book an Social Welfare Statistics*

It is a publication made by the Department of Social Welfare, Ministry of Education and Social Welfare, Government of India. It was brought out first in 1974. It provides valuable statistical informations about the social welfare programmes indicated in India. The statistics that are included in this handbook covers areas like demography, health and family planning, education, employment, housing, backward classes, rehabilitation, levels of living, leisure and recreation, international comparisons, child welfare, women welfare, welfare of physically handicapped, social defense, social work education, training and research, social security etc.

*10. Statistical Statements Relating to Cooperatives*

This is published annually by the NABARD in two Parts; Part-1 contains data regarding the working of agricultural cooperatives in the country. Part-2 deals with non-agricultural co-operatives. District-wise informations are well presented in these statements.

## *Collection and Organsiation of Materials*

*1. Background Reading*

Once the researcher has decided to take a workable project he should go through as many literature as possible to gather useful informations. This is to be done with the main object of knowing whether the reference has nay direct or indirect bearing on the subject under study. For this purpose the researcher can go through the table of contents of the sources. It is on the basis of this that references found useful are to be listed in a bibliography.

*2. Development of a Bibliography*

The next important step is compiling a bibliography. Such a bibliography should be complete, accurate in every detail and consistent in form i.e., following a uniform classification.

A Card index would facilitate easy reference, alterations, additions and save duplication. The sources may be classified with general and specialised data and books, periodicals, news papers and reports-official and non-officials. Each reference should appear on a separate card or sheet with author's name, title of reference, publisher's name, date of publication, page number etc.

*3. Preliminary Outline*

The next step is to prepare a rough outline for what is to be extracted from each source. This depends upon the problem selected, the type of investigation, the researcher's experience and the availability of material.

*4. Evaluation of Material*

Before deciding to include nay information, the researcher should evaluate the materials carefully. The following points are to be kept in mind while evaluating the material.

1. Accuracy and dependability
2. Up-to-dateness
3. Suitability for specific requirements
4. Authority
5. Scope
6. Treatment and style
7. Arrangement
8. Illustrations, tables and diagrams
9. Author
10. Publisher

*Notes-Taking*

After locating the information that the researcher wants, the next problem is to record it for further use. Notes-taking is not an easy job. It requires much time and patience "Method, adequacy and accuracy are the three important ingredients of notes. Good notes should help analysis by isolating facts and synthesis by combining them. The more careful the researcher is in notes-taking the greater will be the benefit from his effort."[9] The notes may be classified into four categories (i) quotations (ii) paraphrases, (iii) summary, and (iv) evaluation.

The researcher may keep in mind the following points while taking notes:

1. Decide what material is to be extracted and recorded.
2. Select the most significant material.
3. Make each note on a separate card. Use always 4 X 6 uniform cards. Different colour cards may be used for different categories of notes.
4. Include only one topic on a card.
5. Make the entries complete and accurate.
6. Place the subject heading on the top of the card.
7. Give a complete and accurate bibliographic citation at he bottom of the card.
8. Distinguish between a direct quotation, a summary and an evaluative statement.
9. Record correctly all the informations that are needed.
10. Keep the notes orderly filed.

# 25

# Metohods of Data Collection for Business Research

## Methods of Data Collection Applied to Business Research

Tolls or techniques of Research are the instruments or devices, which are used to collect data needed for research studies. The type of tool to be used depends on the method of research chosen to approach the problem. The popular tools of research are interview, schedule, mailed questionnaire, observation and scales.

Interview is a process through which a researcher enters into a face-to-face contact with the respondent. Empirical research in Business and Management presupposes to collect data from the primary sources. The primary sources may be the institution or individuals. Interview is not an independent technique. It is used as a supplementary to a schedule.

Hence schedules are to be administered with the help of interview. Preparation of schedule is a technical job and a researcher must be thorough with the intricacies of the construction of schedules. There is a marked difference between a schedule and a mailed questionnaire. The letter is sent through mail and the respondent will fill up the questions. In the former case, the questions will be administered by the Researcher / Interviewer over the respondent and the responses will be recorded. The question framed can be same both for the schedule and mailed questionnaire. The response to mailed questionnaire has been universally poor and the usefulness of this tool has been questioned due to high rate of non-response.

Observation as a tool of data collection has greater use in Business and Management research. The activities of business organizations and the function of individual managers could be studied by observation. Deliberations of Board meetings and conferences could be observed and can be useful to other companies also. Data on these aspect could be collected using observation as a tool. But observation can not be the sole method of data collection. It can be used to supplement other tools of research.

Scales are instruments used by researchers to measure the opinions of the respondents. They are otherwise called as "opinionnaire" also. To construct scales a researcher must have adequate knowledge, experience and background. In Business research opinions are to be gathered to find out the pattern of leadership, personnel behaviors, customer attraction, etc., Scales can be constructed and the opinions could be measured by means of giving weightage to the responses in terms of scores.

# 26

# Editing and Coding

## Introduction

Editing, coding and tabulation are the crucial stages in survey research It is at this the mass of data collected during the survey is processed with a view to reducing them to manageable proportions. Only by such a careful and systematic processing, the data will lend itself for statistical treatment and meaningful interpretation and conclusion.

In other words the data processing which encompasses, editing, coding and tabulation, is an intermediary stage between the collection for data and their analysis and interpretation. Editing is a routine work: yet it has to be carried out with utmost care and devotion. Whereas coding in an operation, which requires judgment skill, Particularly for developing the coding frame. However, major part of the editing and coding involves repetitive and dull work of mechanical nature, which, often times cause monotony and fatigue. Tabulation of data is a common tool in social sciences research used for summarizing the data so that they are amenable for interpretation. Thus, there are three important stages in the processing of social survey data.

They are:

1. Checking the filled questionnaire i.e., editing.
2. Reducing the mass of data into manageable proportion, i.e., coding.
3. Summarizing the data into tabular form.

## Editing

Editing is the first and foremost stage in data processing. According to Pattern; "the process of examining the data collected in a survey to detect errors and omissions and to see that they are corrected and the schedules prepared for tabulation is known as editing." Editing involves routine task of checking the filled questionnaires. By means of careful editing, incorrect and incomplete answers are identified and inconsistencies are rectified. Once an error is left undetected at this stage it becomes rather impossible to rectify the mistake at subsequent stages; which goes unnoticed throughout the report.

Editing thus becomes an obsolete necessity for any large-scale survey researcher, which uses questionnaire or interview schedules for the collection of research data. Moser emphasizes the need for coding thus;

"Before the questionnaires can be regarded as ready for coding, tabulating and analysis they should be checked for completeness, accuracy and uniformity."

### Process of Editing

In the process of editing the following points must be scrutinized:

1. Whether the data is reliable and accurate?
2. Whether the schedules are complete and whether all questions have been answered?
3. Whether the schedules are uniform?
4. Whether the entries have been made in accordance with the instructions
5. Whether there are any inconsistencies in the answers?

The above questions are discussed elaborately in following paragraphs:

### Completeness

At the editing stages it should be verified whether answers have been recorded for all the questions. Sometimes the investigators might have left the question inadvertently. Some questions, which are inapplicable, might have been skipped. The unknown and not applicable categories might have been left without any clear marking. Such gaps should be filled carefully at this stage. If there is any significant omission the reasons for such omissions should be found out. The possible reasons may be: (a) refusal to answer, (b) forgetfulness to record the information, and (c) not applicable. The not applicable cases should be recorded to avoid later confusion; The checking of incomplete answers of open ended question are more difficult. The incomplete information can be gathered either with the information furnished by the interviewer himself of by approaching the respondent himself. Often times the information may e available in the schedules itself.

### Accuracy

It is not enough that the information is complete; but its accuracy and truthfulness is more important. Clerical errors may arise due to carelessness in filling up the schedules. Sometimes the respondents may twist and distort the facts or provide faked information with a view to misleading the researcher or hiding some facts. The entries that are confusing and illegible have to be eliminated. In order to avoid inaccuracies and to ensure the reliability of information following steps should be taken;

1. The answers should as far as possible be pre-coded, as written answers are liable to more inaccurate.
2. Arithmetic such as totaling, subtracting etc., may be done leisurely in the office rather during the course of the interview
3. To ensure accuracy of certain key data, cross checking should be done by means of evolving different questions to elicit the same data information.

### Uniformity

The purpose of editing is to convert the answers into uniform units of measurement before coding.

It is a pre-requisite for accuracy, besides, editing ensures uniform interpretation of questions. At this stage questions are standardized; and the diverse answers will be transformed into uniform, comparable and homogeneous categories. For instance, while entering yearly income, some might have by mistake entered monthly income which have to be converted in to uniform pattern which will facilitate their further treatment, analysis and interpretation.

## Consistency

Editing is a means for ensuring consistency of the data collected, and avoiding contradictions. The inconsistencies in the answers, if any have to be reconciled. For instance, the answers regarding the income of the respondents and the sale proceeds minus the cost of production must normally tally. If not, the inconsistencies and internal disparities may be corrected by examination and comparison of related replies.

## Certain Issues

At the editing stage, certain issues should be clarified so that the operation is completed with efficiency. They are discussed below.

Firstly, it is a common doubt whether the editing work is taken up for each question or for each section or for the complete questionnaire. It is always considered advantageous to edit the whole questionnaire, so that the logical link between various questions are understood and appreciated. Besides, this enables the cross checking of affects and information for ensuring their accuracy.

The second issue raised is whether all or only a sample of questionnaires need to be edited? There is no general rule as to this question

In any large-scale survey, thorough and complete editing scrupulously dome would pay handsomely.

Thirdly, whether the editing should be done immediately or after the completion of the entire survey? In large scale surveys editing is done simultaneously by group leaders i .e., field editor while accepting the completed schedules form the investigators i.e., intake edit. It is always considered advantageous to complete the editing work simultaneously. This would enable the researcher to substantiate and complete the missing information from the fresh memories of the interview situation.

## Coding

### *Introduction*

Coding is considered as the classification process. The purpose of coding is to classify the answers to a question into meaningful categories which in necessary for tabulation. In other words coding aims at summarizing the survey answers, so that the handling of such data is made easy for further analysis; and their essential pattern is brought out. Besides, coding is a useful means of quantifying the qualitative data.

According to Larton: "Coding consists in assigning a number of symbol to each answer which falls in a pre-determined class."[3] Goode and Hatt define coding as follows:

"Coding is an operation by which data are organized into classes and number or symbol is given to each item according to the class in which it falls." Coding thus involves two important operation viz., (i) deciding the categories to be used and (ii) allocating individual answers to them.

The desirability and profitability of coding however depends on the following factors.

1. The number of respondents
2. The Number of question asked and
3. The type of statistical operations planned

The need for coding arises more in the case of qualitative data which is not amendable for pre-coding and structuring of the interview schedule. Besides coding is a mean of quantifying the qualitative data which is a pre-requisite for any meaningful interpretation of social data. The method of coding also vary between the manual and machine processing of data. For manual tabulation any symbol is sufficient: whereas for machine tabulation it must be a numerical symbol. Furthermore, the number of classes is limited to 10 in the case punch cards.

The task of coding may be dispensed with or substantially reduced if questions are pre-coded. By administering pre-coded questions time and money could be saved, and error in coding and transcriptions may be reduced considerably. One great hurdle in pre-coding is that it is not always possible to foresee the type of replies and anwers of the respondents and as a result the classification becomes unrealistic. The answers tend to concentrate in the miscellaneous categories. However, pre-coding is highly useful for mechanical tabulation of data. The widely prevalent practice is to take up coding operation after completion of the collection of data.

## Uses of Coding

1. The difficult task of processing the qualitative information is made easy by means of coding. It serves as a useful

method of utilizing the important sources of data, which cannot be pre-planned or patterned by narrow sets of questions such as historical records, case record, diaries, letters etc.

2. Coding is useful in structuring the questions after preparing the questionnaires/schedules which are done with unstructured questionnaires/schedules.
3. Only by careful coding umpteenth variety of answers to open ended questions are reduced to manageable proportions. For example a question like; " What will you do with your increased income? May generate variety of response. The categorizing and grouping of answers provide a rational basis for classification of data and assigning codes.

## Steps in Codes

### *1. Study the Answers*

Before, commencing the coding operation, it is essential to clarify the meaning and purpose of the question. Unless we are cleat in our minds as to what for the question is being asked, we cannot understand the answer in its proper perspective. The answer should be complete and clear. In case of any ambiguity, it should be developed in such a way as to reflect the intention of the respondents truly. The study of the answer is thus, the first stage in coding. In case of pre-coded questions, coding begins at the preparation of interview schedules.

### *2. Preparation of Coding Frame*

Coding frame is developed by listing the possible answers to each question and assigning code numbers or symbols to each of them which are the indicators used for coding. Such indicators are developed gradually by classifying and grouping of survey data. While developing the coding frames it is always better to retain more number of groups so that it may be easy to amalgamate them later, if necessary, rather than to split to large groups. Such coding frame serves as the basis of coding the diverse answers, which will not fall into neatly pre-arranged classes. Beside assigning code numbers or symbols to each group or category of answers, coding includes the preparation of a set of instructions, which enable others to classify the comments and answers.

### 3. *Fit the Classes to the Data*

After preparing the sample frame the gradual process of fitting the answers to the questions must begin. The answers must be carefully studied, assigning the codes to them. The researcher has to use his common sense and discretion while assigning codes to the answers, which are vague, deviant and difficult to understand. The answers which fall under unclassified categories may be treated as miscellaneous or residual category. The researcher should see that no answer is left uncoded, by proper checking.

### 4. *Transcription*

Transcription means transferring of the information from the schedules to a separate sheet called transcription sheet. Transcription sheet is a large summary sheet, which contains the answers/code of all respondents. It is useful to have an overview of all the illustrations of all respondents. Preparation of tables becomes easy by means of consolidation, grouping and classification of data. It also enables the comparison of variables and preparation of cross tables. Transcription is a time-saving and error preventing device which renders efficient management of data. Transcription may not be necessary when only simply tables are required and the number of respondents are few.

## Principles in Designing Codes

Milred Parten has laid down certain principles in designing codes they are;

1. The classification should be detailed as combining is relatively simple.
2. Codes need not always be in numerical form unless mechanical tabulation is needed
3. For mechanical tabulation, the codes must be numerical and the classes should be limited to10.
4. Items which are pre-coded be prepared to ensure uniform coding.
5. Code instructions should be prepared to ensure uniform coding.
6. Classification must follow certain standards and similar to those used in other studies which will be useful in interpretation of results or for comparison
7. Class intervals should be clear and specific without overlaps.

8. Accuracy and completeness should be checked after coding.
9. Arithmetic computations should be complete before commencing the coding operations

**Problems in Coding**

The Common problems encountered by the researcher while coding are as follows:

1. When the matter to be coder involves certain concepts which are not understood by the respondents in the same sense, the answers will also be diverse and unrelated to the concept. This defect is difficult to rectify at the coding stage.
2. Sometimes the researcher/interviewer fails to elicit the desired data, which is revealed only at the time of coding.
3. Sometimes it is discovered to the dismay of the researcher that the answers to questions are not of uniform type, which defeats the purpose of coding.

# 27

# Tabulation

Tabulation is a means for proper interpretation of the research data. The tabulation is a procedure which involves arranging of assembled data in a logical, concise and systematic manner on the basis of the following criteria: (i) geographical (ii) chronological or temporal (iii) qualitative or attributive (iv) quantitative. On the Basis of the above classifications, the number of cases following in each class is counted and are sorted into relevant classes.

The following principles have to be observed generally while preparing the tables.

1. The pattern of classification is made on the basis of the purpose and objectives of the study and problem in hand.
2. The tables are prepared with reference to the hypothesis, which have a direct bearing on the method of analysis.
3. The tables should properly represent the data collected and their basic features.

### Frequency Distribution

It is the simplest form of tabulation. There will be two columns in the frequency tables. In one column the different qualities of an attribute and different values are entered in the second column. Following are the important considerations in preparing the frequency tables:

(a) Values are entered in the left hand column and the frequencies are entered in the right hand column.

(b) The value or classes should be mutually exclusive; overlapping values will only lead to confusion.
(c) The ordering of data should be logical.
(d) The class intervals should be carefully chosen, ordinarily there should not be less than 8 or 10 classes and more than 20 classes.
(e) The class intervals should be neither too big nor too small, as very small ones becomes irrelevant and very big ones tend to conceal the important characteristics.
(f) They should be of convenient number of 5 or 10 instead of 7 or 9. Definite lower and upper limits should be clearly designated so as to avoid any confusion.

### Mechanical Tabulation

Tabulation may be done either manually or mechanically. For mechanical tabulation the coded answers have to be transferred to the punch cards. Separate card normally contains 80 columns and the code number of each answer is punched by hand operated punching machine. Punching so done is verified by another machine, which assures the accuracy of punching. If there is any discrimination, such cards are verified and in case of mistakes they are replaced. Subsequently these cards are fed to sorting machine, which sort the cards into the number of categories punched in the cards for each question. The sample frequency tables and complicated cross tables are carried in sort time with precision and efficiency. However the need for mechanical tabulation hardly arises in surveys involving small size samples and simple analysis. Following are the circumstances in which the mechanical tabulation is advisable.

If the survey involves large number of samples, tabulation by machine is useful and economical.

If the study aims at complicated cross tabulation and advanced analysis, mechanical tabulation will ensure more accuracy.

Machine tabulation provides lot of flexibility to the researcher. Tabulation can be done within no time as little effort is involved. It gives incentive and scope to try new patterns and methods of analysis.

### Disadvantages

Mechanical tabulation should not be considered as unmixed

blessing. The desirability or resorting to mechanical device is deterred for two important considerations.

The machine tabulation is a costly affair and therefore is out of reach for many a researcher. Its prohibitory cost renders this method unsuited to the low budget researchers.

The machine tabulation requires expert advise.

The researcher has to depend on others for punching, sorting and tabulation, unlike hand tabulation which may be done by the researcher himself.

Thus, neither the advantages nor the disadvantages can be categorically started. As stated by Moser; "For any survey which involves large number or for which a larger number of cross-tabulations are required machine method has much to commend them. These cases apart, hand tabulation has much in its favour."8 The nature of the survey and the needs and requirements of the analysis are the chief factors which determine the need or otherwise of mechanical devices in preparation of tables.

# 28

# Analysis of Data

Analysis and interpretation of data are the most crucial aspects of research. It is considered to be highly skilled and technical job, which should be carried out only by the researcher himself or under his close supervision. The analysis of data requires on the part of the researcher a thorough knowledge about the data, judgment skill, ability of generalization and familiarity with the background, objects and hypothesis of the study.

It is through a systematic analysis that the underlying features of the data are revealed and valid generalizations are arrived at. Facts and figures never speak for themselves. Organized data are more revealing than the facts figures. Only by means of organizing, analyzing and interpreting the research data their salient features, inter-relationship and cause and connections are brought out. The trends and sequences are elicited by means of generalizations.

## Steps in Analysis

While analyzing the research data the analyst is engaged in a series of routine procedures, which have to be undertaken in a sequential manner. According to Herbert Ayman following are the steps in the analysis:

1. The data corresponding to each aspect of the phenomenon that have been conceptualized are tabulated for the aggregate group and provide a general statistical or quantitative description.

2. The data are similarly tabulated for each sub-group i.e., regarded as significant and provide the differentiated quantities description desired as well as descriptions for any redefined population i.e., regarded as especially relevant to the problem.
3. Various modes of consolidating data for the many separate aspects of the phenomenon are employed to provide statistical description.
4. All this data are then examined in the context of related phenomenon so as to improve the evaluation of the finding.
5. A variety of qualitative non-statistical measures are used to supplement the quantitative description.

## Statistical Tools

Statistics is an efficient tool in the analysis of research data. The very purpose of statistic is to aid research. According to Mood: "The statistician is engaged in producing tools for research workers." E.G. Chambers describes the utility of statistical methods as follows:

"Statistical methods are to worker what tools are to the carpenter. The utility of statistics as a tool depends on the knowledge of their use for correct function. The craftsmen will not for instance use a mallet and chisel or a foresaw to plane a plank of wood, not will he use a hammer to drive in a screw, similarly statistical tool must be only used for the specific purposes for which they have been devised.

A basic knowledge about statistics becomes inevitable for research workers, for systematic analysis and accurate and precise interpretation of data. Therefore understanding specific purposes for which different statistical tool are used as if methods of interpretation is a valuable asset to the researcher. Analysis of social data may be broadly classified into four broad categories, they are:

Methods, which aim at summarizing the data and presenting the collective characteristics.

1. Methods used for comparison of two sets of data and assessing their difference.
2. Methods employed to assess the relationship between two or more variable.

3. Methods of predication and forecasting.

The methods of analysis chosen for a particular study depends upon the nature of objectives, hypothesis to be tested and the purpose and use of the study. The commonly used statistical devices in social survey research are discussed in the following paragraphs.

### 1. Summarizing the data

Summarizing the data aims at presenting the collective characteristics of a given body of data. In summarizing the observations we first divide them on the basis of the different characteristics which normally fall in three classes viz., (i) normal characteristics or attributes (ii) ordinal characteristics/qualitative variables (iii) interval variable/quantitative variables. The statistical methods used for assessing the collective characteristics are called the descriptive statistics. Descriptive statistics is concerned with summarizing the information that we have about characteristic no matter how may characteristics there are.6 Normally such analysis relates to a single characteristic such as production, prices, sales etc. Such variables may either be a continuous one or a discrete one. A continuous variable has no break between one value and another (examples: age, weight, temperature etc.); whereas the discrete variables area a series of discontinuous variable without any continuity (example people, houses, automobiles). In other words those variables which cannot be broken into fractional units are discrete variables. Both theses types of variables may be compressed into statistical tables and analyzed for knowing the typical traits and features of such variables. This is known as summarization. There are two distinct sets of variables. This is known as summarization. There are two distinct sets of statistical processes used for summarization. They are: (a) Measures of Central Tendency and (b) Measures of Deviation of Dispersion.

### *A. Measures of Central Tendency*

A set of statistical indexes are applied to find out the central tendency of the distribution. They are concerned as to how scores tend to cluster in a distribution. The commonly used measures of central tendency are; Mean, Median and Mode. Mean refers to the average value of the distribution which is arrived at by dividing the sum of scores in the distribution by number of observations.

Median is the mid-point of the array of scores. It is that value or point which divides the distribution equally. The scores are arranged in order of magnitude; and the middle point above and below which equal number of scores fall, is regarded as the median. In the case of grouped data the median position is located by means of identifying the class interval within which the middle value falls and then estimating the value of median. This method is called interpretation. Mode is that score which most frequently occurs in a distribution. Normally, mode can be located by means of inspection, in simple series. In a frequency distribution the mode is that point on the scale of variable where the frequency is the greatest.

*Advantages of Measures of Central Tendency*

1. The measures of central tendency reduce the common characteristics of a given data into a simple representative number.
2. The center of concentration of the scored and the most typically occurring scores are identified by means of these measures.
3. They enable us to derive some meaning from the otherwise disorganized data, which is the basis for generalisation.
4. Measures of central tendency of a distribution help to forecast, estimate or determine the value that may occur in a given situation.

***B. Measures of Dispersion***

The purpose of the measures of dispersion or deviation is to describe how the scores are scattered or dispersed across the scale. Dispersion exists when the individual values of the observations are not identical to the mean value. The extent of dispersion, then, can be visualized as the extent to which the observation deviate from the mean"7 Some distributions may have the same average but greatly differ in their variability. In such a situation, the measures of dispersion will better represent the characteristics of the distribution that measures the central tendency. The Range, Mean Deviation, Standard Deviation and Quartile Deviation are the most common measures of dispersion.

**Range**

Range is the difference between the highest score and the lowest scores in a distribution i.e., Range is H-L. This is simple tc calculate. Since it is based on only two vales, it may not present a true picture of the characteristics of data. Extreme cases in either side may alter the value considerably.

### Mean Deviation

It is statistical device intended to measure the extent of deviation of individual scores from the mean. The mean deviation or the average deviation is defined as the mean of the deviations of the individual scores from some measure of central tendency. It is arrived at by summing up the deviations irrespective of signs and dividing it by the number of observations.

### Standard Deviation

The measures of variability is widely used. It is the square root of the sum of squared deviation divided by the number of observations. It is the standard measure of viability in most statistical procedures. A modified formula is used for calculating the Standard Deviation in a grouped data.

### Quartile Deviation

It is also known as Semi-Inter-quartile Range. The distribution is divided into four equal parts. It is defined as the average amount by which the quartile point Q1 and Q3 deviate from the mean. Q1 is the point below which 25 percent of the scores fall and Q3 is the median which divides the scores equally.

### 2. Comparison and Assessing the Differences

Comparison of a bi-variate distribution and assessing the difference in two sets of observation is a common method of analysis in research. Generally a bi-variate table represents a joint distribution of two variable and a list of categories in each variable. A bi-variate distribution arises in either of two circumstances; Firstly, two characteristics of the same population say age and sex or income and employment are represented in a single table, one variable in the row and another in the column. This helps to assess the joint occurrence of the two characteristics. In the second category of bi-variate table, the universe is divided into two categories of characteristics that must be present in every member of that category which is referred to as constant or condition. For instance the universe is divided into two parts on the basic geographic region and within each such region there are different characteristics such as income or education, which are present in both population and are comparable. The comparative analysis of two sets of data are made by means of the following tools.

*(i) Ratio*

It is a common method of comparing frequencies. It is "merely an indicated or actual quotient which relates the size of one number to another". If there are two sets of figures to be compared, usually the figure in the right hand side of a distribution is reduced to 1 an thus allowing comparison to be made easy.

*(ii) Proportion*

"This measure is a fraction such that the numerator is one of two observed frequencies and the denominator the sum of observed frequencies." Proportion of two observations will be expressed in fraction of 1 and the total is always 1.

*(iii) Percent*

A proportion multiplied by 100 is called a percent. While reporting percentages, original frequencies must also be represented.

*(iv) Rate of Change*

It aims at comparing number with the number of potential events, i.e., number of individuals exposed to the risk of events. The comparison is accomplished by dividing the number of occurrences by the by dividing the number of occurrences by the number of individuals exposed. This fraction is called the rate of occurrence.

*(v) Percentage Change*

The change that had taken place over a given period between the beginning year and terminal year is expressed in terms of percentage. The actual change is divided by original frequency and its multiplied by 100, to arrive at the percentage change.

The purpose of using the above methods of comparison is to simplify the problem of comparison. They all serve to put qualitative characteristics into quantitative form. We are able to condense the information by the process of division. The basic difference in all these methods primarily lies in the method of selection of the base or denominator.

## Testing the Difference between Two Groups

Testing the significance of the difference becomes a useful statistical method. It helps to solve an important and frequently occurring problem namely, whether there is real difference between two observational means or not? This type of analysis is highly useful in impact studies, hypothesis testing and in experimental researches. Both in experimentation and testing it serves as a useful tool. One fundamental difference between and testing is in experimentation we keep our subject constant and vary the subjects. In other words in experimentation we give our initial and final tests to the same group of objects by introducing the experimental factors. In the testing, on the other hand the conditions are kept constant and the standard measuring stick is used for variety of subjects. If conditions are not kept constant we may not be sure that changes observed between the two groups is due to the factor under study or due to other factors. Since experimentation is a remote possibility in social science research, the testing of different groups under identical condition is an accepted method of studying effect or impact of certain factors. In order to ascertain whether the difference observed between two groups or two experiments are significant or not, the following statistical tools are used.

### *1. Testing the Difference between two Means*

By obtaining the mean and standard deviation of the groups, we can calculate 't' statistics. It is essentially the ratio of the mean to its standard error; or it may be the ratio of a difference between means to its standard error."11 It is a most important statistical tool; as some such test is crucial in most researches. There are several methods of testing the difference between two means. The test may be for a single group tested before and after the introduction of an experimental factor or when two groups have been carefully equated for comparison. The four types of 't' test which are commonly used are; (a) test for large uncorrelated samples (b) test for large correlated samples (c) test for small uncorrelated sample and as (d) test for small correlated sample.

## 2. *Significance of the Difference Between Two Percentages*

Sometimes it happens that it is not possible to measure the presence or absence of quality but we know the percentage of those who possess a particular attribute. Testing the significance of the differences in two percentages will help to examine whether the proportion of one group possessing the same quality. This test is also based on the calculation of possessing the same quality. This test is also based on the calculation of standard error of difference between two percentages and the calculation of 't' on the basis. A different formulae is applied for this test.

## Analysis of Variance(ANOVA)

The 't' test is a statistical method used for testing. The significance of the difference lies between two groups or two sets of observation. When the group to be compared are more than two, a different analysis is used for such comparison. The analysis of variance is a test of variability of a set of data. In any experiment, several factors may be at work which may result in the variability of the observations. The causes for such variability is isolated and their contribution on the variability is measured by means of this analysis, we may be able to ascertain whether the different groups represent a homogeneous population or are drawn from the heterogeneous population.

While grouping the observations into several independent classification, it is seen that the classification is made on the basis of the characteristics we want to isolate as a causative factor for the variability. For example, if we want to analyze the variability of the loans obtained by farmers belonging to different size of holdings, from institutional agencies, we have to necessarily base the classification, on the farm size.

The test of analysis of variance is based on the following three assumptions:

1. that the data are normally distributed
2. that the separate estimates are independent
3. that the variance in each class is the same.

## Multiple Factor Analysis of Variance

In the single factor analysis of variance, the variability of a single independent variable is tested. Whereas in multiple factor analysis the variability of more than one independent variables at different levels is tested. Thus, multiple factor analysis of variance provides methods for testing. Whether different sub-groups or various combinations of sub-groups, represent different populations in terms of what is being measured as the dependent variable12. For example the variance in I.Q. of the children of a particular class belonging to three different schools are measured. It is a simple analysis of variance involving only one factor. If a second factor, say, sex is introduced and further classification is made on that basis, there arises the multiple factor analysis of variance. Similarly, a third factor say, family background / social status may be introduced. Thus, the different causes for the variability in the dependent factor namely I.Q. is brought out by means of this analysis.

**3. Test of Analysis**

Research is largely concerned with the identification of casual connections between different variables and studying the inter-relationship between them. The hypothesis framed by researchers are generally of statements of relationship between variables. Several techniques are used to test the extent of association between variables. Correlation is one such analysis which is more frequently used. When the two variables are numerical and normally distributed, the Product Moment Correlation analysis is the best.

When the actual value of two correlations cannot be accurately measured, and the distribution is not a normal distribution, we can rank the distribution and the correlation co-efficient is calculated on the basis using Spearman's Rank Order Correlation technique. Though this is an approximate estimate of correlation, it is simple to calculate. This correlation cannot be employed for further statistical analysis like partial and multiple correlation, factor analysis etc. In any correlation analysis a significant correlation co-efficient does not always prove a cause and effect relationship has to be supported by the researcher's interpretation, for a significantly high correlation may be due to either or all of the following reasons.

1. Cause and effect relationship between the two;
2. Both the variables may be influenced by a third variable; and

3. Co-variance may be accidental without any causative relationship.

When the test of association relates to some attributes or quantitative variables, the Chi square test of null hypothesis is used to determine the extent of association between variables.

## Multi-Variable Relationship

It has been started that one of the causes for the simple correlation may be the influences of a common variable. Such influences are not eliminated in the simple correlation analysis. In practical life situation problem, direct cause and effect relationship is a rare phenomenon to occur. Often times more than two variables are involved and nay meaningful explanation for such phenomenon should take into account all those factors. Co-efficient of partial and multiple Correlations are the indexes used ot measure the extent of correlation between two variables are kept constant; whereas the multiple correlation is the measurement of the combined effect of a group of indepent variables on a dependent variable.

## 4. Prediction and Forecasting

Analysis of trend and forecasting the future is one of the purpose of research. Production and forecasting has greater relevance of disciplines like Economics, Commerce, Management and Co-operation. The basic requirement for the trend analysis and forecasting is the time series data for sufficiently long period. The prediction is a risk task and yet with the appropriate statistical device forecasting may be made with reasonable degree of accuracy. Here are some of the commonly used methods of trend analysis and forecasting.

### *Time Series Analysis*

Time series is the data classified chronologically in terms of days, months or years, of a given variable. The fluctuation in the variable under study is due to the combined effect of four components viz., (1) secular trend (2) cyclical variation (3) seasonal variation and (4) irregular or random fluctuation. It is usually presented in the form of an equation.

O = T X C X S X I

The analysis of Time Series consists in separating these constituent parts by holding the other components constant. A measure of one of these components can be obtained by eliminating the remaining elements from the original data of the time series by the process of division. The model given above should be represented in percentages. If the absolute values are used the model is applied in the additive form i.e., O = T+C+S+I. Analysis of time series is useful in predicting the future tendencies. It is an essential aid in planning, allocation of resources and budgeting.

### *Measurement of Trend*

The trend may be described in different methods. These methods aim at separating the trends by eliminating fluctuations. Prediction in such methods is made possible by means of extrapolation i.e., by projecting the trend line. It is possible by the following methods.

### *Curve by Inspection*

It is the easiest method of all. The scribes is plotted on the graph and a smooth curve is drawn by inspection in such a way that the line lies between the points. The short term fluctuations are ignored; and it is seen that fluctuations are equal in both sides.

### *Semi Average Method*

In this method the original series is divided into two equal parts, the value of each part is summed up and the average is arrived at separately. These two values are plotted on the graph at the central period of the part from which they have been calculated respectively. These are two values are then connected by a straight line.

### *Moving Average Method*

It is another simple method in which the short term fluctuations are smoothened. The moving average may be calculated either for 3 years, 5 years, 7 years. The process of totaling and averaging starts in the middle year. For instance, if the average is for 5 years the averaging starts from 3rd year. The values of first two years of the first five year cumulative total is arrived at by adding 6th year value and deleting the value of the first year. This process is repeated for the whole series. To arrive at the average value, each year value is divided by a constant, the number of years for which moving average is calculated.

### *Least Square*

If the data is linear the least square is an appropriate method. A graph of the series will be required to enable the decision to be made as to the curve to be fitted. The formula used is Y = a + bx; where y is the trend value or independent variable, 'a' is the constant, 'b' is the value determines the slope of the curve and 'x' denotes the year to which it pertains. It is most commonly employed and a satisfactory method.

### *Regression*

Regression is an effective statistical tool to predict a bi-variate situation. It tells us the predicated value of a dependent variable 'x' and the constant 'a' and the regression co-efficient, 'b'. The formula used for linear regression is

$$Y = a + bx$$

This method is a logical extension of the correlation analysis, which implies co-variance. High correlation between 2 variables i.e., x and y will imply that predication is possible by means of regression analysis.

# 29

# Interpretation of Data

After collecting and analyzing the data, the researcher's duty is to draw inferences from the data. This has to be done very carefully, otherwise, misleading conclusions may be drawn and the whole purpose of conducting the research will be defeated.

## Meaning of Interpretation

Interpretation refers to the task of drawing inferences from the collected data after an analytical or experimental study. It is a search for broader meaning of research findings. The task of interpretation has two major aspects.

1. The effort to establish continuity in research through linking the results of a given study with another study.
2. The establishment of some explanatory concepts.

According to William Emory, "In one sense, interpretation is concerned with relationships within the collected data, partially overlapping analysis. Interpretation also extends beyond the data of study to include the results of other research, theory and hypothesis".

Thus interpretation is the device through which the factors that seem to explain what has been observed by the researcher can better be understood and it also provides a theoretical conception, which can serve as a guide for further research.

## Need for Interpretation

1. *For the right findings*—Interpretation is essential for the usefulness and utility of research findings on a right direction.
2. *Continuity in research*—It is through interpretation that the researcher can understand the principles that work beneath his findings. Through this, he can link up his findings with other research studies.
3. *Establishment of explanatory concepts*—Interpretation leads to the establishment of explanatory concepts that can serve as a guide for future research studies. It opens new avenues of knowledge and stimulates the researcher
4. *Significance of research findings*— Only through proper interpretation, the researcher can come to know what are his research findings, how are they, and how can others understand the real significance of his research findings.
5. *Hypothesis*—Through proper interpretation, a research study may result in hypothesis, which will be useful for the researcher to lead the further course of research.

## Requirements of Interpretation

1. *Explanations*—The researcher must give reasonable explanations of the relations, which he has found between variables and must interpreted the lines of relationship properly. This is the technique of how generalization should concepts be formulated.
2. *Extraneous information*—Any additional information collected during the study must be collected while interpreting the final results of the study. It may prove to be a key factor in understanding the problem under consideration.
3. *Consultation*—Before entering into the interpretation, it is better for the researcher to consult some experts who have insight into the area. They can guide the researcher on the right way.
4. *No hesitation*—While interpreting the data, the researcher should not be in a hurry in interpreting the data. He must be cautious at every stage to come out with right conclusions.

## Precautions in Interpretation

1. *Adequacy of data*—Before starting the interpretation, the researcher must satisfy that the data are sufficient, they are accurate, appropriate and trustworthy.
2. *Errors*—The researcher must be cautious about the errors that may arise in the process of interpreting the results. Errors may arise due to false generalization or due to wrong interpretation of statistical tools.
3. *Avoiding broad generalizations*—The research work undertaken by the researcher has limited scope and broad generalizations of his findings cannot be made. This caution a researcher must keep in mind.
4. *Interaction between theory and practice*—In the course of research, there may be constant interaction between hypothesis and theoretical conceptions. It is in this area the researcher must try to gain originality in his interpretation.

# 30

# Uses of Research for Business and Management and its Limitations

## Uses of Research in Business and Management

The following are the uses of research for cooperatives.

1. *To solve the problems of the corporate sector*—Private sector face problems in their day-to-day operations. Number of managerial and administrative tools are available for them to solve such problems. But through research, they can solve the problems scientifically and accurately.
2. *To evaluate the performance of Individual companies*—Companies and firms have to evaluate their performance once in few years. A stock taking of their operational efficiency will give continuity to their working. Companies can use research as a tool to measure their performance.
3. *To study the past*—Studying the past is necessary to analyze the limitations and problems faced by the companies. By using historical method of research, business research can study their past. The past of the individual companies at local, regional, national, and international level could also be studied.
4. *To find out the causes for success and failure*—Private corporate sectors are running successfully and in certain cases many individual firms have become sick. Both success factors and failure factors must be found. This is possible by

means of undertaking research.

5. *To build viable Business*—Viability denotes the self-reliance of firms in their resources and rendering service to the community at a lower cost. For this purpose, research would be helpful to business..
6. *To improve their operational efficiency* —Companies have to improve their operational efficiency by means of reducing the cost of operations, improving customer service, and applying various management techniques. To operate these variable, research will be helpful to them.
7. *To face competition*—Individual firms have to face competition from within the private sector, as well as public sector. Liberalization of the economy has further intensified the competition. Such competition is both a challenge and an opportunity for the corporate sector. Research can come to the help of business under such circumstances.
8. *Facing the future*— Corporates have to focus their attention to the future also. Expansion programs, opening of new offices and branches, etc are part of such programs. By means of feasibility research studies, the future could be predicted.
9. *To compare performance* —Performance of one company can be compared with others to find out difference in their operations. Such performance appraisal and comparison can be done by research.
10. *Leadership strength*—Various leadership styles could be studied and applied by means of research.
11. *To study various functions of management*— Companies apply various functions of management like planning, organizing, staffing, directing, and controlling. This could be analyzed by research.
12. *To study the functional areas*—Functional areas like production management, materials management, marketing management, financial management, etc could be examined by research.

## Limitations of Research in Business and Management

Business and management provide immense scope for research. Easy availability for primary and secondary data, reliability of data, inter disciplinary approach, etc., are certain merits of doing research in usiness.. At the same time business research have certain limitations to research. They are as follows:

*1. Lack of Theories*

Theories are necessary to develop a social science and to do research. Theories explain various concepts in a research problem and the scope of research is widened by theories. But business and management, though have developed theories, yet they lack theories. At present it borrows theories from other social science like, economics, psychology, etc., Hence, there is need to build theories in business by researchers.

*2. Lack of Literature*

Researches in business heavily depend on journals. Literature in the form of books, is not sufficient. Availability of books from foreign countries is another limitation.

*3. Figures are Not Uniform*

Data relating to the corporate sector are provided by federal and regional Governments, such figures are not uniform in nature. So the researcher is in a dilemma to use the right type of data.

*4. Delay in Getting Latest Data*

Latest data will not be available from agencies. The reports issued by such agencies are 2 or 3 years old. This puts the researcher to certain difficulties.

*5. Repetitive Nature of Selection of Research Topics*

Though corporate sector provides enormous scope for selecting new topics of research, researchers choose areas which are already done by many scholars. This leads to repetition. Such repetition should be avoided by researchers.

*6. Certain Firms Boost the Figures*

Certain firms, including public sector organisations boost their financial data. Performance areas like recovery of loans by banks are boosted by means of book adjustments. Such manipulation will increase the recovery position.

### *7. Lack of Uniform Measures*

Measures of weight, land holdings, agricultural production are not shown uniformly. In certain states weights are shown in bags and in other states in tones and quintals. In the case of land holdings local measures are used. One state gives land holdings in hectares and other states in acres. This is again a confusion area for researchers.

### *8. Difficulties in the Field*

While undertaking survey a business researcher has to face field problems like non – co-operation of the respondents, etc., Such difficulties can be overcome by sufficient.

## Scope / Areas of research in Business and Management

Research is expected to improve the quality of business decisions, but what business decision topics benefit from research efforts? Figure 1.3 lists several major topics for research in business. (This Figure follows the logic found in Thomas C. Kinnear and Ann Root, eds., 1994: survey of Marketing Research (Chicago, America Marketing Association, 1995).

**Figure 1.3: Major Topics for Research in Business**

*General business, Economics, and Corporate Research*

- Short-range forecasting (up to one year)
- Long-term forecasting (over one year)
- Studies of business and industry trends
- Inflation and pricing studies
- Plant and warehouse location studies
- Acquisition studies
- Studies of global environments

*Financial and Accounting Research*

- Forecasting of financial interest- rate trends
- Stock, bond, and community value predictions
- Capital formation alternatives
- Research related to mergers and acquisitions
- Risk-return trade-off studies
- Impact of taxes
- Portfolio analysis
- Research on financial institutions
- Expected rate-of-return studies

Capital asset pricing models
Credit risk
Cost analysis

*Management and Organizational Behavior Research*

Total quality management
Moral and job satisfaction
Leadership style
Employee productivity
Organizational effectiveness
Structural studies
Absenteeism and turnover
Organizational climate
Organizational communication
Time and motion studies
Physical environment studies
Labor union trends

*Major Topics for Research in Business (continued)*

---

*Sales and Marketing Research*

Measurement of marketing potentials
Market-share analysis
Market segmentation studies
Determination of market characteristics
Sales analysis
Establishment of sales quotas, territories
Distribution-channel studies
New-product concept tests0
Test-market studies
Advertising research
Buyer-behavior/ consumer satisfaction studies

*Corporate Responsibility Research*

Ecological impact studies
Legal constraints on advertising and promotion studies
Sex, age, and racial discrimination worker-equity studies

---

# 31

# Planning Research Report

## Introduction

Report writing is the culmination of any research investigation as the research worker is obligated to report his study on its completion. Only at this stage the researcher assembles the findings of the study, draws conclusions and evaluates his own findings.

By means of the research report the researcher is able to communicate to the readers his findings and conclusions in a form which is readily understood and assessed, as also the validity verified by the evidence produced in support of the conclusions. Reporting is thus the end product of a research activity. It is a highly skilled work, which is both interesting as well as challenging. Report writing is a technical activity which "requires considerable though" effort, patience, skill and penetration and an overall approach to the problem data, and analysis as well as firm control over language and greater objectivity.[1] Considerable amount of planning and preparation is necessary for organizing and writing the report. Besides, perfection in the research report is achieved by continuous and perfection thought and creative and intelligent writing. It is a time consuming process, and normally about 25 to 30% of the budget time of a research should be earmarked for writing the reports.

## Issues to be Clarified

Before actually planning for writing the report, the researcher should clarify certain issues.

Firstly, the researcher should be clear about the point whether the report is meant for publication? Who will undertake the publication? Who will meet the cost? Whether the agency sponsoring the research is interested in publishing the report?

Secondly, the researcher should have a prior knowledge about the process of reproduction of the research report that is whether the report is to be typed? Mimeographed? Printed? Or photo lithographed? This will enable the researcher to adapt his plan accordingly, as each method has certain do's and don'ts. For instance in photolithograph, last minute changes cannot be made as on other methods of duplication. Generally the method of reproduction depends on : (a) size of report, (b) type of readers, (c) number of copies likely to sell, (d) the desired format, and (e) financial budget etc.

Thirdly, the researcher should be clear about the point who will read the report or of whom the report is meant? There are three broad categories of such readers: (i) the layman and the general public (ii) the administrator and the project sponsor and (iii) the fellow researcher and the technical expert.

### Report for Layman

The preparation of research report for layman is a trying task. It must be interesting, simple and lucid. It must avoid all technical jargons and details as to the methods of investigation.

### Report for the Administrator

Such reports should neither be too general nor too technical. It may contain some technical aspects, but on the whole simple and direct. The recommendations must be specific for the administrator to give effect to.

### Technical Report

In such report the researcher is expected to give a full account of the technical aspects both in the sampling methods and subject matter. Fellow professionals are more concerned about the methods, as they want to know the accuracy of the investigation. Conceptual and analytical frame work and sample design should be adequately explained. M.H. Gopal points out four distinguishing facts of technical report.

1. The problem and its nature.
2. The method and its scientific accuracy.
3. The data and their dependability.
4. The logical relationship of the data and the interpretation.

These facts have to be presented logically and sequentially with simplicity, clarity and brevity. The research report is not usually presented to the popular lay audience, since this task is taken over by the journalists.

## Objectives of Report

According to the American Marketing society, the purpose of a research report is, "to convey to interested persons the whole result of the study, in sufficient detail and so arranged as to enable each reader to comprehend the data and to determine for himself the validity of the conclusion".

1. The main object of research report is to present the data and analysis in scientific form. This forms a record and which can be used in future also.
2. Report is the index of a researcher's efficiency. The quality of the research work is judged on the basis of the report.
3. Research report is the quintessence of a research study and it can be easily referred by the executives or users. Hence, it aids or quickens the process of decision making.

## Principles of Report Writing

1. *The Audience:* As stated earlier, the researcher must bear in mind the type of audience who uses the report. Accordingly he can decide the language, etc.
2. *Easy to Follow:* The topic contents and the style of writing must be easy to follow. Headings and sub-headings must be used.
3. *Clarity:* Clarity in writing is essential in order to communicate easily. "To the report writer, clarity of exposition must be the first objective, taking priority over all else, including elegance of expression and style".
4. *Sentence Construction:* Sentence construction must be simple and easy to follow. There must be the continuity in matter and flow in the language and sentences.
5. *Subject Matter:* The subject matter, if it is technical in nature must be made simple. As Britt pointed out that, "the readers

of your reports are busy people and very few of them can balance a research report, a cup of coffee and a dictionary at one time". The statistical tool like correlation, linear equations, etc must have descriptive explanations.

6. *Briefness of the Report:* The report must be brief and need not run to pages for the sake of quantity. "The report should be long enough to cover the objectives of the study. Highlight major points by stressing the big issues and taking them up first. Omit details unless it is really needed to comprehend significant points. Write concisely and to the point. Value clarity rather than impressing the reader with your expertise and vocabulary."

Using Visual Aids: Graphs, charts, maps and diagrams can be incorporated in relevant pages of the report.

## Planning and Organizing the Report

Before starting the report writing a good deal of planning is necessary. Planning and organizing the study materials from the basis of organizing the research report. While commencing the report writing, the researcher, particularly the beginners do not know how to start writing. Researcher would have at this stage accumulated volley of data and information, which have to be prudently used in the study. The author's mind is crowded with ideas and a jumble of thoughts. A well conceived planning and organizing the report facilities report writing with proper emphasis to different aspects. Planning permeates the entire report-to each chapter, aspects and paragraph. It is nothing but arrangement of ideas in a logical and coherent manner within the frame work of the overall structure laid down. Following are the advantages of planning and organization of the report:

1. Ideas and facts which are relevant to the study alone are included in the report by screening them at the stage of planning.
2. The report gets greater clarity and unity.
3. Research findings and result can be easily communicated to the readers.
4. It facilitates the transition of ideas, ease in passing from one idea to another.
5. Planning ensures unity and sequence in presentation of facts i.e., one idea at a time, and a series of ideas one after another.

6. The planning results in an integrated and comprehensive research report.

## Steps in Organization

Planning and organization of the research report involve the following three steps; (A) Organizing the research notes (B) Reflective thinking and (C) Formation of an outline.

### *(A) Organizing the Research Notes*

Notes taking is the core activity in social research. The process of notes taking starts even before the selection of research topic. Such notes are helpful in every stage of research from the selection of topic till the completion of the final report. The accuracy and utility of the notes taken from wide ranging literature as also from field observation had to be put to optimum use while writing the report. Methodical and systematic organizing of notes is a prerequisite for effective writing. Following points have to be adhered to while organizing research notes.

1. For taking down notes, it is always better to use cards rather than sheets of paper. Writing in sheets of paper may not ensure accuracy and adequate control over the facts and may lead to confusion.
2. The cards have to be assorted and arranged topically. Such arranging of notes and putting them under major heads is necessary before commencing the writing.
3. After organizing the notes under different heads the researcher should review them, and consider their adequacy. If the researcher finds any notes being inadequate he has to gather additional information.

### *(B) Reflective Thinking*

Research is a thinking process. It is not a mechanical work of gathering information and presenting them. Instead it is a lively, thrilling, soul satisfying experience. The thinking process starts even before choosing a research topic. Reasoning power of the researcher is the efficient tool for research decisions, interpretation and generalization and giving meaningful recommendation. Besides, defining and delimiting different concepts, choosing the right methodology and tool are all the result of deep, continuous and lively thinking. At the writing stage it is all the more necessary, as clear thinking alone results in clear writing. As Whitney puts it: "There is a highly positive correlation between good thinking and effective writing." The reasoning process helps to present a clear and straightforward exposition of the ideas.

According to M.H. Gopal. "Research is not merely the accumulation, evaluation and assimilation of facts; it is also and more so re-building them into meaningful whole. This demands patient, deep and alert thinking."4 The researcher must therefore develop his thinking faculty and train himself in the thinking process.

### *(C) Outlining*

Drafting an outline is a natural sequence and an outcome of thinking. The outline of the research study is made at two stages. One at the beginning of the study, which serves as a design of the study and the second before writing the report. The outline prepared for the purpose of reports writing should be elaborate so as to include all important aspects which should find a place in the report. Such an elaborate report renders the drafting easy and gives direction to the writing. In the words of Parten: "Generally the report secures greater clarity and unity if the entire report is first outlined under large heading and then filled in by more and more detailed outline," To make the outline elaborate, it should be prepared at three stages; topical outline, paragraph outline and broad aspects outline. Topical outline includes the chapters and broad aspects to be included in each chapter. It is a skeleton outline. Paragraph outline includes all major paragraphs, indicating the central idea of each paragraph. It is merely composed of points to be included in sentences. M.H. Gopal suggests the following points to be observed while planning an outline.

1. It should be as detailed as possible and should enable continuous writing.
2. It should not be as vague, and should not include, such vague phrases as 'introduction 'body' conclusion etc, which give no direction to the report writing.
3. It should fulfill the considerations of chronology, topical unity, coherence and transition.
4. Each paragraph should contain one major idea.

# 32

# Outline of Research Report

**I. Pre-Factory Material**

1. Title Page
2. Table of contents
3. List of illustrations, tables and charts
4. Preface or foreword.

**II. Text or body of report**

***1. Introduction***

(a) Objectives of the study, statement of the problem, definition of concept and hypotheses.
(b) Time, place and material of the survey,
(c) Scope, assumption and limitations,
(d) Organization and sampling procedures,
(e) Methods, tools and techniques employed for data collection.

***2. Analysis and Presentation of Results***

(a) Report of facts-nature, volume and dimension,
(b) Statistical analysis of data,
(c) Interpretation, generalization and conclusions,
(d) Summary of findings and recommendations.

**III. Supplementary Material**

1. Appendices–questionnaires, statistical tables, techniques
2. Bibliography
3. Index
4. Glossary of terms

The title page contains the title of the report, name of the author, sponsoring organization, place and data of publication and publishers. The table of contents includes outline of the topic, headings and sub-headings. Some authors suggest the inclusion of summary of findings and recommendations in the prefatory material, but it is customary to present them at the end of the report.

## Contents of a Report

A report generally contains three important parts namely; the preliminaries, the text, and the preference materials.

### *1. The Preliminaries*

The preliminaries contain the following sub-divisions:

i. Title page
ii. Preface
iii. Table of Contents
iv. List of Tables
v. List of illustrations

I. *Title Page:* The title page should be simple and should show the subject of the report, the author, date of submission and sponsoring agency, if any. The title should be centered in the upper side of the page.

II. *Preface:* The preface or the forward can be crisp and brief. The preface must be written only after completing all works connected with the report. Acknowledgement recognizes the names of individuals and institutions who have helped the researcher in wring the report, collecting data or any other manner.

III. *Table of Contents:* The table of contents is an outline of all the chapter and their contents in sub-divisions. The main chapter and the sub-divisions must be shown in separate letters to distinguish them separately.

IV. *List of Tables:* All the tables that appear in chapters must be given title and number. Hence, the tables must be shown according to title and number used inside the report. The tables can also be given chapter-wise.

V. *List of Illustrations:* The list of illustrations can be presented in the same form of list of tables. Illustrations include the charts, graphs, maps and diagrams used.

## 2. The Text

The second major aspect of the report is the text. The text contains the chapters of the report. Each chapter will contain tables, their interpretation and suitable illustrations. "The text is the most important part of the thesis as it is in this section that the writer presents his facts or the basic tents of his argument. The writer should devote the greater part of his energies to a careful organization and presentation of his findings or general argument."

I. *Introduction:* In very many research reports introduction forms the first chapter. In the introduction the writer has to introduce the subject and scope of research. The introduction will include few pages of historical development or orientation of the subject. Other aspects of the research design namely statement of the problem, objectives, scope of the study, definition of concepts, methodology and sampling, limitation f the report, period of study, budget and chapter scheme will be found.

II. *Body of the Report:* The body of the report is presented in various chapters. The number of chapters of divisions of chapters is based on the title of the study. According to the demands of the study the researcher must divide chapters. Inclusion of too many chapters must be avoided. Every chapter must contain a brief introduction. While writing the chapter, subject-matter sequence and continuity and flow of language must be followed. Interpretation for every table must follow below the tables. Statistical tools must be used in appropriate places.

III. *Conclusion:* Conclusions are drawn from the findings of the report. A separate chapter, normally the last chapter is meant for conclusions and suggestions. Conclusions must also be drawn in order and sequence. Conclusions must be unbiased and must be based on facts. Conclusions may be drawn chapter-wise. Suggestions or recommendations can follow the conclusions immediately or they can be given separately. The suggestions offered must be valid and practicable for implementation. Theoretical or sterile suggestions must be avoided.

### 3. Reference Materials

Reference materials used must come at the end of the chapters. The materials used are bibliography, appendix an index.

Bibliography is an integral part of the report and the researcher must mention the books, research journals, research reports, and newspapers used.

In appendix, supportive facts or information can be included.

Index can be prepared and presented in alphabetical order. Important concepts that appear in the report can be culled out and presented. Against each concept or terms, the page numbers in which they appear must be given.

There are certain scientific sets of procedures in writing the footnotes or quoting materials from other sources. Procedures are also there in numbering tables, drawings, diagrams and charts. The researcher has to follow certain laid down procedures in numbering pages and giving headings and sub-titles in chapters.

### Conclusion and Generalization

The primary task in social surveys is that the data presented in tabular from should first be discussed and explained. At the same time the researcher should avoid repeating the whole data that the table contains. One has to be selective in explaining the table. While explaining tables it is always necessary to cite relevant column numbers and row numbers for the convenience of the readers. The statistical materials presented in the tables should be systematically checked for accuracy. Besides explaining the tables, the researcher has to interpret the data on the basis of the evidences. Such interpretation is the basis of generalization. It should be honest and straight forward exercise. He should prefer understatement instead of overstatement in order to retain readers confidence. While drawing conclusions he has to follow certain principles as laid down by Parten.7 Data should be scrutinized to see whether: (i) it is possible to come to opposite conclusions with the same material (ii) other persons on the staff would reach the same conclusions with the evidence shown (iii) conclusions are consistent with the one another and with other known facts (iv) they seem to sense and if not why? (v) they are colored by the writer's personal biases (vi) their meaning is unmistakable (vii) they could be accounted for by the survey techniques used.

### Arrangement of Ideas

Arrangement of ideas and the methodical and or the systematic presentation is an aid to draw the attention and evoke the interest of the readers. According to Carter V. Goode: "the skilful writer leads his reader step by step through a well organized analysis of problem, method, data and conclusions." Headings should be specific, brief and represent the content. Such headings and sub-headings call the attention of readers as to the materials presented. In the opinion of Parten: "Logical relationship of various points can be brought out by organizing the points, by appropriately employing center heading, sub-headings, under lining bold face type etc." Besides there must be uniformity and consistency in presentation of ideas. Punctuation, capitalization, abbreviations, footnotes, quotations, acknowledgement and bibliography must follow a uniform pattern. Frequent paragraphing, topical and summary sentences at the beginning and end of paragraphs, capitalization of key phrases and sentences will make the presentation meaningful and logical.

### Writing Style

Utmost attention should be paid for writing the research report. The report is a communication process between the researcher and the reader. The report should be clear, easy to read and accurate in information and statements. Vagueness, generalization and presumptions will make the report incomplete and uninteresting. The essence of communication is clarity in presentation. According to M.H. Gopal the following factors influence good write-up (a) the reader in view; (b) how technical the problem is ; (c) the researcher's hold over his facts and techniques; (d) his command over language; and (e) the form and fullness of the notes i.e.., of the data and (f) documentation.

The first step in clear presentation is clear thinking. The poor writing is largely due to hazy thinking on the problem in question. Only by thinking the researcher develops originality, which is reflected in his report. Research report writing is a reasoning process and without clarity of thought there won't be clarity in writing.

Next the researcher should have a good command over the language. Often, a poor writing is the result of the researcher's inadequate command over language "Too frequently faulty sentence structure, illogical paragraphing, poor punctuation, incorrect spelling and other variations of English render an otherwise promising manuscript virtually worthless." At the same time the researcher should not use complex high sounding language at the cost of clarity and straight forward presentation. Researcher is often, tempted to write with an eye more towards style than clarity, drama than facts and persuasiveness than incisiveness." The researcher should always remember that he is writing a scientific report and not a magazine article.

Brevity is another point the researcher should keep in mind while writing his report. He should take care of the economy of words and concentration of ideas, which will lead to density and poignancy. Repetition and superfluousness will obstruct the lucidity of the report and will interfere with precision and clarity.

Objectivity is yet another principle in report writing. The report writer should write an unbiased, objective report fortified by facts. It should convince the audience of the truth of the ideas present.

The research report normally goes through three drafts. The objectives of the first are comprehensiveness and fullness of facts. The first draft should be written as rapidly as possible and without any break. An uninterrupted period is conducive for integrated presentation. In the subsequent drafts the report should be improved both in the form and the language, by considerable trimming, pruning and chiseling. Ideas and sentences have to be realigned by cutting and joining, so that the report gets clarity, order, logic, unity, coherence and naturalness.

By patient review of the written materials, improving the draft and by giving more thought and effort, the write up could be made effective and poignant. Before giving final touch up to the report, it is better to keep the manuscript aside foe a while so that it gets cold. The gaps and weakness come to limelight only after a lapse of time when the material is carefully re-examined and re-edited.

## Graphic/Diagrammatic Presentation

Presentation of research data in the form of charts and diagrams is a method of attracting the attention of the readers. Besides, this enables the complex facts to be grasped more readily. Bar charts, component bar charts, pie diagram and pictogram are the methods more commonly used. Bar chart is useful in comparing two groups each having sub-strata which are components of the whole. Pie chart, like the component bar chart shows the relationship of parts to the whole. Pictogram has greater appeal and represents the data in small symbols or simplified pictures and is useful in visual comparison as in the case of bar chart. Besides the chart, the graph is also one of the most common devices for providing trend. The map is useful in ecological analysis to show the position of natural barriers or , location of industries, and traffic etc.

Such aids, according to Goode and Hatt "not only present the data in readable form but also help the reader to understand the more complex tabulations." These are common aids to clarify and are explained in any book on business or research statistics.

## Footnotes and Bibliography

Documentation is one of the important components of research report. Footnotes and bibliography are the reference to the sources from which ideas, data facts and opinions are borrowed from previous or current works. It makes the citations more authoritative, adds to the growth and continuity of knowledge and an acknowledgement of the benefits the researcher received from other's writings. Footnote serves the following specific purpose:

1. It gives credit to previous authors who have tackled the problem.
2. The larger context of the problem is indicated to the reader.
3. The researcher's contribution is distinguished from those of others.
4. The researcher is protected from being attacked by others.
5. It provides a reference to the sources, which may be consulted for more details.

While citing references the researcher must keep in mind certain points. Well-known facts need not be cited. It is always better to cite scholarly editions than the ordinary sources. If the content of the citation has already appeared in the text, such citation should be avoided lest it results in repetition. Too lengthy and controversial quotations should be relegated to the appendix. The footnotes must be relevant and the researcher must avoid the tendency to overwhelm the reader with quotations. As M.H. Gopal puts it: Over-documentation is bad; but under-documentation is worse. The citations should fit in with the text, relevant, clear and factual and sources must be cited fully and correctly.

# Glossary of Research Terms

**accuracy:** one of the considerations in determining sample validity: the degree to which bias is absent from the sample—the underestimators and the overestimators are balanced among members of the sample (i.e. no systematic variance).

**alternative hypothesis:** that a difference exists between the sample parameter and the population statistic to which it is compared; the logical opposite of the null hypothesis used in significance testing (notation: HA ).

**analysis of variance (ANOVA):** a statistical test for testing the null hypothesis that the means of several populations are equal; test statistic is the F ratio; used when you need k independent samples tests.

**applied research:** research with a practical problem-solving emphasis, where a problem is a negative circumstance or an opportunity.

**basic research:** research that aims to solve perplexing questions of a theoretical nature, with little direct influence on actions, performance, or policy decisions (a.k.a pure research).

**business research:** a systematic inquiry that provides information to guide business decisions

**case study:** emphasizes the full contextual analysis of fewer events or conditions and their interrelations for a single subject or respondent; a type of preexperimental design (one-shot case study).

**categorization:** a type of scale in which the respondents put themselves or property indicants in groups or categories.

**causal hypothesis:** statement that describes a relationship between two variables with respect to some case, one variable leads to an effect on the other variable (a.k.a. explanatory hypothesis).

**causal study:** attempts to reveal the relationship between variables; a.k.a. causation (A produces B or causes B to occur).

**census:** a count of all the elements in a population.

**central limit theorem:** for sufficiently large samples (i.e. n = 30+), the sample means of repeatedly drawn samples will be distributed around the population mean approximately in a normal distribution.

**central tendency:** a measure of location, most commonly the mean, median, and mode.

**closed question/response:** a type of measurement question that presents the respondent with a fixed set of choices (nominal, ordinal or interval data).

**cluster analysis:** a technique that identifies homogeneous subgroups or clusters of study objects or people, then displays the relevant clusters in a diagram (dendogram); viewing the data by segmented or groups of data cases.

**cluster sampling:** a sampling plan that involves dividing the population into clusters or subgroups, then drawing a sample from each subgroup in a single-stage or multi-stage design.

**clustering:** a data mining technique that assigns each data record to a group or segment automatically by clustering algorithms that identify the similar characteristics in the data set and then partition them into groups.

**code of ethics:** a comprehensive source that contains the firm's policies with respect to ethical conduct; effective codes are regulative, protect the public interest, are behavior specific, and are enforceable.

**codebook:** contains the coding rules for assigning numbers or other symbols to each variable; a.k.a. coding scheme.

**coding:** assigning numbers or other symbols to answers to that responses can be tallied and grouped into a limited number of classes or categories.

**content analysis:** a flexible, widely applicable tool for measuring the semantic content of a communication—including counts, categorizations, associations, interpretations, etc. (e.g. used to study the content of speeches, ads, newspaper and magazine editorials, etc.); contains four types of items: syntactical, referential, propositional, and thematic.

**control group:** a group of subjects that is not exposed to the independent variable being studied but still generates a measure for the dependent variable.

**control situation:** a classification of management questions that includes monitoring or diagnosing various ways in that an organization is failing to achieve its established goals.

**control variable:** extraneous variable that is assumed or discounted in a study; in data analysis, a variable introduced to help interpret the statistically significant relationship between variables.

**convenience samples:** a low-cost but less reliable nonprobability sample where element selection is unrestricted or left to those elements easily accessible by the researcher.

**data:** facts (attitudes, behavior, motivations, etc.) collected from respondents or observations (mechanical or direct) plus published information; categorized as primary and secondary

**data analysis:** editing and reducing accumulated data to a manageable size, developing summaries, looking for patterns, and applying statistical techniques

**data entry:** the process of converting information gathered by secondary or primary methods to a medium for viewing and manipulation; usually done by keyboarding or optical scanning.

**data mining:** the process of extracting meaningful knowledge from volumes of data contained within internal data marts or data warehouses; purpose is to identify valid, novel, useful, and ultimately understandable patterns in data.

**deduction:** a form of inference in which the conclusion must necessarily follow from the reasons given; a deduction is valid if it is impossible for the conclusion to be false if the premises are true.

**dependent variable (DV):** the variable measured, predicted, or otherwise monitored by the researcher, expected to be affected by a manipulation of the independent variable.

**depth interview:** An extensive one-on-one objective-driven and orchestrated conversation with a participant, usually lasting 1 or more hours.

**descriptive hypothesis:** states the existence, size, form or distribution of some variable.

**descriptive statistics:** display characteristics of the location, spread, and shape of an array of data.

**descriptive study:** attempts to describe or define a subject, often by creating a profile of a group of problems, people or events, through the collection of data and the tabulation of the frequencies on research variables or their interaction; the study reveals who, what, when, where, or how much; the study concerns a univariate question or hypothesis in which the research asks about or states something about the size, form, distribution, or existence of a variable.

**discriminant analysis:** the joining of a nominal dependent variable with one or more independent internal or ratio variables into an equation that is used to predict the classification of a new observation.

**"don't know" (DK) responses:** a response provided by respondents when they have insufficient knowledge to answer the question, when the instrument fails to provide an understandable operational definition for a construct, when the respondents have not formed a judgment on an issue, are reluctant to provide an answer, or feel the issue is too unimportant to formulate an answer.

**double-barreled question:** a type of multiple question that includes two or more questions in one that the respondent might need to answer differently to preserve the accuracy of the data.

**dummy variable:** nominal variable used in multiple regression and coded 0, 1 as all other variables must be interval or ratio measures.

**editing:** a customary first step in analysis for detecting errors and data omissions, correcting them when possible, and certifying that minimum data quality standards are achieved.

**equal-appearing interval scale:** an expensive, time-consuming type of consensus scaling which resulted in an interval rating scale for attitude measurement, a.k a Thurstone scale.

**explanatory hypothesis:** statement that describes a relationship between two variables with respect to some case, one variable leads to an effect on the other variable (a.k.a. causal hypothesis).

**exploratory research:** research undertaken to expand understanding of the research dilemma, identify alternative ways to address a problem, gather information to refine the research question, and identify sources for and actual research questions and sample frames; a.k.a exploratory study.

**ex post facto design:** researchers have no ability to manipulate the variables, but can report what has happened or is happening to the variables.

**external validity:** when an observed causal relationship can be generalized across persons, settings, and times.

**factor analysis:** techniques for discovering patterns among the variables to determine if an underlying combination of the original variables (a factor) can summarize the original set.

**factor scales:** types of scales that deal with multidimensional content and underlying dimensions, such as scalogram, factor, and cluster analyses, and metric and non metric multidimensional scaling.

**factors:** in principal components analysis, the result of a transformation of a set of variables into a new set of composite variables (factors) that are linear and not correlated with each other.

**filter question:** a question used to qualify the respondent's knowledge about the target questions of interest.

**focus group:** an information collection approach widely used in exploratory studies involving a panel of subjects led by a trained moderator that meets for 90 minutes to two hours; the moderator uses group dynamics to explore ideas, feelings, and experiences on a specific topic; can be conducted in person or via phone.

**free-response question:** a type of measurement question in which the respondent provides the answer to without the aid of an interviewer (either in phone, personal interview or self-administered surveys); a.k.a. open-ended question (nominal, ordinal or ratio data).

**frequency table:** a device for arraying data from lowest value to highest value, with columns for percent, percent adjusted for missing values, and cumulative percent.

**halo effect (error):** a systematic bias that the rater introduces by carrying over a generalized impression of the subject from one rating to another.

**hypothesis:** a proposition formulated for empirical testing; a tentative or conjectural declarative belief or statement that describes the relationship between two or more variables.

**independent variable (IV):** the variable manipulated by the researcher, which causes an effect or change on the dependent variable.

**in-depth interview:** a type of interview, usually unstructured and in an unconstrained environment, that encourages the respondent to talk extensively, sharing as much information as possible.

**index:** secondary data source that helps identify and locate a single book, journal article, author, etc. from among a large set.

**induction:** to draw a conclusion from one or more particular facts or pieces of evidence; the conclusion explains the facts.

**internal validity:** the ability of a research instrument to measure what it is purported to measure; when the conclusion(s) drawn about a demonstrated experimental relationship truly implies cause.

**interview schedule:** an alternative term for the questionnaire used in an interview (phone or in-person communication approaches to collecting data).

**interviewer error:** error that results from interviewer influence of the respondent; includes problems with motivation, instructions, voice inflections, body language, question or response order, or cheating via falsification of one or more responses.

**intranet:** a company's proprietary computer network.

**investigative questions:** questions the researcher must answer to satisfactorily arrive at a conclusion about the research question.

**judgment sampling:** a type of purposive sampling in which the researcher arbitrarily selects elements to conform to some criterion.

**leading question:** a measurement question that assumes and suggests to the respondent the desired answer (nominal, ordinal, interval or ratio data).

**leniency (error):** an error that results when the respondent is consistently an easy rater.

**level of significance:** the probability of rejecting a true null hypothesis.

**Likert scale:** a variation of the summated rating scale, this scale asks a rater to agree or disagree with statements that express either favorable or unfavorable attitudes toward the object. The strength of attitude is reflected in the assigned score and individual scores may be totaled for an overall attitude measure.

**literature review:** recent or historically significant research studies, company data or industry reports that act as the basis for the proposed study.

**literature search:** a review of books, articles journals or professional literature, research studies, and web-published materials that relate to the management dilemma, management question, or research question.

**management dilemma:** a symptom of a management problem or an early indication of a management opportunity; a problem or opportunity that requires a management decision.

**management-research question hierarchy:** process of sequential question formulation that leads a manager or researcher from management dilemma to investigative questions.

**manager-researcher relationship:** Describes the responsibilities of and conflicts between the manager contracting for the research and the firm providing or conducting the research process.

**multiple question:** a question that requests so much content that it would to be better if separate questions were asked.

**multiple regression:** a descriptive tool used to (1) develop a self-weighting estimating equation by which to predict values for a dependent variable from the values of independent variables, (2) control confounding variables to better evaluate the contribution of other variables, or (3) test and explain a causal theory.

**multivariate analysis:** those statistical techniques that focus upon and bring out in bold relief the structure of simultaneous relationships among three or more phenomena.

**multivariate analysis of variance (MANOVA):** a technique that assesses the relationship between two or more dependent variables and classificatory variables or factors; frequently used to test differences among related samples.

**nonprobability sampling:** a nonrandom and subjective procedure where each population element does not have a known nonzero chance of being included, as the probability of selecting population elements is unknown.

**null hypothesis:** that no difference exists between the sample parameter and the population statistic to which it is compared; notation: HO.

**numerical scales:** a scale where equal intervals separate the numeric scale points, while verbal anchors serve as labels for the extreme points.

**objects:** Concepts of ordinary experience, like people, books, autos, genes, or peer-group pressures.

**observation:** the full range of monitoring behavioral and nonbehavioral activities and conditions (including record analysis, physical condition analysis, physical process analysis, nonverbal analysis, linguistic analysis, extralinguistic analysis, and spatial analysis).

**open-ended question:** a type of measurement question in which the respondent provides the answer without the aid of an interviewer (either in phone, personal interview, or self-administered surveys); a.k.a unstructured or free response question (nominal, ordinal, or ratio data).

**operational definition:** a definition for a variable stated in terms of specific testing criteria or operations, specifying what must be counted, measured, or gathered through our senses.

**participant:** a term used to describe the respondent, subject, or sample element in a research study.

**participant observation:** when the observer acts as both observer and participant with the subject; the observer can be known or concealed.

**pie charts:** a statistical presentation technique that uses sections of a circle (slices of a pie) to represent 100 % of a frequency distribution of the subject being graphed; not appropriate for changes over time.

**pilot test:** a trail collection of data to detect weaknesses in design and instrumentation and provide proxy data for selection of a probability sample; see also pretesting.

**population:** the total collection of elements about which we wish to make some inferences.

**precoding:** Assigning codebook codes to variables in a study and recording them on the questionnaire, thus eliminating a separate coding sheet.

**pretesting:** an established practice for discovering errors in questions, question sequencing, instructions, skip directions, etc.; see also pilot test.

**primary data:** original research where the data being collected are designed specifically to answer the research question.

**primary sources:** original works of research or raw data without interpretation or pronouncements that represent an official opinion or position; include memos, letters, complete interviews or speeches, laws, regulations, court decisions and most government data, including census, economic and labor data; the most authoritative of all sources.

**Probability sampling:** a controlled, randomized procedure that assures that each population element is given a known nonzero chance of selection.

**probing:** techniques for stimulating respondents to answer more fully and relevantly to posed questions.

**process (activity) analysis:** the detailing of process steps and the collection of data on the effectiveness and efficiency of the steps and process as a whole, including time-motion studies in manufacturing, traffic flow within distribution centers and retailers, paperwork flow, customer complaint resolution, etc.

**proximity:** an index of perceived similarity or dissimilarity between objects.

**pure research:** research that aims to solve perplexing questions of a theoretical nature, with little direct influence on actions, performance, or policy decisions (a.k.a. basic research).

**qualitative techniques:** a fundamental approach of exploration, including in-depth interviews, participant observation, videotaping of subjects, projective techniques and psychological testing, case studies, street ethnography, elite interviewing, document analysis, and proxemics and kinesics. See also content analysis.

**quota sampling:** a type of purposive sampling in which relevant characteristics are used to stratify the sample in an attempt to improve the representativeness of the sample.

**ranking scale:** a measurement approach that asks the respondent to make comparisons among two or more objects or properties in relation to each other using a numeric scale, thus providing a relative order of those factors (ordinal or interval data ); a.k.a ranking question; see also ranking question.

**rating question:** a measurement question that asks the respondent to position each property or object on a companion verbal, numeric, or graphic scale.

**rating scale:** a measurement approach that asks the respondent to score an object or property without making a direct comparison to another object and thus position each factor on a companion scale, either verbal, numeric, or graphic (ordinal or interval data); see also rating question.

**relevant population:** the definition of those elements in the population most likely to have the information specified in the investigative questions.

**reliability:** a characteristic of measurement concerned with accuracy, precision, and consistency; a necessary but not sufficient condition for validity (if the measure is not reliable, it cannot be valid).

**research design:** the blueprint for fulfilling research objectives and answering questions.

**research process:** various decision stages involved in a research project, and the relationship between those stages.

**research question(s):** the choice hypothesis that best states the objective of the research; the answer to this question would provide the manager with the desired information necessary to make a decision with respect to the management dilemma.

**research variable:** an event, act, or characteristic measured by research; a.k.a. variable.

**respondent:** another term for a participant in a communication study.

**response error:** error created when the data reported differs from the actual data.

**sample:** a group of cases, respondents, or records comprised of part of the target population, carefully selected to represent that population; see also pilot testing, data mining.

**sample statistics:** descriptors of the relevant variables computed from sample data

**sampling:** the process of selecting some elements from a population to represent the population as a whole

**sampling error:** a reflection of the influences of chance in drawing the sample from the population; the error not accounted for by systematic variance

**sampling frame:** a list of elements in the population from which the sample is actually drawn

**scaling:** the assignment of numbers or symbols to an indicant of a property of objects to impart some of the characteristics of the numbers to the property

**scientific method:** disciplined procedures for generating quality research including direct observation of phenomena; clearly defined variables, methods, and procedures; empirically testable hypotheses; the ability to rule out rival hypotheses; and statistical rather than linguistic justification of conclusions.

**secondary data:** studies done by others and for different purposes than for which the data are being reviewed.

**secondary sources:** interpretations of primary data generally without new research.

**self-administered questionnaire:** a survey delivered to the respondent via personal (intercept) or non-personal (computer-delivered, mail delivered) means that is completed by the respondent without additional contact with an interviewer.

**simple random sample:** a probability sample in which each element has a known and equal chance of selection.

**stratified random sampling:** a probability sampling technique where the sample is constrained to include elements from each of the mutually exclusive segments or strata within a population

**stratified random sampling-disproportionate:** A probability sampling technique in which each stratum's size is not proportionate to the stratum's share of the population; allocation is usually based on variability of measures expected from the stratum, cost of sampling from a given stratum, and size of the various strata.

**stratified random sampling-proportionate:** a probability sampling technique in which each stratum is properly represented so the sample drawn from it is proportionate to the stratum's share of, the population; higher statistical efficiency than a simple random sample

**structured question:** a type of measurement question that presents the respondent with a fixed set of choices (nominal, ordinal or interval data); a.k.a structured response; see also closed question.

**survey:** a means of questioning a respondent via a collection of questions and instructions for both the respondent and the interviewer; a.k.a questionnaire, instrument, or interview schedule.

**systematic sampling:** a complex probability sampling technique in which the population (N) is divided by the desired sample (n) to obtain a skip pattern (k). Using a random start between 1 - k, each kth element is chosen from the sample frame; usually treated as a simple random sample but statistically more efficient.

**theory:** a set of systematically interrated concepts, definitions and propositions that are advanced to explain or predict phenomena (facts); the generalizations we make about variables and the relationships among variables.

**unstructured question:** a type of measurement question in which the respondent provides the answer to without the aid of an interviewer (either in phone, personal interview or self-administered surveys); see also open-ended question or free response question (nominal, ordinal or ratio data).

**validity:** a characteristic of measurement concerned that a test measures what the researcher actually wishes to measure; that differences found with a measurement tool reflect true differences among respondents drawn from a population.

**variable:** a characteristic, trait, or attribute that is measured; a synonym for a construct or the property being studied; a symbol to which values are assigned; includes several different types: continuous, control, decision, dependent, dichotomous, discrete, dummy, extraneous, independent, intervening, and moderating variables; see also research variable.

# Select Bibliography


1. Abrams Mark, *Social Surveys and Social Action*, London: William Heinemann Ltd., 1951.
2. Alan Bryman, *Business Research Methods*, Amazan.Co, UK, 2008
3. Anderson, R. and Zelditch, Morris Jr. *A Basic Course in Statistics with Sociological Application*. New York: Holt, Rinehart and Winston INC., 1975.
4. Best, John, *Research in Education*, New Delhi: Prentice Hall of India Pvt. Ltd., 1963.
5. Blalock Jr., Herbert M. and Blalock, Ann B., *Methodology in Social Research*, New York: McGraw Hill Book Company, 1968.
6. Borg, Walter R. *Educational Research, An Introduction*, New York; David Mckay Company, 1976.
7. Chou-Ya Lun, *Statistical Analysis*, New York: McGraw Hill Book Company, 1968.
8. Chambers, E.G. *Statistical Calculation for Beginners*, London: Cambridge University, 1955.
9. Cooper, Donald et.al, *Business Research Method*, McGraw Hill, New York, 2003.
10. Cordasco, Fransisco and Gatner Elliot, *Research and Report Writing*, New York: The Dryden Press, 1953.

11. Festinger, Leon and Katz, Daniel, *Research Methods in Behavioural Sciences*, New York: The Dryden Press, 1953.

12. Goode and Scates, *Methods of Research*, New York: Appleton-Century Crofts, 1954.

13. Goode, Carter V. *Essentials of Educational Research*, New York: Appleton Century Crofts, 1966.

14. Goode, William J. and Hatt, Paul K., *Methods in Social Research,* London: McGraw Hill Book Company, 1964.

15. Gopal, M.H., *An Introduction to Research Procedure in Social Sciences,* Mumbai, Asia Publication House, 1964.

16. Gopal, M.H., *Research Reporting in Social Science,* Dharwar: Karnatak University, 1965.

17. Hyman Herbert, *Survey Designs and Analysis,* Illinois: The Free Press Publishers, 1955.

18. Hillaway, Tyrus, *Introduction to Research,* Boston: Hougton Mifflin Co., 1965.

19. Macdougall, Curits D, *Interpretative Reporting,* New York: The Macmillan Company, 1961.

20. Mark Saunders, et al, *Research Methods for Business Students.*

21. Moser, C.A., *Survey Methods in Social Investigation,* London: William Hienemann Ltd., 1959.

22. Murdick Robert, G., *Business Research – Concepts and Practice,* Florida, international Book Company, 1959.

23. Nakkiran, S., *An Introduction to Research Methods in Social Sciences,*AbhijeetPublications,NewDelhi, 2009.

24. Nakkiran, S., *Research Methods in Rural Development,* Deep and Deep Publications,New Delhi, 2009.

25. Nakkiran, S., *Cooperative Management,* Deep and Deep Publications, New Delhi, 2007.

26. Parten Mildred, Surveys, *Polls and Sample; Practical Procedures,* New York: Harper and Row, John Weatherhill Inc, 1965.

27. Rummel, J.F. and Ballaine, W.C. *Research Methodology in Business,* New York: Harper and Row, 1963.

28. Selltiz Clarire, Jahoda Maria, et. al. *Research Methods in Social Relations*, USA: Methuen & Co., 1967.

29. Travers, Robert M.V., *Introduction to Educational Research*, New York: the Macmillan Co., 1958.

30. Whitney, F.L. *The Elements of Research*, New York: Asia Publishing House, 1961.

31. Young, P.V., *Scientific Social Surveys and Research*, New York: Asia publishing House 1962.

32. Cordasco and Catner, *Research and Report Writing*, New York: Barnes Noble INC., 1956.

33. Krishnasami, O.R., *Research Methodology in Social Sciences*, Himalaya Publishing House, Mumbai.

# Model Questions

**Short Questions**

1. Give the definition of Research.
2. Examine the characteristics of Research.
3. Explain the need for research in Business and Management.
4. Define 'concept' and 'theory'.
5. Explain the importance of hypothesis.
6. Discuss various types of hypothesis.
7. How to test a hypothesis.
8. Compare pure and applied research?
9. What is problem oriented research.
10. Explain the features and uses of feasibility research.
11. Discuss the use of feasibility studies in Business..
12. Discuss the steps involved in historical research?
13. Explain the steps in case study? What are its uses?
14. How can case study be useful in Business research?
15. Discuss the features of survey?
16. What are the purposes of survey?
17. What is a research problem?

18. How will you identify a research problem?
19. Explain the need to review literature.
20. what are the forms of interaction?
21. Define a seminar and workshop.
22. Differentiate a schedule and a questionnaire.
23. Explain the questions to be avoided in a schedule.
24. What are the advantages of an interview?
25. What are the qualities of an interviewer?
26. Define observation. What are its contents?
27. Explain a scale.
28. Define sampling.
29. Define the features of random sampling.
30. What are the essentials of a research design?
31. Define mean and mode.
32. What is ANOVA?
33. What is time series analysis?
34. What is coding?
35. Explain various methods of coding.
36. What are the limitations of research in business?

**Essay Questions**

1. Define social research and explain its importance to Business Research
2. Explain the role of theory and hypothesis in social research.
3. Give an account of various methods of research that could be applied to Business Research.
4. Explain the areas and types of evaluation studies.
5. Define action research.
6. What are the uses of historical research?
7. Explain the role of historical research to Business research.
8. Define and explain the significance of case study.
9. Explain in brief the social survey.

10. What are the advantages of surveys?
11. How do surveys help Business Research in improving the quality of their operations?
12. What is experimental research?
13. Explain the sources of a research problem in Business research.
14. Explain the significance of research gap.
15. Discuss the need and mode of interaction with research experts.
16. What is the relevance of seminars to a Business researcher?
17. Explain the steps in preparing a schedule.
18. What are the limitations of a questionnaire? How will you overcome them?
19. Explain the steps involved in conducting an interview.
20. Discuss various forms of observation. What are its uses in Business Resaerch?
21. What are the uses of scales to social research?
22. Explain the uses of library in Business Research .
23. Discuss in brief various methods of sampling.
24. Explain the body of a research design.
25. Discuss in brief the importance of editing.
26. Explain the contents of a research report.
27. Discuss various areas of research in Business management.

■■■